Archaeology on Medieval Knights' Manor Houses in Poland

WYDAWNICTWO
UNIWERSYTETU
ŁÓDZKIEGO

Anna Marciniak-Kajzer

Archaeology on Medieval Knights' Manor Houses in Poland

WYDAWNICTWO UNIWERSYTETU JAGIELLOŃSKIEGO

WYDAWNICTWO UNIWERSYTETU ŁÓDZKIEGO

Łódź—Kraków 2016

Anna Marciniak-Kajzer – University of Łódź, Faculty of Philosophy and History
Institute of Archaeology, Chair of Historical Archaeology and Weaponry
91-137 Łódź, 3 Uniwersytecka 3 St.

© Copyright by University of Łódź, Łódź 2016
© Copyright for this edition by Jagiellonian University Press

All rights reserved

No part of this book may be reprinted or utilised in any form or by any electronic, mechanical or other means, now known or hereafter invented, including photocopying and recording, or in any information storage or retrieval system, without permission in writing from the publishers

Published by Łódź University Press & Jagiellonian University Press

First edition, Łódź–Kraków 2016

ISBN 978-83-8088-002-3 – paperback Łódź University Press

ISBN978-83-233-3921-2 – paperback Jagiellonian University Press

ISBN 978-83-8088-003-0 – electronic version Łódź University Press

ISBN 978-83-233-9202-6 – electronic version Jagiellonian University Press

Łódź University Press
8 Lindleya St., 90-131 Łódź
www.wydawnictwo.uni.lodz.pl
e-mail: ksiegarnia@uni.lodz.pl
phone +48 (42) 665 58 63

WYDAWNICTWO UNIWERSYTETU ŁÓDZKIEGO

Distribution outside Poland

Jagiellonian University Press
9/2 Michałowskiego St., 31-126 Kraków

phone +48 (12) 631 01 97, +48 (12) 663 23 81, fax +48 (12) 663 23 83

cell phone: +48 506 006 674, e-mail: sprzedaz@wuj.pl
Bank: PEKAO SA, IBAN PL 80 1240 4722 1111 0000 4856 3325
www.wuj.pl

JAGIELLONIAN UNIVERSITY PRESS

CONTENTS

I. Author's Preface 7

II. Foreword 11

1. Introduction 13

2. Development of Views 21

III. Archaeology and Relics of Medieval Knights' Manor Houses 31

1. Where Did the Knights Build their Manor Houses? 33

2. Buildings within Knights' Residences 49

3. Furnishings and Interior Fittings of Manor Houses 66

4. Other Artefacts 85

IV. An Attempt to Reconstruct the Image of a Medieval Knight's Manor House in Poland 121

V. The Ending 147

VI. Short Bibliography for Concerning Archaeological Stes 173

VII. Bibliography 183

I. AUTHOR’S PREFACE

The Middle Ages is a period that has been inspiring our imagination for a long time. Even contemporary *fantasy* literature, especially in its film versions, draws most frequently from the medieval climate, with the buildings, everyday objects and clothing styled after the fashion of the Medieval period. The greatest of emotions and interest are aroused by knights and castles. Some of the medieval strongholds have survived in their entirety to this day and have been changed to a smaller or lesser extent by the following generations, others enrapture with their picturesque ruins. However, not many people ask themselves the question where did the medieval knights actually live when they were not accompanying their master in war, or were not staying in their lord's impressive castles. Where did they spend their time with their families whilst bringing up the next generation of knights? Most certainly the majority of them, at least in Poland, did not reside in such mighty castles.

So where did the medieval knights actually live? The answer to this question may vary taking into consideration the extensive territories of Europe. Even the issue of the duration of the Middle Ages causes many difficulties and differs for the various regions of our continent. In this book, however, I would like to concentrate on the fortified manor houses of knights that functioned in medieval Poland, that is within Central Europe. Our country was, at the time, overgrown with widespread forests cut with marshy river valleys and with mountain ranges in the south. Such a landscape had a considerable influence on the form and specificity of settlements and homesteads.

In the major part of Europe the motte and bailey residence, with its tower buildings on top of an artificial mound, was the initial form of settlement dwelt in by the knight. However, it is not my intention to study the origins of this type of fortified manor house. This is a huge issue and it is extremely popular among scholars, not only archaeologists.

Above all, I would like to make an attempt at the reconstruction of the appearance of such a manor house, including the objects that could be found inside. In this work the reader will not come across any attempts at creation of a typology, which is so popular among archaeologists. I would like to give a glimpse into what we may refer to as 'everyday life' in the Middle Ages, and in particular focus on how the fortified manor house functioned. The manor houses of knights, and later those of the nobility, found within the territories of Poland are indeed a real phenomenon. The geographical location of Poland, situated between East and West, resulted in a melting pot of cultural impacts and given the unsettled times a safe fortified settlement was a necessity. Subject to only slight changes, the shape of such settlements survived well into the 17th century, with some remaining even into the 18th century. It would not cause us any great astonishment if we were talking here of palaces of brick or stone, however, in this case we are talking of small wooden manor houses, frequently hidden among wet meadows. As such the fortified manor houses within the territories of Poland need be considered as a unique phenomenon that really finds no parallel in other regions of Europe.

II. FOREWORD

1. Introduction

For the majority of historical researchers, the manor houses of knights belong to the past and are something that has been and gone forever. For an archaeologist, however, they still exist, albeit in a heavily modified form. Therefore, the basic question is what is the state of the manor house today, or in reality, what are its remains, and how to identify, verify and investigate them? The most common response of the archaeologist to this question is that the designation of a manor house is a fortified residence, that is an archaeological site with distinct land features. In Poland most frequently it is the so-called motte-type residence, in the form of a mound often surrounded with a moat. Another form, typical of more mountainous regions, is the cutting off the end of a headland by a ditch, often referred to as a dry moat. The strict typological classification into upland, headland and lowland etc. fortifications was not successful. In principle we are still using the old nomenclature and saying it is a ring-shaped fortified town if it is surrounded with embankments, or a motte and bailey residence if the courtyard is situated on a raised earthwork. Misunderstandings are sometimes caused by the fact that these terms intuitively have chronological associations, that is ring-shaped fortifications are of early medieval construction whereas the motte and bailey residences have late medieval origins.

The presumption that the seat of the dominant social class, or knights, should stand out against the background of peasant households, is certainly well-grounded. In general it is emphasized that these seats were most frequently fortified. In the case of motte and bailey settlements or residences located on headlands, defence was ensured by the elevated location. In other cases, surrounding embankments or moats formed part of the defence system. It is obvious that sites with distinctive land features are easier to be discovered. Excavations of such sites provide artefacts typical of manor houses that differ from findings discovered within rural settlements in terms of quality, diversity and the high standard of workmanship. This fact supports the classification of such sites as relics of settlements occupied by representatives of the privileged social classes - knights or nobility. However, reliance only on the presence of a distinct land feature, deprives us of the possibility of learning about the full range of the types of seats affiliated to this social group. Sometimes, archaeological field surveys reveal 'courtly material' which is not reflected by any land feature that we could expect according to the accepted norms. Of course, there is always the possibility that such a structure had existed, and that it was completely destroyed leaving only the artefacts to remain[1]. Unfortunately, we are really not able to answer these doubts at the moment.

After many years of research, much can be said about the location of manor houses and their form of construction. It seems that no strict rules or trends existed that determined the choice of the location for construction of a safe residence. Our ancestors simply made use of the most suitable land features available within the boundaries of their landed estate. As can be observed, manor houses built on artificial mottes situated in river valleys prevail over constructions located on hills surrounded by ditches or embankments. Most likely it results from the fact that in the greater part of our country it was easier to find a marshy river valley than an isolated hill that could be lined with a defensive system without any difficulties.

Another issue that must be addressed at the beginning of this work is the question of ownership of these objects. The title of this work mentions 'the knight's manor' implying private ownership. In principle then, in this work properties owned by the church or rulers will be excluded, as long as they have been identified properly. Is this procedure justified? We can presume that both part of the clergy and the knighthood – nobility, as well as a duke or king to a lesser extent, used similar objects, such as utensils, weapon, tools and ornaments and so on. Royal locations or private residences of wealthy clergymen spread around the country most likely did not differ in form or furnishing from the manor house of the knight. The existing studies done allow us to make such a conjecture[2]. However, in order to turn the speculations into an assertion, it would be necessary to conduct a comparative analysis. I hope that this work on the knight's manor house will be the first element that renders such deliberations possible in the

1 The examples of such sites are Żerniki near Kórnik and Pomorzany.

2 T. J. Horbacz, *Nowożytny dwór w Brodni Dolnej koło Łasku*. In: Między północą a południem. Sieradzkie i Wieluńskie w późnym średniowieczu i czasach nowożytnych, (ed.) T. J. Horbacz, L. Kajzer, Sieradz 1993, pp. 303–307.

future. Unfortunately it will not be an easy task to perform. Above all, due to the lack of historical studies in the case of many sites it is impossible to determine the ownership. Still, the possibility of incorrect classification of particular facilities does not seem to be of such a crucial importance. According to estimates by L. Kajzer in relation to Central Poland, private estates accounted for more than 90% of all fortified manor houses built prior to the year 1500[3].

In the seventies and eighties of the 20th century studies of the fortified residences of knights reached their peak. Inventories were taken and verifications of late medieval defensive residences were carried out in many regions of the country. As a result, a significant database was developed providing information on the number, location and state of preservation of such sites. However, since no compilation has ever been published it can only be estimated that approximately five hundred such structures are affiliated with the Late Middle period on the territories of contemporary Poland. Different scale excavations were carried out on approximately 200 sites, including stationary excavations for a few seasons on some, to surveys which were limited to one trench and a few test boreholes.

A significant difficulty is the assignment of specific objects to subsequent owners as a result of problems with the precise dating of archaeological sites. Hence, the determination of the founder or even the successive users is not easy. The case becomes even more complicated when we have to deal with estates that used to be owned by the king or a duke and subsequently were transferred to private owners. An excellent example is the stronghold in Rozprza, undoubtedly it was initially a state-owned residence, the title to which was later assigned to a knight. In the case of the manor house in Zduny, nominally it remained the property of bishops from Wrocław, however it was leased to a knight during the entire period in question[4]. In such cases, especially when the objects under study resulted in extremely interesting data, I have tried to take them into account even as analogies.

3 L. Kajzer, *Archeologiczny rodowód dworu. Przemiany siedzib obronno-rezydencjonalnych Polski centralnej w późnym średniowieczu i czasach nowożytnych*, Łódź 1988, p. 19.

4 T. Jurek, *Właściciele rezydencji*. In: R. Grygiel, T. Jurek, Zduny. Późnośredniowieczne i nowożytne rezydencje właścicieli miasta, Łódź 1999, p. 243 et seq.

There is one more debatable issue concerning the term 'the knight's manor', namely who actually belongs to the circle of 'knights'[5]. In this context, the question seems of particular importance for archaeologists, the majority of whom were brought up on the views of Janina Kamińska, published until this day, that associate the so-called motte and bailey constructions with the average knight."[6] L. Kajzer made an attempt at solving this issue on the basis of considerably more extensive materials obtained both from exploration and archive sources[7]. He demonstrated that fortified keeps situated on a raised earthwork were initially constructed by the social elites. However, gradually they were becoming more and more popular and available even for minor knights, especially from the end of the 14th century, when the nobility started to build private brick castles. Hence, the owners of the buildings in question were representatives of all strata of the privileged class, yet different at different times. Here the most important problem is the fact that the earliest manor houses most likely belonged to magnates and were not owned by knights. Unfortunately, chronology determined with little accuracy and very few dates obtained by means of physico-chemical dating methods or dendrochronology, do not allow for such distinction.

5 The term 'knight' usually refers to a person who served as a mounted warrior and was a landholder. However, the variatey of this definition is reflected e.g. in monographs that have been published in the past years; cf. R. Barber, *Rycerze i rycerskość*, Warsaw 2000; J. Flori, *Rycerze i rycerstwo w średniowieczu*, Poznań 2003; cf. Polish publications: K. Buczek, *Prawo rycerskie i powstanie stanu szlacheckiego w Polsce*, "Przegląd Historyczny", vol. 69, 1978, no. 1, pp. 23–46; A. Bogucki, *'Strennus' jako tytuł rycerzy pasowanych (XIII–XV w.)*, "Przegląd Historyczny", vol. 77, 1986, no. 4, 1987, pp. 625–647; J. Bieniak, *Tytuł rycerski jako kryterium identyfikacji osób w średniowieczu*. In: Personae–colligationes–facta, Toruń 1991, pp. 66–73; A. Bogucki, *Rycerz i panosza w źródłach polskich XIV i XV wieku*. In: Społeczeństwo Polski średniowiecznej, S. K. Kuczyński (ed.), vol. 7, Warsaw, 1996, pp. 165–200; H. Samsonowicz, *Struktura społeczna późnego średniowiecza Polski w badaniach historycznych*, ibid., pp. 267–282.

6 J. Kamińska, *Grodziska stożkowate śladem posiadłości rycerskich XIII–XIV w.*, "Prace i Materiały Muzeum Archeologicznego i Etnograficznego w Łodzi", Seria Archeologiczna, no. 13, 1966, pp. 43–78.

7 L. Kajzer, *Czy tzw. gródki stożkowate były fundacjami „średniego rycerstwa"?*. In: Średniowieczne siedziby rycerskie w na tle badań podobnych obiektów na ziemiach polskich, A. Kola (ed.), Toruń 1987, pp. 105–126.

With a broad definition of knighthood and treating the term 'manor house' more as a cultural concept than a material phenomenon, it would be also necessary to discuss the residences of magnates, when they abandoned the small household situated on raised mounds and moved inside brick-walled castles. However such a procedure does not seem to be well-founded. This phenomenon is commonly observed in Poland in the 15th century. At that time however, the stratification of the knighthood, especially the widening differences in wealth, resulted in a considerable diversification of furniture and objects found in the residences occupied by the richest and the poorest knights. This should also become a subject for future research. Therefore, in this study private castles will not be considered, although ideologically they were 'knights' manor houses', formally they were significantly different from them. Clearly we have come to another problematic issue, namely how to distinguish between a manor house and a castle in the material sense. Fortunately, this questions has been answered by the authors of *Leksykon zamków w Polsce [Lexicon of Castles in Poland]*[8]. So the objects or constructions which are listed in the *Lexicon* will not be discussed in this study.

The arrangement of artefacts in particular parts of this book was an essential decision to be made, which had a significant impact on the presentation of the study results. According to archaeological practice, raw material is the main criterion for the organization of artefacts obtained within excavations. Archaeologists describe objects as pottery, metal, bone and 'other'. Most likely such a practice derives unconsciously from the historical division into Stone Age, Bronze Age and Iron Age based on the criterion of raw material. Classification suggested by S. South, who was one of the first theoreticians of historical archaeology, was not adopted in Poland. The criteria for division are not really uniform here and the legitimacy of classification into certain groups is disputable[9]. The classification proposed by V. Brych[10] seems to be

8 L. Kajzer, S. Kołodziejski, J. Salm, *Leksykon zamków w Polsce*, Warsaw 2001.

9 It should be emphasized that the deliberations of this author refer mainly to historical times in North America; S. South, *Method and Theory in Historical Archaeology*, New York 1977, tab. 3 and 4, cf. remarks of K.M. Kowalski. In: *Artefakty jako źródło poznania*, Gdańsk 1996, pp. 29–34.

10 V. Brych, *Hmotná kultura středověké tvrze v Čechách*. In: Encyklopedie českých tvrzí, vol. 1, Praha 1998, pp. 47–83.

more suitable in our realities, although this method is unlikely to be instilled in Polish archaeology in the light of different research traditions.

Methodological reflection in Polish archaeology has been developing mainly based on studies of prehistory. Apart from artefacts, historical archaeology deals with text and it lacks separate proposals for methodological reflection. I have also observed an even more peculiar fact. When presenting their views, methodologists more and more frequently speak of prehistory instead of archaeology. It is encouraging that they distinguish the specific character of the archaeology of historical times[11].

It seems in practice that a particular research approach usually depends on the changeable fate of the discussion between Polish methodologists trying to answer the question whether archaeology is the study of artefacts or past societies[12]. It should be noted at this point that although the majority of archaeologists are aware of the fact that any manifestation of human activity may be a potential archaeological source, still the spectrum of typical forms of activity described, ergo identified by archaeologists, is relatively small. This is not a consequence of the lack of appropriate source facts, but our limited ability of observation. It seems that when exploring a site, we are searching for the traces of human activity that we expect. Moreover, it often happens that some of the observations made during excavations, especially not standard ones and difficult to interpret, are written only in the field diary. For fear of criticism of our explanations, we do not present our remarks to the readers and at the same time we narrow the discussion and limit the possibilities of broadening our potential expectations. Hence, this book includes only those manifestations of human activity that were described by researchers.

For archaeologists, certain objects (or most frequently their relicts discovered during excavations) are integral elements of knights' manor houses. Such objects are usually referred to as 'artefacts or material culture'. The latter term is obviously used here with a narrow meaning.

11 On disintegration of relations between researchers within one branch of knowledge and the actual division into practitioners and theoreticians cf. A. Zalewska, *Teoria źródła archeologicznego i historycznego we współczesnej refleksji metodologicznej*, Lublin 2005, especially part I/1 *Refleksje nad źródłem–polem spotkania teorii i praktyki*, pp. 13–18.

12 Cf. remarks: H. Mamzer, J. Ostoja-Zagórski, *Orientacje badawcze w polskiej archeologii*, "Nauka", no. 1, 2007, pp. 131–148.

In Poland, the issues related to comprehension, definition and finally the study of material culture (with a broad meaning) were the subject of extensive discussion over fifteen years ago in *Kwartalnik Historii Kultury Materialnej [Quarterly History of Material Culture]*[13]. The discussion concerning both theoretical background and particular research was very broad and we shall not refer to it in this work. We will focus in particular on material culture meaning "the structures of everyday life", as defined by F. Braudel[14] and limited only to the functioning of knights' manor houses. As this work is an archaeological study, it is obvious that particular emphasis is placed on artefacts discovered during excavations. As archaeologists have access only to a small number of objects used in manor houses, it is necessary to support with written sources or iconography to get the full picture of material culture created on the basis of excavated artefacts.

Finally, as a formality it should be emphasized that the archaeological sites referred to in this book are located on the territory corresponding more or less to the territorial range of Poland during the reign of the last Polish king from the Piast dynasty, i.e. Casimir III the Great (+1370). Other territories that are within the present borders of Poland, i.e. Chełmno Land, Pomerania and Silesia will be discussed here as a valuable comparative background.

In the case of our considerations, the chronological limits of the phenomena referred to in this book are much less controversial. The lower time limit is naturally determined by the emergence of private knights' manor houses, i.e. starting from the second half of the 13th century[15]. The upper time limit is more difficult to define. As demonstrated by L. Kajzer in many of his publications, the model of the motte-and-bailey residence or settlement with defensive embankments was so attractive that it lasted longer than the Middle Ages,

13 J. Topolski, *Fernand Braudel a koncepcja historii kultury materialnej*, "Kwartalnik Historii Kultury Materialnej", vol. 42, 1994, no. 2, pp. 159–165; W. Wrzosek, *Braudelowska idea kultury materialnej…*, ibid., pp. 167–172; L. Kajzer *Archeologia a historia kultury materialnej*, ibid., pp. 173–175; J. Ostoja-Zagórski, *W kwestii znaczeniowych treści kultury materialnej*, ibid., pp. 177–179.

14 This is the subtitle of the first volume: F. Braudel, *Kultura materialna, gospodarka i kapitalizm XV–XVIII wiek*, vol. 1, *Struktury codzienności. Możliwe i niemożliwe*, J. Kochanowicz (ed.), Warsaw 1992.

15 A. Wędzki, *Ze studiów nad rezydencjami możnowładczymi i rycerskimi na ziemiach polskich w XI–XII wieku*, "Slavia Antiqua", vol. 25, 1978, pp. 173–187.

i.e. at the conventional turn of the 15th and 16th centuries[16]. Therefore, the disappearance of manor houses cannot determine the upper time limit, as it occurred much later. When studying the medieval residences in Lesser Poland, S. Kołodziejski introduced a very accurate and convincingly well-grounded end date of medieval residences owned by magnates[17]. Relying on previous proposals as regards the periodization of the development of castles by B. Guerquin[18], he considered that the year 1530 to be the end date. Kołodziejski reckoned that the most essential reason in support of such a dating is the decline of medieval defensive-residential constructions in the first quarter of the 16th century and at the same time the development of new modern residences compatible with Renaissance trends[19]. The work of S. Kołodziejski is based on written sources and archaeological studies to the same degree. Hence the need for the determination of a specific year on the timeline that would limit the preliminary source research. In our case such exact precision is not required, mainly due to little accuracy in the dating of archaeological sites subject to exploration. Traditional dating methods based mainly on the determination of the age of pottery, tiles or arms allow for a precision of about twenty-five years. However, especially in the case of older studies, it would be necessary to verify the chronological terms defined by researchers. Unfortunately, in order to re-define the age of some of the sites it would be necessary to undertake separate studies. In such situations the dating quoted is by the authors of studies or excavations. On a few occasions, I took the liberty to express my doubts, whether the chronology of particular structures should not be changed in the light of the up-to-date findings. To recapitulate, it should be assumed that our deliberations are related to the period ending in the widely understood early 16th century.

16 L. Kajzer, *Studia nad świeckim budownictwem obronnym województwa łęczyckiego w XIII–XVII wieku*, "Acta Universitatis Lodziensis, Folia Archaeologica", no. 1, Łódź 1980, pp. 147–160; L. Kajzer, *Grodziska średniowieczne i nowożytne*, "Prace i Materiały Muzeum Archeologicznego i Etnograficznego w Łodzi", Seria Archeologiczna, no. 36, 1989–90, p. 35 et. seq.

17 S. Kołodziejski, *Średniowieczne rezydencje obronne możnowładztwa na terenie województwa krakowskiego*, Kraków 1994, pp. 15–17.

18 B. Guerquin, *Zamki w Polsce*, Warsaw 1984, pp. 25–26.

19 S. Kołodziejski, *Średniowieczne rezydencje obronne...* p. 17.

2. Development of Views

It is interesting that the history of excavations of medieval fortified seats in Poland dates back to the times when they were erected. It was as early as in the year 1390 that Louis I the Fair of Briest (1311–1398) ordered that excavations of the fortified residence in Ryczyn in Silesia be carried out[20]. No sources exist that could explain the intentions of the duke. I. and J. Kramarek believed that he was searching for the remains of the bishop residences from Wrocław, who most likely inhabited Ryczyn for many years in the 11th century, following the destruction of the country due to invasion of the Czech Duke of Bohemia, Bretislaus I. L. Kajzer was of a different opinion. He reckoned that the reason for the excavations was the search for mortal remains – relics that were so desired and valued in the Middle Ages[21]. The actual intentions of the duke were possibly taken to the grave. Nevertheless we can take pride in an over six-hundred-year-old history of the studies of fortified residences. These interests continued to be shared by the Enlightenment and by positivist enthusiasts of antiquity[22].

Curiosity about the relics of medieval knights' manor houses in Poland has a long tradition. W. Łęga used the term motte-and-bailey for the first time already in 1930[23]. However G. Leńczyk should be considered as a precursor of systematic archaeological works aiming at the study of medieval fortifications. Leńczyk started making a planned inventory of fortified households and castles in 1932 and his works were interrupted only by the outbreak of World War II[24]. G. Leńczyk was also the first archaeologist in Poland to conduct a fully

20 J. Kramarek, *Pierwsze wykopaliska archeologiczne na Śląsku*, "Z Otchłani Wieków", vol. 24, 1958, no. 1, pp. 25–33; I. J. Kramarkowie, *U źródeł archeologii*, Wrocław 1972.

21 L. Kajzer, *Wstęp do archeologii historycznej w Polsce*, Łódź 1996, pp. 33–34.

22 This subject is discussed in detail in A. Marciniak-Kajzer, *Średniowieczny dwór rycerski w Polsce. Wizerunek archaeologiczny*, Łódź 2011.

23 W. Łęga, *Kultura Pomorza we wczesnym średniowieczu na podstawie wykopalisk*, part. II, "Rocznik Towarzystwa Naukowego w Toruniu", vol. 36, 1930, pp. 295–327.

24 Search works resulted in description of particular structures together with drawings, schemes and sections. The author focused on the area considerably larger than historical Lesser Poland. The result of his studies were published in more than ten articles; cf. G. Leńczyk, *Katalog grodzisk i zamczysk z terenu Małopolski*, monograph by S. Kołodziejski, Cracow 1983.

methodological exploration of the medieval motte and bailey residence in Piekary near Cracow[25]. The subsequent publication of these works[26] proved that the excavations were carried out comprehensively and that typical archaeological analysis were correlated with the interpretations of written sources by the historian[27].

After World War II there was an attempt at the coordination of the subject in matter and the range of the excavation works. The Committee of Research on the Origins of the Polish State was established in 1949 and it operated until 1953. The most significant achievement of the Committee was the initiation of closer cooperation between archaeologists and historians, which resulted in an expanded range of interest of the representatives of both disciplines. There was also an attempt at cataloguing all fortified constructions in Poland. *Mapa grodzisk w Polsce [Map of fortified settlements in Poland]* was published in 1964[28]. Although it covered as many as 2312 sites, it was only the initial stage of research. W. Antoniewicz and Z. Wartołowska claim in this publication that chronology was determined only in the case of approximately 10–15% sites, and just 2% of them were explored. In this situation all the objects were identified only on the map, without giving even an approximate dating.

In Greater Poland in 1950, W. Hensel started publishing *Studia i Materiały do osadnictwa Wielkopolski Wczesnohistorycznej [Studies and Materials of Early Historical Settlements in Greater Poland]*[29], that included also information concerning medieval fortified residences. In 1976 Z. Kurnatowska and

25 G. Leńczyk, *Grodzisko w Piekarach w powiecie krakowskim*, "Z Otchłani Wieków", vol. VII, 1932, pp. 77–85; G. Leńczyk, *Tymczasowe sprawozdanie z badań terenowych na grodzisku w Piekarach pod Krakowem*, "Sprawozdania Polskiej Akademii Umiejętności", vol. 37, 1932, pp. 23–24.

26 R. Jamka, G. Leńczyk, K. Dobrowolski, *Badania wykopaliskowe w Piekarach w powiecie krakowskim*, "Prace Prehistoryczne", no. 2, Cracow 1939.

27 K. Dobrowolski, *Uwagi o grodach wczesno-historycznych w Polsce ze szczególnym uwzględnieniem grodziska w Piekarach*, "Sprawozdania Polskiej Akademii Umiejętności", vol. 37, 1932 (1933), pp. 24–26.

28 *Mapa grodzisk w Polsce*, W. Antoniewicz, Z. Wartołowska (eds.), Wrocław 1964.

29 W. Hensel, *Studia i materiały do osadnictwa Wielkopolski Wczesnohistorycznej*, vol. 1–3, Poznań 1950, 1953, 1959; The following volumes: W. Hensel, Z. Kurnatowska, *Studia i materiały do dziejów Wielkopolski wczesnohistorycznej*, vol. 4–6, 1972, 1980, 1987.

A. Łosińska commenced the verification of fortified settlements in Greater Poland (Wielkopolska). Their work resulted in two very interesting publications[30], which provide a starting point for further exploration and give a view of the state of research. In 1988 E. Krause published a study of knights' manor houses in Greater Poland and Central Poland[31], which includes the author's attempt at systematizing the existing state of knowledge. Among other things, a catalogue of fortified settlements in Poznań Province was issued in 1995 on the basis of the above mentioned publications[32]. For more than ten years G. Teske and J. Tomala[33] have been verifying fortified settlements in the vicinity of Kalisz.

Apart from the above mentioned studies of G. Leńczyk[34], the majority of fortified sites in Lesser Poland were explored within the works carried out by the *Carpathian Archaeological Expedition* established by A. Żaki[35]. Defensive settlements, including knights' manor houses, aroused at that time the interest of many people from various parts of Lesser Poland: e.g. A. Jodłowski[36] conducted

30 Z. Kurnatowska, A. Łosińska, *Weryfikacja grodzisk wielkopolskich na półmetku*, "Fontes Archaeologici Posnanienses", t. 32, 1981(1983), s. 25–62; Z. Kurnatowska, A. Łosińska, *Sprawozdanie z weryfikacji grodzisk wielkopolskich w latach 1983–1984*, "Fontes Archaeologici Posnanienses", vol. 34 (1982–1985), pp. 77–84.

31 E. Krause, *Średniowieczne siedziby rycerskie w Wielkopolsce i Polsce środkowej*. In: "Rocznik Przedsiębiorstw Państwowego Pracownie Konserwacji Zabytków", vol 2 (1987), Warsaw 1988, pp. 44–60.

32 B. Kirschke, A. Prinke, *Grodziska w województwie poznańskim. Katalog stanowisk archeologicznych,* "Poznańskie Zeszyty Archeologiczno-Konserwatorskie", no. 2, Poznań 1995.

33 J. Tomala, *Budownictwo obronne powiatu kaliskiego w XIV–XVIII wieku*, Poznań 1995.

34 G. Leńczyk, *Na śladach miejsc obronnych*, "Dawna Kultura", vol. 3, 1956, pp. 122–127; G. Leńczyk, *Na śladach miejsc umocnionych*, "Z Otchłani Wieków", vol. 27, 1961, pp. 108–109; G. Leńczyk, *Elementy obronne w miejscach umocnionych*, "Studia Archeologiczne", vol. 2, 1967, pp. 73–116.

35 Recently, the works of *Carpathian Archaeological Expedition* have been referred to in detail in the following publications: J. Machnik, *Legenda Karpackiej Ekspedycji Archaeologicznej*. In: Polonia Minor Medii Aevi. Studia ofiarowane Panu Profesorowi Andrzejowi Żakiemu w osiemdziesiątą rocznicę urodzin, Z. Woźniak, J. Gancarski (eds.), Cracow–Krosno 2003, pp. 65–82; J. Kurczab, *O działalności Karpackiej Ekspedycji Archaeologicznej*, ibid., pp. 83–120.

36 A. Jodłowski, *Osadnictwo obronne w dolinie Dunajca*, "Materiały Archeologiczne", vol. 8, 1967, pp. 5–23.

research in the Dunajec River Valey, M. Szope[37] in the Tarnów district, A. Kunysz and J. T. Frazik[38] in the Rzeszów district, J. Reyniak[39] in the south-western territories, Z. W. Pyzik and E. Gąssowska[40] in the Kielce district, M. Cabalska[41], in the Sądecki district, W. Błaszczyk in the Polish Jurassic Highlands, and E. Ćwiertak[42] in the Radom region. Publications regarding sites in the Carpathian Mountains we owe to J. Marszałek[43], to M. Florek[44] as regards to Rzeszów Land, to A. Hunicz[45] concerning the Lublin district, to E. Banasiewicz[46] about the Zamość district, whereas B. and M. Gedl[47] wrote about the south-western borderland of

37 M. Szope, *Grodziska i zamczyska województwa tarnowskiego*, Tarnów 1981; cf. L. Kajzer, [review] M. Szope, *Grodziska i zamczyska województwa tarnowskiego*, Tarnów 1981, "Z Otchłani Wieków", R. 48, 1982, no. 4, pp. 191–192.

38 A. Kunysz, *Grodziska w województwie rzeszowskim*, "Materiały i sprawozdania Rzeszowskiego Ośrodka Archeologicznego za rok 1966", 1968, pp. 25–87; J. T. Frazik, *Zamki i budownictwo obronne ziemi rzeszowskiej*, Cracow 1971.

39 J. Reyniak, *Osadnictwo obronne w dorzeczu górnej Wisły*, "Acta Archaeologica Carpathica", vol. 20, 1980, pp. 73–92; J. Reyniak, *Dawne miejsca obronne w dorzeczu górnej Wisły*, "Karta Groni", no. 9–10, 1980, pp. 55–74.

40 E. Gąssowska, *Wojewódzki Ośrodek Archeologiczno-Konserwatorski w Kielcach. Plan działania*, "Peregrinus", no. 1, 1990, pp. 5–26.

41 Cf. Bibliography.

42 E. Ćwiertak, *Wyniki weryfikacji grodzisk w oparciu o badania na terenie województwa radomskiego*, "Biuletyn Kwartalny Radomskiego Towarzystwa Naukowego", vol. 22, 1985, no. 1–2, pp. 63–100; E. Ćwiertak, *Ze studiów nad wiejską siedzibą obronną w ziemi radomskiej w XIII–XVIII w.*, "Prace i Materiały Muzeum Archeologicznego i Etnograficznego w Łodzi", Seria Archaeologiczna, no. 34, 1987, pp. 241–249.

43 J. Marszałek, *Katalog grodzisk i zamczysk w Karpatach*, Warsaw 1993.

44 M. Florek, *Rozpoznanie grodzisk na terenie województwa Podkarpackiego*. In: Rzeszowska Teka Konserwatorska, vol. 2, Rzeszów 2000, pp. 7–39.

45 A. Hunicz, *Katalog wczesnośredniowiecznych i średniowiecznych grodzisk południowo-wschodniej Lubelszczyzny*, "Biuletyn Informacyjny Pracowni Konserwacji Zabytków", vol. 5, no. 19, 1970, pp. 163–179; cf. J. Gurba, *Grodziska Lubelszczyzny*, Lublin 1976.

46 E. Banasiewicz, *Grodziska i zamczyska Zamojszczyzny*, Zamość 1990.

47 B. Gedl, *Erforschung der mittelalterlichen Wehraulangen im nördlichen Teil des schlesischkleinpolnischen Grenzgebietes*, "Zeszyty Naukowe UJ", Prace Archaeologiczne, vol. 23, Cracow 1976, pp. 97–103; M. Gedl, *Studien bei die Entwicklung der Frühmittelalterlichen Besiedlung im Nordteil der kleinpolnisch-schlesischen Grenzgebiete*, Raports du IIIe Congres International d'Archelogie Slave, Bratislava 1979, vol. 1, pp. 271–276.

Lesser Poland. S. Kołodziejski[48], who has been studying the subject since many years, has definitely contributed immensely to our knowledge on magnates' seats in Lesser Poland, and in particular in Cracow Province.

In Masovia and the neighbouring territories, studies on fortified residences were carried out mainly within the works of the Polish Historical Atlas Team at the Institute of Material Culture of the Polish Academy of Sciences that continued the studies conducted within the *Pracownia Inwentaryzacji Grodzisk* [*Inventory of Fortified Settlements*]. The works of scholars from Warsaw resulted in the publication of a catalogue of fortified settlements in Warsaw Province in 1976[49].

In the 1940s Janina Kamińska commenced her studies in Central Poland. Undoubtedly she can be considered to be a precursor of the innovative research of fortified enclosures, including motte and bailey residences in Poland. J. Kamińska implemented completely new standards into her studies and the results of her excavations conducted in Siedlątków in 1965–66 constitute the foundation for archaeological research and created the idea of a fortified mound as the seat of *middle class knights* [50]. An attempt at depicting small

---

48 S. Kołodziejski, *Rezydencje obronne możnowładztwa…*, and many other publications.

49 I. Górska, L. Paderewska, J. Pyrgała, W. Szymański, L. Gajewski, Ł. Okulicz, *Grodziska Mazowsza i Podlasia (w granicach dawnego województwa warszawskiego)*, Wrocław 1976; A. Gieysztor [review], "Kwartalnik Historii Kultury Materialnej", R. 25, no. 4, pp. 550–551); cf. L. Gajewski, J. Górska, L. Paderewska., J. Pyrgała, W. Szymański, *Badania sondażowe grodzisk Mazowsza i Podlasia w latach 1966–1968*, "Sprawozdania Archeologiczne", vol. 22, 1970, pp. 151–172.

50 J. Kamińska, *Grody wczesnośredniowieczne ziem Polski środkowej na tle osadnictwa*. Łódź 1953; M. Młynarska, [review] "Kwartalnik Historii Kultury Materialnej", R. 4, 1956, pp. 131–140; Z. Hilczerówna, [review] "Studia i materiały do dziejów Wielkopolski i Pomorza", vol. 2, no. 1, 1956, pp. 307–313; J. Kamińska, *Sprawozdanie z badań nad grodami i osadnictwem otwartym wczesnego średniowiecza na terenie Polski środkowej w 1955 r.*, "Sprawozdania Archeologiczne", vol. 5, 1959 pp. 185–188; J. Kamińska, *Siedlątków, obronna siedziba rycerska z XIV wieku*, "Prace i Materiały Muzeum Archeologicznego i Etnograficznego w Łodzi", Seria Archaeologiczna, no. 15, 1968, pp. 15–88; A. Wędzki, [review] "Slavia, Antiqua", vol. 18, 1970, pp. 312–314; J. Kamińska, *Radomsko-Dobryszyce*. In: *Na granicach archaeologii*, A. Nadolski (ed.), Łódź 1968, pp. 67–72; J. Kamińska, *Sprawozdanie z badań archeologicznych na grodziskach typu „stożkowatego" w pow. Poddębickim, w 1965 r.*, "Sprawozdania Archeologiczne" vol. 6, 1968, pp. 216–219; J, Kamińska, A. Golczyńska, *Kopiec w Witowie*. In: Rozwój osadnictwa w rejonie Burzenina nad Wartą VI–XIV w., J. Kamińska (ed.), Wrocław 1970, pp. 162–165.

keeps occupied by knights in the economic and political context of the region and the country is an essential element of her publication. With the stratigraphic patterns of the burnt construction preserved in excellent condition, the abundance of artefacts and a model publication, the 14th-century knight's manor residence in Siedlątków dominated the imagination of the majority of archaeologists who explored similar sites and it became a kind of a benchmark to which more up-to-date studies refer.

L. Kajzer is the successor of J. Kamińska. Together with his colleagues he verified the majority of late medieval fortified settlements in the area of Kuyavia, Dobrzyń Land, as well as the Wieluń, Łęczyca and Sieradz districts[51].

J. Kamińska was the first to connect motte and bailey constructions with knights' residences[52]. She defined the typical list of formal features peculiar to such settlements:

a – situated in a river valley or at the edge of a river valley
b – a circular or near-circular base with the diameter of approximately 30 m
c – a hollow or almost flat surface at the top of a truncated mound
d – a moat and circular embankments (not always preserved)[53]

At the same time, when analysing the studies of the castles in Silesia and Western Pomerania, J. Kamińska observed that considerably smaller fortified mounds are similar to brick defensive keeps, especially in the territories of

51 L. Kajzer, *Z badań nad budownictwem rezydencjalno-obronnym ziemi łęczyckiej i sieradzkiej w XVI w.* "Kwartalnik Architektury i Urbanistyki", vol. 24, 1979, no. 4, pp. 373–382; L. Kajzer, *Studia nad świeckim budownictwem obronnym województwa łęczyckiego…;* L. Kajzer, *Dwory obronne wieluńskiego w XIII–XVII w.*, "Acta Universitatis Lodziensis", Folia Archaeologica, no. 6, 1984; L. Kajzer, J. Augustyniak, *Wstęp do studiów nad świeckim budownictwem obronnym sieradzkiego w XIII–XVII/XVIII wieku*, Łódź 1986; L. Kajzer, *Budownictwo obronno-rezydencjonalne Kujaw i ziemi dobrzyńskiej*, part II, T. J. Horbacz, L. Kajzer, T. Nowak, L. Wojda, *Siedziby obronno-rezydencjonalne w powiecie kowalskim na Kujawach w XIII–XVIII wieku*, L. Kajzer (ed.), Łódź 1991; L. Kajzer, *Pałace i dwory w dawnym województwie sieradzkim*, vol. 2. In: Materiały do dziejów rezydencji w Polsce, T. S. Jaroszewski (ed.), Warsaw 1994; L. Kajzer, A. Horonziak, *Archeologiczna weryfikacja grodzisk i kopców podworskich na obszarze Kujaw Brzeskich i ziemi dobrzyńskiej*, "Zapiski Kujawsko-Dobrzyńskie", vol. 11, 1997.

52 J. Kamińska, *Grodziska stożkowate śladem posiadłości rycerskich…*, pp. 43–78.

53 Ibid, p. 43.

Silesia. This analysis brought her to the conclusion about what archaeologist may expect during exploration:

a – traces of wooden, or alternatively brick or stone, constructions in the central part of the mound

b – external fortifications in the form of a palisade, moats, and embankments

c – remains of adjacent settlements, fulfilling the role of a farmstead, in relation to the modest size of its defensive structure[54]

The extraordinary intuition of Kamińska is worthy of admiration. She formulated such a list of expectations at the very beginning of studies conducted in relation to fortifications in Poland.

The second essential question posed by J. Kamińska was the issue of the origins of knights' manor houses, identifying with motte and bailey residences. In her work published in 1966 she presented excavations of similar constructions in Europe, especially in the territories of Germany and the Czech Republic[55]. As L. Kajzer[56] refers to these issues in detail in some of his publications, this work quotes only the most crucial findings. In Western Europe the origins of private small keeps date back sometimes to the turn of the 8th and 9th centuries. The earliest traces were recorded in the Rhineland, where they appeared in large numbers only between the 11th and 12th centuries and in the 12th century in the Czech Republic. Gradually, the most typical form of a private fortified seat became a motte type construction, i.e. a keep situated on a raised earthwork, most often surrounded by a moat or pond.

In 1972 L. Kajzer published an article dedicated to the genealogy of a rural defensive residence in Poland. Based on conducted excavations, the author put forward the following conclusions. The size of the keeps built on mounds in Poland does not differ from similar constructions erected on the territories of the neighbouring countries. Similarly, the layout of the building and reconstructed functions of particular rooms are comparable. As a rule, these were single-space buildings. Downstairs and upstairs there were utility and service rooms for residential and representative purposes. These observations

54 Ibid, pp. 47–48.

55 Ibid…

56 L. Kajzer, *Studia nad świeckim budownictwem obronnym województwa łęczyckiego…*, pp. 25 et seq., 135 et seq.

led to further conclusions: keeps erected on mounds were typical for vast areas of Europe and their emergence and functioning can be connected with a particular stage of development of the feudal society. It was a certain peculiarity that in Poland, and especially in the Lowland (except from Silesia), wooden constructions were predominant[57]. In a further part of his work L. Kajzer dealt with the evolutionary development of the defensive seats of the knighthood, starting from a wooden keep built on a mount, followed by a brick manor house with a tower and finally to the early modern fortified mansions of the gentry.

The next works worthy of discussion in more detail are the publications of S. Kołodziejski[58]. The author drew attention to the fact that due to the geomorphologic features of the Lesser Poland, which is a mountainous area, there is a lack of the typical motte and bailey constructions in that area. Private fortified residences were situated in places that had natural defensive features, such as elevated planes or branches of mountain chains entering the flood plains. S. Kołodziejski called for, among other things, an analysis of the selection criteria for the preferred location to build the seat within the boundaries of the estate, taking into consideration the number and type of land features available on the plot of land. He emphasized that there was a close correspondence between the location of the keep and availability of the body of water, most frequently from a relatively small watercourse in the vicinity. In the case of uplands, he pointed that the preferred location was most often not a hill summit, but slopes with southern or south-western exposure. Areas with relatively fertile soil were of preference. As regards the location, S. Kołodziejski agreed with the earlier views that the residences were situated in the vicinity of major roads. Up to this point keeps had

57 L. Kajzer, *W sprawie genealogii wiejskiej siedziby obronnej w Polsce*, "Kwartalnik Historii Kultury Materialneji", vol. 20, 1972, no. 3, p. 454.

58 S. Kołodziejski, *Średniowieczne rezydencje obronne w zachodniej Małopo*lsce. In: Średniowieczne siedziby rycerskie w ziemi chełmińskiej na tle badań podobnych obiektów na ziemiach polskich. Materiały z sesji archeologiczno-historycznej. Bachotek 3–4 maja 1985, A. Kola (ed.), Toruń 1987, pp. 167–179; This is the extended version of the article written by this author: S. Kołodziejski, *La problématique des études sur les résidences fortifiées feodales sur le territoire de la Petite-Pologne occidentale*, "Acta Archaeologica Carpathica", vol. 22, 1983, pp. 161–198; S. Kołodziejski, *Średniowieczne rezydencje obronne…*

been attributed the function of watchtowers along communication routes. S. Kołodziejski claimed that the location of seats in their vicinity was utilitarian in nature. Roads leading to neighbouring towns, that is local trade areas, rendered the possibility of the convenient transport of surplus production. In favourable circumstances it rendered the possibility of customs houses rental, which guaranteed significant profits. S. Kołodziejski also suggested that blacksmiths' forges and metallurgical workshops often operated in fortified residences.

Another important issue pointed out by L. Kajzer[59] is the double function of towers as both defensive and residential. Apart from purely utilitarian functions, they also bore ideological significance. Together with the development of heraldic symbols, such keeps manifested the ambitions and exceptional position of knights as a privileged social group. In the same publication, when recapitulating the existing views on the genesis of motte and bailey residences, the author pointed that the issue of their disappearance is much less known. Based on the analysis of explored or verified sites, L. Kajzer presented a scheme of the changing forms of the motte and bailey households. In the 14th century, when safety was of the utmost importance, keeps erected on steep coniform elevated mounds predominated. In the second half of the 15th century, when the medieval knighthood evolved towards landowners and agricultural producers, the comfort of the residents and their needs became more important than the seemingly defensive character of their seat. The manor houses of that time had a horizontal layout and were located on larger and flatter mounds together with outbuildings. L Kajzer also pointed out the extended life of such residences, even until the 18th century.

The last decades have brought changes in the policy concerning the protection of archaeological monuments with the emphasis on rescue excavations. It has resulted in a considerable decline in the number of field researches of medieval fortified residences. At the same time we can observe significant progress as regards interdisciplinary research. On the one hand medievalists or historians of art and architecture have become more interested in the results of archaeological studies, and on the other hand, archaeologists have started to appreciate in full the significance of professional queries of

59 L. Kajzer, *Grodziska średniowieczne i nowożytne,* "Prace i Materiały Muzeum Archeologicznego i Etnograficznego w Łodzi", no. 36, 1989–90, pp. 33–43.

written sources, which has resulted in closer cooperation with historians. As a consequence, there is an increased number of publications in which history from written sources and excavation results complement each other and give a full picture of the manor houses in question[60].

60 L. Kajzer, *Średniowieczna i nowożytna Kościelna Wieś w świetle archeologicznych badań terenowych*. In: Kościelna wieś na Kujawach. Studium osadnicze, L. Kajzer (ed.), Łódź 1994, pp. 107–158; R. Grygiel, T. Jurek, *Doliwowie z Nowego Miasta nad Wartą, Dębna i Biechowa. Dzieje rezydencji i ich właścicieli*, Łódź 1996; R. Grygiel, T. Jurek, *Zduny...*; M. Proksa, *Studia nad zamkami i dworami ziemi przemyskiej od połowy XIV do początków XVIII wieku*, Przemyśl 2001; A. Nierychlewska, *Budownictwo obronne powiatu radomskiego w okresie od XIII do XVIII wieku*, Radom 2002.

III. ARCHAEOLOGY AND RELICS OF MEDIEVAL KNIGHTS' MANOR HOUSES

> "The one who desires to be called *dominus* needs to build up the prestige of one's *domus*, rising it higher and enclosing it with a moat to highlight one's extraterritoriality, and building a tower to support one's status as master; the estate itself must also be built in a solid way."*
>
> D. Barthelemy

* D. Barthelemy, *Zagospodarowanie przestrzeni prywatnej XI–XIII w.* In: Historia życia prywatnego, vol. 2, Od Europy feudalnej do renesansu, G. Duby (ed.), Wrocław 1998, p. 448.

1. Where Did the Knights Build their Manor Houses?

In the case of late medieval settlement studies the issue of geographic determinism seems to be less significant when compared with earlier periods. I feel obliged from the chronicler's point of view only to mention that these issues have been the subject of consideration in historical studies at least since the times of F. Ratzel[1]. A criticism of the monist approach to settlement studies was expressed mainly by the French school of social geography[2], which led to further discussions evolving between environmental and humanist determinism[3], that gave rise to modern historical geography[4]. A concise overview of the issues concerning the relationship between man and the environment in the Middle Ages can be found in the works of J. Tyszkiewicz[5]. Without going into further methodological considerations, we can say that throughout history, environmental resources were the most significant factor that determined the choice of the site for settlement. Environmental resources shall be very widely understood as the climate, soil quality, access to water and building materials, as well as food availability and also the exploitation of natural resources. In the Late Middle Ages the choice of location for a residence was considerably limited due to the private ownership of land.

Even the social elites referred to in this book had restricted choice options as to the land they owned. Certainly the choice was all the greater when the larger landed estates were in possession of a particular family or individual. When analyzing the preferences in the choice of the location for the seat, one should pay attention to what forms of terrain were actually available within a particular

1 F. Ratzel, *Antropogeographie*, Bd. 1–2, Stuttgart 1921 (first published in 1882) *non vidimus*.

2 P. Vidal de la Blache, *Principes de geographie humaine*, Paris 1948 (first published in 1922)

3 H. Łowmiański, *Początki Polski*, vol. 3, Warsaw 1967, p. 15.

4 G. Labuda, *Uwagi o przedmiocie i metodzie geografii historycznej*, "Przegląd Geograficzny", vol. 25, 1953, pp. 5–56.

5 J. Tyszkiewicz, *Człowiek w środowisku geograficznym Polski średniowiecznej*, Warsaw 1981, pp. 7–33.

landed estate. Here, however, our possibilities are considerably limited. Hardly ever are we able to identify the founder of the residence that is being excavated. Even if we narrow down the group of potential founders to a particular family, it is still difficult to establish the boundaries of their landed estate, in which their seat was located. There are even more difficulties in determining the number and distribution of all the landed estates possessed by a given family at a particular time and it requires cooperation with historians. Only after all such information has been collected, can we get any idea about which land was available when the decision concerning the location for building the family hearth was made. Such knowledge would provide a basis for a fuller discussion of the preferences as regards the choice of the optimal place for a settlement. Monographs concerning particular families, written by historians of the Medieval period, turn out to be incredibly useful for archaeologists in such cases. Mention must be made here even, as among the first, the dissertations of W. Semkowicz[6], Z. Wdowiszewski[7], or S. Kozierowski on knights in Greater Poland[8], S. Gawęda on nobility in Lesser Poland[9], W. Dworzaczek on the coat of arms of Leliwa[10], as well as monographs on the Tęczyński family by J. Kurtyka[11], on the Łabędź coat of arms by J. Bieniak[12], on the Grzymała coat

6 W. Semkowicz, *Ród Awdańców w wiekach średnich*, "Roczniki Towarzystwa Przyjaciół Nauk Poznańskiego", vol. 44, 1917; W. Semkowicz, *Ród Pałuków*, Cracow 1907.

7 Z. Wdowiszewski, *Ród Bogoriów w wiekach średnich*, "Rocznik Polskiego Towarzystwa Heraldycznego", vol. 9, 1928/1929.

8 S. Kozierowski, *Studia nad pierwotnym rozsiedleniem rycerstwa wielkopolskiego*, published successively in *Miesięcznik Heraldyczny* in the years 1913–1920.

9 S. Gawęda, *Możnowładztwo małopolskie w XIV i pierwszej połowie XV wieku*, "Zeszyty Naukowe UJ". Prace historyczne, vol. 18, 1966; S. Gawęda, *Początki i rola rodziny Lanckorońskich do końca średniowiecza*, Ibid vol. 89, 1989.

10 W. Dworzaczek, *Leliwici Tarnowscy. Z dziejów możnowładztwa małopolskiego wiek XIV–XV*, Warsaw 1971; W. Dworzaczek, *Hetman Jan Tarnowski. Z dziejów możnowładztwa małopolskiego*, Warsaw 1985; W. Dworzaczek, *Leliwici Tarnowscy od schyłku XVI wieku do czasów współczesnych*, Tarnów 1996.

11 J. Kurtyka, *Tęczyńscy. Studium z dziejów polskiej elity możnowładczej w średniowieczu*, Cracow 1997.

12 J. Bieniak, *Ród Łabędziów*. In: Genealogia. Studia nad wspólnotami krewniaczymi i terytorialnymi w Polsce średniowiecznej na tle porównawczym, Toruń 1987.

of arms by A. Szwed[13], on the Lis of Krzelów coat of arms by B. Śliwiński[14], on the Lanckoroński family of Brzezie by S. Cynarski[15], the Rawicz family by J. Wroniszewski[16], and many others. Publications with the records of the properties that belonged to particular families in a given territory are also of essential importance. Owing to the excellent works of S. M. Zajączkowski and A. Szymczak[17], Sieradz Land is the most fully elaborated. There are also publications concerning Łęczyca and Dobrzyń Land[18].

Unfortunately, even to obtain the complete information on the status of possessions held by historical owners is not sufficient in this case. Over the past centuries the intensive economic activity of man has caused extensive changes in the environment. A reconstruction of the picture of the environment from the Middle Ages involves vast expenditures of time involving a whole team of naturalists and geographers versed in various fields of study.

13 A. Szwed, *Ród Grzymałów w Wielkopolsce*, Toruń 2001.

14 B. Śliwiński, *Lisowie Krzelowscy w XIV–XV w. i ich antenaci*, Gdańsk 1993.

15 S. Cynarski, *Dzieje rodu Lanckorońskich z Brzezia*, Warsaw–Cracow1996.

16 J. Wroniszewski, *Ród Rawiczów. Warszowice i Grotowice*, Toruń 1992; J. Wroniszewski, *Ród Rawiczów. Współrodowcy Warszowiców i Grotowiców*, Toruń 1994.

17 S. M. Zajączkowski, *Wielowioskowa własność szlachecka w dawnych ziemiach łęczyckiej i sieradzkiej w drugiej połowie XIII i w XIV w.*, "Rocznik Łódzki", t. 9 (12), 1964, s. 119–143; S. M. Zajączkowski, *Studia nad wielowioskową własnością szlachecką w Łęczyckiem i Sieradzkiem i jej rolą w osadnictwie*, "Kwartalnik Historii Kultury Materialneji", vol. 14, 1966, no. 2, pp. 179–208; S. M. Zajączkowski, *O wielowioskowej własności szlacheckiej w województwie łęczyckim w XV i pierwszej połowie XVI w.*, "Zeszyty Naukowe UŁ" series I, vol. 60, 1969, pp. 79–104; S. M. Zajączkowski, *Sieć osadnicza i struktura własnościowa osadnictwa dawnych ziem łęczyckiej i sieradzkiej w początkach XVI wieku*, "Slavia Antiqua", vol. 19, 1972, pp. 19–80; S. M. Zajączkowski, *Wielowioskowa własność szlachecka w województwie sieradzkim (XV i pierwsza połowa XVI w.)*, "Rocznik Łódzki", vol. 18 (21), 1973, pp. 23–50; A. Szymczakowa, *Urzędnicy łęczyccy i sieradzcy do połowy XV wieku*, "Acta Universitatis Lodziensis". Folia Historica, vol. 20, 1984; A. Szymczakowa, *Szlachta sieradzka w XV wieku. Magnifici et generosi*, Łódź 1998.

18 T. Nowak, *Własność ziemska w ziemi łęczyckiej w czasach Władysława Jagiełły*, Łódź 2003; J. Bieniak, *Elita ziemi dobrzyńskiej w późnym średniowieczu i jej majątki*. In: Stolica i region. Włocławek i jego dzieje na tle przemian Kujaw i ziemi dobrzyńskiej. Materiały z sesji naukowej (9–10 maja 1994 roku), O. Krut-Hozonziak, L. Kajzer (ed.), Włocławek 1995, pp. 23–60.

This list of mounting up difficulties is not intended to be an excuse, as to why such deliberations are not very popular in archaeology. However, I would like to draw attention to the existing conditions that need to be examined, if possible. The most important thing, however, is perhaps the realization of the fact that we are trying to find reasons for actions and decisions that led to the construction of the residences that we are investigating, based on a considerably limited amount of information. This should encourage more the search for alternative explanations.

S. Kołodziejski conducted a thorough analysis of preferences as regards the options to locate a residence in the territories of the historical Cracow Province. In his opinion access to water was most desired, followed by safety aspects[19]. Although as regards geomorphology, Lesser Poland is considerably different from the remaining parts of our country, the observations of the author should be considered as applicable to the whole Poland.

It is a cliché to quote the well-known views that motte and bailey residences, considered to be the relics of knights' manor houses, were located in places by nature defensive and difficult to access. To summarize existing studies, it needs to be emphasized that natural land features were usually utilized to build a raised earthwork. Boggy valleys with small flowing bodies of water are considered to be the most typical location. Such a placement of the seat both provided access to water and ensured safety. However, it caused many inconveniences in relation to the investment process itself. Building an artificial mound to a few meters in height with a diameter often exceeding 40 m required the supplying of substantial amounts of construction materials. I do not mean soil, as it was obtained during the building of a moat. According to his observations, A. Pawłowski worked out that the amount of soil dug up during the construction of a moat corresponded approximately to the amount of soil needed for forming the mound[20]. However, a newly-built motte was not usually very stable, unless it was constructed of clay. Hence the frequent attempts at the stabilization of the mound using wooden or stone constructions. If the area was boggy, it was necessary to pave a road used

19 Ibid, pp. 30–31.

20 A. Pawłowski, *Jak budowano obronne siedziby rycerskie?*, "Z Otchłani Wieków", vol. 46, 1980, no. 1, s. 80; cf. T.J. Horbacz, Z. Lechowicz, *Fikcja czy rekonstrukcja? (w związku z artykułem A. Pawłowskiego),* "Z Otchłani Wieków", vol. 48, 1982, no. 4, s. 175–177.

for the supply of the construction materials. Wooden footbridges were most likely used for that purposes, but they had to be dismantled after the end of the building works and replaced with a construction that was easy to be destroyed in the face of a hostile invasion. Therefore it was a reasonable action to search for slightly elevated locations within wetland sites. Unfortunately, archaeological reports do not always provide such information as to whether the mound was built directly on wet terrain or on a slight elevation, or at least on a sandbank.

Now, let us take a closer look at typical mottes located in wetlands, but not necessarily in the valleys of small flowing bodies of water.

Most frequently the diameter of the base of artificial mounds is between 25 and 35 m, whereas the upper surface is between 18 and 25 m. It is difficult to determine the original height of a motte, mainly due to the destruction of its upper section, the boundaries of which are hard to identify. We can only come to the conviction that the height depended on the original form, which was decided to take advantage of. Most frequently the mounds that we can observe today are between 2 and 5 m high. The earthworks are almost always enclosed with a lowering in the ground that is interpreted as the relics of a moat. Most likely these are traces of the location from which the builders removed soil for the construction of the mound. Some of them were filled with water permanently and some of them only periodically. The change of hydrographic conditions due to subsequent land reclamation is an impediment when it comes to determining the presence of water in the Middle Ages. The examples of such hillforts are the sites in Będzieszyn, Golice, Karmin or Dziankówek, Pełczyska and Wilkanów[21].

The width and depth of moats also varied. Most frequently the moats were rather shallow and their average depth was 1–2 m. Sometimes, there are small uplifts on the external side of the moat, which may be interpreted as an additional defensive line in the form of a rampart. However, it cannot be precluded that these small embankments were formed as a result of the periodical cleaning of moats, when soil was taken out and discarded outside. Occasionally there is a visible lowering outside the moat that can be interpreted as an additional water obstacle (Dziankówek).

Large earthworks in hillforts are considerably less frequent. The present height of the mound in Nabyszyce is approximately 12 m, whereas the diameter

21 Academic papers with reference to archaeological sites can be found at the end of the book.

reaches circa 65 m. The current diameter of the base in Oleksów is 56 m, whereas the top *plateau* is 24 m and the height amounts to 5 m. The whole site was surrounded with a moat of approximately 10 m.

It was possible to make very good use of the defensive character of water obstacles, in locating fortified manor houses not only in wetland meadows but also at the confluence of two rivers (Taczów).

Very often the relics of medieval residences are located in the vicinity of modern manor–park complexes which were placed in the uplands (Ktery, Małków, or Strzałków). This demonstrates an adherence to the originally selected location. However, subsequent works connected with the construction of the more modern seats, especially in the organization of farm outbuildings or parklands may have changed the lie of the land to a considerable extent, which hinders a reconstruction of the geomorphological situation in the Middle Ages. Still it can be observed that moats surrounding motte residences were often enlarged and converted into ponds.

Now let us focus on residences the shape of which is slightly different from that referred to above. Still their location is similar, that is in valleys with bodies of water, most frequently in wetlands. Such settlements were encircled with ramparts, as a result of which they resemble ringforts. However, they are usually larger than typical motte and bailey residences. The diameters of baileys enclosed with ramparts reached up to 50 m (Książ Wielki).

In the foregoing paragraphs we have discussed the typical 'lowland' strongholds, commonly found in marshy areas near natural bodies of water. Another very popular method of constructing a mound was the use of a fragment of upland terrain, most often a promontory, jutting into a river valley. Such structures are most often referred to as 'promontory' forts. Obviously, this term is conventional. The site in Bebelno can be taken as an example. Undoubtedly it is located on a promontory between two river valleys, but it was built in the same way as lowland residences. The natural slopes were not utilized, rather a moat was dug and a mound constructed. [22]. What term should be used in such a case so as not to mislead the reader?

22 C. Hadamik, *Bebelno koło Włoszczowy. Wieś i siedziba rycerska w wiekach średnich*, Kielce 2004, pp. 72–127; C. Hadamik, *Średniowieczne dwory obronne w powiecie włoszczowskim*, Włoszczowa 2005, pp. 15–16.

In general, typical promontory forts were created by cutting off a fragment of a promontory jutting into a river valley. Such location of residences is relatively common. In many cases, it was possible to reduce the work to making only a ditch. Sometimes, an additional rampart or one more moat was built. Usually everything depended on the existing local situation.

The more important issue, however, is the declaration as to why a particular promontory was chosen for the construction of the defensive residence. The answer is seemingly simple, namely such a location was to ensure security because access to the household was difficult. And here, it seems, that there were a few possibilities. First of all, the constructors utilized the existence of water obstacles, such as a river, lake or, as mentioned above, wetlands with difficult access. Very often however, a promontory jutted out into a river valley or lake basin, but it was so high that the presence of the water obstacle did not really matter. Security was ensured above all else by the considerable height and steep slopes.

Examples of lowland manor houses that were situated on a promontory in order to utilize a water obstacle are: Kłocko, Orszymowo, Wistka, Zagórz (Sosnowiec) and Wola Książęca.

There also exists a large group of residences located on promontories that have a considerably more complicated defensive system. For example, the manor house in Krzykawka is situated on a promontory jutting into wetland meadows. It is cut off by a 7-meter-deep and 28-meter-wide moat with ramparts on both sides. The cone-shaped tip of the promontory is cut off with a smaller moat (4.2 m wide and 1.5 m deep). The diameter of the base is approximately 15 m. The second larger element has a shape more similar to an isosceles triangle with a side length amounting to about 40 m[23].

Medieval strongholds were hardly ever located, so it seems, by using headlands on lakes. Perhaps this was due to the lack of appropriate forms of terrain. However, the manor houses in Głuszynek and in Mrówki are situated on such peninsulas. Two other forts in Lubień Kujawski and Kleszczyn Stary

23 J. Pierzak, D. Rozmus, *Średniowieczny gródek rycerski w Krzykawce gm. Bukowno, woj. Katowice*, "Śląskie Prace Prahistoryczne", vol. 3, 1994, p. 125; S. Kołodziejski, *Średniowieczne rezydencje obronne możnowładztwa na terenie województwa krakowskiego*, Kraków 1994, pp. 152–153

are currently located on promontories that originally seem to have been islands not far from the lake shore[24].

We know of very few manor houses built on islands in natural bodies of water. The only one discussed among our sites, which is still located on an island today, is Ledniczka Island. The relics of the manor house comprise a mound with the diameter of 40.5 m located on a 150-meter-long oval island. In Petrykozy the manor house was situated on an island surrounded by branches of the Drzewiczka river.

The manor house in Zduny is yet another type of location. At present this is a flat oval elevation rising approximately 1.5 m above the surrounding area, with the diameter of the base of circa 40 and 46 m. It was built amidst wet meadows on the right bank of the Borownica river. However, initially the residence was surrounded with water banked up by a dike constructed on the river[25]. In written sources there is a mention that the manor house was reached by boat[26].

So far we have discussed the location of manor houses, in which water was an important part of the defensive system. Let us now focus on strongholds that enthusiasts of strict classification would refer to as 'highland manor houses'. In such cases, the elevated location of the residence in contrast to the surrounding area was of essential importance as regards the defensive character of the place.

Here we also have the 'promontory location' type, however in this case a headland was used from part of the hills towering over the area, which was then cut off by a ditch. We know a few examples of such sites. Some of them had more complicated defense systems. Most frequently these were additional ramparts built from the side of the upland as in Kopaliny Pogwizdowskie, Chrostowa, Łączki Jagiellońskie, Będkowice, Mrukowa, Słupia, Sobolów etc.

Sometimes convenient land features were utilized to gain much more terrain protected by fortifications. Most likely that was the place for outbuildings. The manor house in Mymoń is one of these examples. It is located at the tip of a promontory (60 x 120 m, height: 30–35 m) formed by the Wisłok river and its

24 L. Kajzer, A. Horonziak, *Budownictwo obronne Ziemi Dobrzyńskiej. Wstęp do badań*, Włocławek 1995, pp. 148–149.

25 R. Grygiel, *Wyniki badań archaeologicznych rezydencji*. In: R. Grygiel, T. Jurek, Zduny. Późnośredniowieczne i nowożytne rezydencje właścicieli miasta, Łódź 1999, pp. 28–29.

26 T. Jurek, *Właściciele rezydencji...*, Ibid, p. 255.

tributary. The width of the promontory at the narrowest eastern end amounts to 26.5 m. Within a distance of approximately 40 m from the tip of the promontory there is the first line of ramparts, the height of which is between 1–1.5 m. Behind this line there is a wide moat with the depth of circa 8 m. This separated eastern part of the hill is known as 'The Castle'. Further west at a distance of 85 m there are the remains of the second line of ramparts with a four-meter deep moat behind. At a distance of between 20 and 40 m in the same direction there is an elevation, referred to by researchers as the third line of ramparts[27].

Construction site preparation methods as regards manor houses located on upland promontories are much more diverse. Starting with the separation of a certain upland area by a ditch, through to the use of a dry moat, even the construction of a multiple system of ramparts or cuttings/moats. As regards the territories referred to in this book, such location of manor houses and utilizing unique land features were peculiar to Lesser Poland and Kuyavia. Compared to houses built on lowlands, such residences more often have irregular shapes due to the specifics in adapting the terrain available. Even more diverse are the size of such manor houses. Large, or even very large settlements were predominant, e.g. Kopaliny Pogwizdowskie with a courtyard of 48 x 60 m, Łączki Jagiellońskie with a courtyard diameter of 50 m or Mrukowa with a courtyard of 22 x 50 m.

Still the most typical 'highland' position for the manor house was in the use of a hill dominating the surroundings. With this type of location we are dealing with a number of strongholds such as Janków Dolny, Kowala Stępocina, Rzeczków, or Sromowce Wyżne. Similar to those residences referred to earlier, it is also necessary to classify strongholds located on hills as large in size.

Apart from the above listed sites, it is hard to determine the initial location of many landed estates due to the extensive transformation of the region by human activity, especially if subsequent residences were built at the same location or in the close vicinity. Most frequently such buildings were located within the confines or along the edge of a park enclosing the manor house. Garden arrangement works affected the flow of watercourses extensively and also changed the location of ponds. Old moats disappeared and new ones were built in places where none had existed before.

27 J. Marszałek, *Katalog grodzisk...*, pp. 149–50.

An example of such a site is the manor house in Kalinowa. The modern palace is surrounded with canals running into a large pond from the garden elevation. In this pond there is an island (with a diameter of circa 36 m) on which a fortified residence was built in the Middle Ages.

The foregoing deliberations are an attempt at analyzing the preferences as regards the choice of land features that were adapted in order to build a safe residence. Now it is necessary to devote a few words about the forms, how the place was chosen for the intended construction site as a result of direct investment activities.

Most frequently the shape of the mound bases was circular or oval, but we also come across descriptions about households built on a quadrilateral plan. The majority of such constructions are described as "an irregular quadrilateral with rounded corners". Examples of such strongholds are found in Czułczyce, Borówek, Orłów, and Kościelna Wieś. My studies have demonstrated however, that it is only the base that has a quadrilateral shape. So far I have not come across a geodesic plan of a residence with the mound or ramparts built along quadrangle plans with a quadrangle top plateau, the dating of which would be indisputably medieval and that was not transformed during subsequent periods. The fact that some strongholds currently have bases that are close to a quadrilateral might have been caused as a result of the ploughing up of slopes during the cultivation of land in present times or in the past. It seems, therefore, that mounds built on a quadrilateral plan with a quadrangular plateau emerged on these territories only in the early modern era. However, it is hard to take a stance on similar descriptions of Silesian or Pomeranian strongholds or to propose typological classification for them[28].

It is obvious that the majority of manor houses were surrounded with moats and sometimes even with ramparts. However, it needs to be emphasized that it is hard to differentiate between the actual remains of intentionally built ramparts or a dumping site for the disposal of soil from the construction of a moat, especially if the relics are barely visible. We are aware of the fact that

28 J. Olczak, K. Siuchniński, *Typologische Klassifikation der frühmittelalterlichen Burganlagen in Mittelpommern,* "Ethnografisch-Archäologische Zeitschrift", vol. 16, 1975, pp. 443–474; A. Pawłowski, *Z badań grodzisk średniowiecznych województwa wrocławskiego,* "Sprawozdania Archeologiczne", vol. 30, 1978, pp. 241–257.

the material used for the construction of the mound came from the moat. Yet, we should not forget that the ditch, even if irrigated periodically, would fill gradually with silt and needed to be cleared and deepened from time to time. This is how such embankments might have occurred and which we interpret today as the remains of ramparts.

Apart from the most frequent forms mentioned above, there were also defensive forts built on a more complex plan or strongholds with solid embankments constructed instead of a mound. In such a situation, additional embankments were often built to also secure outbuildings, such as in Kępno or Kozłów, where the oval earthwork (60 x 80 m) raises at present 1 m above the surrounding land. The actual residence was situated on the mound with an elliptical base (30 x 50 m), surrounded by a 16-meter-wide moat. It was accompanied by a bailey at the south side and enclosed with a moat. The entire settlement was encircled with ramparts connected with two causeways to ensure access to the seat. A wooden bridge was used for communicating between the two parts of the settlement[29]. On the other hand, the settlement in Sobota was most likely surrounded by three moats. However, more strongly developed defensive systems were rather rare.

Excavations provide us with information on the various methods of mound construction. Most frequently it was built of sand with clay or stone admixture. Various internal constructions were implemented to prevent the slopes from subsiding. Nevertheless, detailed descriptions of such constructions are relatively rare in archaeological excavation reports, most likely due to the limited range of exploration. As a consequence, the information provided sometimes needs to be treated with a certain amount of distrust. A description of the mound construction method based on one or two small trenches is not always reliable. A narrow survey trench cutting through the entire mound does not necessarily give us the full picture of stratigraphy. For me personally, an extreme learning experience were the excavations of a 'typical motte' residence in Gruszczyce. Not until the second season of exploration, did archaeologists manage to observe and interpret correctly the accumulation of layers, and that was only after they uncovered a place with barely visible thin streaks of rotten

29 S. Kołodziejski, *Obronne rezydencje Lisów w północnej Małopolsce. Uwagi do problematyki badań*, "Acta Universitatis Lodziensis", Folia Archaeologica, vol. 18, 1994, p. 68.

wood separated with sand-clay material that differed only in color. Thorough observation of traces of the wooden construction we were led to the conclusion that the mound was built of trapezoid boards in the shape of 'boxes' arranged in a radial pattern at the edges of the slopes[30].

The excavations of 'typical motte' residences have provided a lot of interesting information as regard their construction. The fact that the mound was reinforced with a wooden filling was demonstrated in the course of excavation works carried out on numerous sites. Most frequently the filling was constructed of horizontal logs and piles driven into marshy land. In many places sandy mounds were often reinforced with clay.

Sometimes excavation reports inform of the reinforcement of a mound with stones, we are dealing with this situation in the case of Karmin, Jarocin and Kłocko.

We are least likely to encounter planned residences erected on landforms which are almost entirely man-made. An example of such a situation is the manor house in Szydłowiec, which was located amidst backwaters of a river on an artificial island reinforced with thick board planking and reinforced piles.

In the Late Middle Ages, it is not very often that we can observe the 'journey' of a manor house within a single estate. An example of such a site maybe the residence in Kościerzyn. The earlier manor house, dating back to the first half of the 14th century, was located among riverside meadows on a typical motte, with the approximate diameter of 15 x 18 m, and was surrounded with a ditch. During excavation works it was determined that at the end of the 14th century the manor house was destroyed as a result of fire. Shortly afterwards, probably around the year 1400 another motte residence with a wide moat was built in the same village, but on a more elevated location (currently the manor park). This time the diameter of the *plateau* exceeded 32 m.

Lack of precision dating of particular structures hinders the possibility of investigating how the form of mounds for the construction of medieval manor houses was changing through time. We can only take a closer look at certain phenomena, but cannot be certain that they represent general trends.

30 A. Marciniak-Kajzer, T. J., Horbacz, *Sprawozdanie z badań archeologicznych przeprowadzonych w roku 1995 w miejscowości Gruszczyce gm. Błaszki woj. sieradzkie*, "Sieradzki Rocznik Muzealny", vol. 10 (1995–96), p. 122.

And so among the oldest fortified manor houses considered, that is those with origins that date back to the 13th century, and those which have not subsequently seen dramatic conversions in the following periods, the classic cone-shaped mounds seem to prevail. As a general rule the diameter of the mound was between 25–35 m and the present altitude is between 2 to 5 m. Almost all settlements were surrounded with a moat. As the mound is the element that is most prone to rapid damage, the widths and depths quoted by archaeologists seem to depict the state of preservation rather than their original height. Of course, this refers to sites in which examined moats were not excavated and relevant publications include only the description of relics visible on the surface. Amongst these typical mounds dating back to the 13th century, mention can be made of strongholds which include: Biskupice, Gniazdkowo (2nd stage), Golice, Jarocin, Karmin, Kiełbów, Klwów, Stary Koniecpol, Mokrsko Dolne, Radzymin, Sędziszów, Szczekociny and Wilkanowo.

Despite the very small amount of source materials, both as a result of limited excavation works and the fact that the majority of objects have undergone considerable transformation in the modern era, we know that the evolution of land features, on which the medieval knights constructed their manor houses, was very slow. In general we can only observe that the construction site was increasing in size. The diversity of form did not really change. The only visible difference is that smaller residences, initially surrounded with embankments, were converted into households on typical mounds.

As was already written by L. Kajzer[31] in his publications, the evolution of mounds was caused by the changing form of the manor house itself, which was considerably more distinct during the Early Modern Period and which is not within the framework of our deliberations.

The above mentioned construction site preparation methods for the fortified manor house prove that such undertakings required considerable investment, good organization of works and appropriate tools.

31 L. Kajzer, *Grodziska średniowieczne i nowożytne*, "Prace i Materiały Muzeum Archeologicznego i Etnograficznego w Łodzi", vol. 36, 1989–90, p. 33–43.

Fig. 1. The motte at Kiełbów Stary. Photo. A. Marciniak-Kajzer

Fig. 2 The motte at Trzemsze. Photo. M. Kociński

Fig. 3. The motte at Bebelno. Photo. W. Siudowski

Fig. 4. The motte at Witów. Photo. A. Marciniak-Kajzer

Fig. 5. The motte at Małków. Photo. A. Marciniak-Kajzer

Fig. 6. The motte at Kurzeszyn. Photo. A. Nierychlewska

2. Buildings within Knights' Residences

Let us focus firstly on archaeological sites in which excavations have revealed the remains of wooden manor houses and begin with the already mentioned residence in Siedlątków. Janina Kamińska reconstructed the buildings on the mound as a residential keep on a square plan with sides of 6 m. It was constructed of oakwood with the use of a log building technique[32]. In addition, the author suggested that the entrance to the keep was built with the use of post-and-plank technique. However, she did not specify exactly how these two types of constructions were combined together[33]. Presumably the keep was a three-floor building with the height of approximately 9–10 m. It was built partly with a basement, the dimensions of which were 2×2 m. The basement was recessed 1 m below the contemporary ground level[34]. Well-preserved log constructions were also discovered in Pęczniew, Chłapowo, Czarnuszka, Gruszczyce and Popów.

Excavations of the settlement in Kłocko revealed a rather more complicated building situation. The building located in the south-western part of the *plateau* of the mound had the dimensions of 4.5×6 m and its longer walls were oriented along a NW-SE axis. Its southern and western walls were erected with the use of a log building technique, while the northern wall was of a wattle construction. We have no knowledge as regards the eastern wall[35].

Much less frequently discovered are the remains of buildings with vertical constructions, indicated by wooden traces found in post-holes. Sometimes due to the small amount of wooden construction elements discovered during a field survey, it is impossible for a more precise reconstruction of the buildings.

A wooden house built on a square plan with sides of 5 m and erected with the use of a frame building technique is the oldest structure in the settlement in Stryków. It dates back to the period between the end of the 14th century and the second half of the 15th century. Another building located to the south-

32 J. Kaminska, *Siedlątków, obronna siedziba rycerska z XIV wieku*, "Prace i Materiały Muzeum Archeologicznego i Etnograficznego w Łodzi", vol. 15, 1968, p. 44.

33 Ibid, p. 39.

34 Ibid, p. 34.

35 B. Głowacka-Fronckiewicz, T. J. Horbacz, *Późnośredniowieczne grodzisko stożkowate w Kłocku pod Sieradzem*, "Sieradzki Rocznik Muzealny", vol. 8, 1992, p. 136.

west of the above mentioned house was constructed of horizontally placed boards. This is dated to the end of the 15th and beginning of the 16th century. Yet, there is a lack of more precise characteristics concerning the construction of the walls[36].

Excavation studies of the settlement in Trzemsze contributed to an interesting reconstruction of the manor house. Exploration of the extensive mound revealed the outline of a residential building (8×10 m), the shorter sides of which were built along a NS axis. Based on the analysis of the spatial distribution of artefacts, the interiors were divided into two parts and four rooms. Most likely the northern part of the building housed a workshop, utility space and a kitchen. In the western part of the northern side of the manor house there was a small workshop with a domed stove in the north-western corner of the house, where food could have been prepared. The southern part was interpreted as residential space. Official chambers were located on the eastern side, where the majority of metal objects were discovered. In the opinion of the scholar, the south-western part housed a bedroom[37]. Analysing this research M. Kociński, who performed the studies, suggested also that the attic was used for storage. Therefore craftsman's objects could be found in the southern part of the house after the building collapsed. It is possible that the southern part of the house was built with a basement[38].

The motte in Biskupice revealed the remains of clay foundations of a quadrilateral building (5×5 m). A similar situation was found in Orenice, where traces of the building erected on the mound had the form of sheets of wood strengthened and bedded in clay, with dimensions of 6 by 6 m and a thickness to approximately 0.6 m. The excavations of the settlement in Orszymowo revealed fragments of continuous footing 1.3 m wide and made of

36 B. Muzolf, *Stryków, st. 5–siedziba obronne właścicieli miasta Strykowa*, "Prace i Materiały Muzeum Miasta Zgierza", vol. 5, 2003, pp. 80–83.

37 However, the existence of bedrooms as separate chambers has not been confirmed in the course of studies over medieval houses, even in Western Europe; cf. P. Ariès, *Historia dzieciństwa. Dziecko i rodzina w dawnych czasach*, Gdańsk 1995, pp. 20–21; P. Contamine, *Problemy XIV–XV wiek.* In Historia życia prywatnego, vol. 2. Od Europy feudalnej do renesansu, G. Duby (ed.), Wrocław 1998, pp. 451–458.

38 M. Kociński, Późnośredniowieczna siedziba obronna w Trzemszach w woj. konińskim, Łódź 1995 (Master's dissertation in the archives of the Institute of Archaeology at the University of Łódź), p. 74 et seq.

stone and soil. This discovery was interpreted as the foundations of a wooden quadrangular keep coated with clay, with the side length of circa 6 m, embedded at least 1.5 m in the ground[39].

Small mounds were most frequently built up with a single building. The manor house in Gniazdków is an isolated case. It revealed the remains of five log houses. The floor area of two houses was circa 18–20 m^2 and their approximate dimensions were 2.6–3 m x 6.5–7 m. Two other buildings seem to have been similar. The buildings inside had two rooms and they were connected with gable walls and encircled the round bailey, the diameter of which was approximately 14–15 m. Most likely there were around eight buildings. Archaeologists also discovered the remains of a well and furnace[40].

The author of the studies of the site excavated in Borówek also mentions outbuildings accompanying the residential building. The remains explored at the site were interpreted by archaeologists as a smithy and possibly a pottery workshop[41]. Two log buildings were found in Staw (Szczytniki commune). They were 4 m away from each other and one of them was located in the central part and built of oak-wood. The thickness of wooden elements used for construction reached 50 cm and its NS wall was 6.2 m long. The second building was erected southwards and it was built of pine-tree logs with the diameter of ca. 15 cm. The length of its NS wall measured 5.6 m. The authors of the studies suggested that these are the remains of an oak-wood manor house and a pinewood outbuilding[42]. The site in Zduny revealed a similar situation. During the first phase of occupation there were two wooden buildings: one was slightly recessed in the ground (5.5×7 m) and it was interpreted as a manor house. The smaller

39 W. Szymański, *Przyczynek do badań nad problematyką grodzisk stożkowatych (Orszymowo i Wilkanowo w pow. płockim)*, "Kwartalnik Historii Kultury Materialnej", vol. 16, 1968, no. 1, p. 64; W. Szymański, *Sprawozdanie z badań sondażowych grodzisk w Miejscowościach: Biała, Orszymowo, Parzeń, Wilkanowo i Wyszogród (D. Drwały), pow. Płock w 1966 roku*, "Sprawozdania Archeologiczne", vol. 20, 1966, p. 233.

40 Z. Lechowicz, *Wyniki badań na stanowisku 1 w Gniazdkowie gm. Chotcza, woj. radomskie w latach 1985–86*, "Materiały Konserwatorskie. Badania archeologiczne w woj. radomskim – 1986", part II, Radom 1987, pp. 5–7.

41 A. Kosiorek, *„Dwór na kopcu" w Borówku wyniki badań archeologicznych*, "Prace i Materiały Muzeum Miasta Zgierza", vol. 3–4, 2002, p. 232.

42 J. Tomala, *Budownictwo obronne powiatu kaliskiego w XIV–XVIII wieku*, Poznań 1995, p. 135.

building (3.5×4.5) was located 10 m away along the NS axis and it was referred to as an outbuilding[43].

The site in Ledniczka Island, where archaeologists discovered the relics of three houses, revealed a very interesting building development. One of them with the dimensions of 4 by 5 m was located in the northern part of the mound. Archaeologists uncovered walls up to the height of 0.8 m that were erected out of three layers of stones bound with clay. However, there are no remains that would allow for the reconstruction of the higher sections of the building. The floor was made of compact clay on a stone foundation. The construction of the second building (5×8 m) was most likely done in the same way. It was located in the central part and it was 1 m away to the south from the first. The eastern walls of both buildings ran along the same axis. The floor in this house was made of stones and it was recessed 1.1 m below the ground level. The third building was 4 m away from the second one. It was an oval half-dugout (4–6 m^2) embedded 0.6 m deep in the ground. Archaeologists also discovered fragments of two walls built of stone bound with clay. However, their function was not determined. It was suggested that these might have been the remains of an unfinished building or fragments of a fence or even a low wall protecting the earthwork from sliding[44].

To recapitulate, taking the above mentioned observations concerning wooden buildings, it should be noted that log constructions were definitely predominant. The site in Dobrzyca is the only isolated case, where the authors were confident that they had identified a post-and-plank construction. In the case of three buildings the traces of posts implied an unspecified vertical building technique, for example, with the house in Dąbrówka. The only remains of a wattled wall were found in Kłocko, whereas wattle and daub construction was suggested only in Dmosin. The only reports as regards to frame construction come from Stryków.

The vast majority of the buildings were sunk below the contemporary ground level. Researchers have different interpretations of this fact. The first issue that should be addressed here, is in what way the houses were connected to the ground and what were possible foundations in the case of buildings erected on natural or artificial landforms. Claims about cellars sunk into artificial

43 Ibid, pp. 43–44.

44 J. Górecki, M. Łastowiecki, J. Wrzesiński, *Gródek na Ledniczce*. In: Studia Lednickie, vol. 4, Poznań–Lednica 1996, pp. 208–210.

mounds should be considered as completely anachronistic. As a matter of fact such opinions are only met occasionally. The vast majority of authors agree that as early as the stage of construction, houses were covered on their sides with soil from the earthwork that was built simultaneously. We do not know much about foundation practice in the case of wooden buildings. Only in a few cases have archaeologists managed to uncover additional structures that strengthened the foundations of houses. Walls were further reinforced by sinking vertical stabilizing posts, as for example in Gruszczyce. In the case of the manor house in Popów, the authors allow for the possibility that the entire bottom floor was buried and it served as foundations. In Chłapowo and Orszymowo glacial erratic boulders were used for construction, including for the foundations that were built without the use of mortar.

The type of wood used for construction was rarely identified and hardly ever can we find any mention on this subject in the studies. Based on very few references, we can conclude that oakwood was the most popular. Such material was identified, for example, in Siedlątków, Pęczniew, Gruszczyce and Popów[45]. In Popów archaeologists discovered mainly oakwood, but pinewood was also identified, which may imply that pinewood, the quality of which is worse, might have been used for repairs or reconstructions. The same situation was in Wola Piekarska, whereas in Gozdowo poplar was identified other than oakwood. In Jeziorsko, Trzemsze and Kakawa the buildings were constructed of pinewood. The settlement in Staw (Szczytniki Commune) revealed the remains of two buildings, one built of oakwood and the latter of pinewood. Hence the interpretation that the manor house was constructed of oakwood, whereas pinewood was used for an outbuilding[46].

The above mentioned deliberations show that a reconstruction of the building plan or wall constructions, especially from wood, evidently cause considerable difficulties. Yet, attempts at roof reconstruction are even more problematic. Hardly ever archaeologists encounter artefacts that allow for reliable reconstruction, as it was in Gozdowo, where two clusters of well-preserved pine

45 T. Łaszkiewicz, P. Wawrzyniak, *Popów – przyczynek do dyskusji nad funkcją niektórych gródków stożkowatych*. In: Średniowieczne siedziby rycerskie w ziemi chełmińskiej na tle badań podobnych obiektów na ziemiach polskich. Materiały z sesji archeologiczno-historycznej. Bachotek 3–4 maja 1985, A. Kola (ed.), Toruń 1987, p. 142.

46 Ibid., pp. 134–136.

shingles were discovered. Their length ranged from 69 to 81 (with the majority of 70–71 cm) and width from 12 to 15 cm. The thinner part of the shingles was approximately 0.5 cm thick whereas the thicker part reached up to 1.5 cm[47].

As regards the form of the roof, we can only make assumptions based on indirect premises, such as a large number of nails that might have been used for a shingled roof. For example, the roof on the building in Siedlątków, where archaeologists discovered 800 nails, was reconstructed as a shingled roof[48]. A draw-knife for shaping shingles was also found there as a confirmation of the assumption concerning the form of the roof. Similarly, the roof in Popów was reconstructed as a shingled roof due to a large number of nails discovered on the site[49]. The finding of roofing tiles is also rare. They are usually fragmented and their dating, that is, assigning them to a particular residential phase of the site, causes additional difficulties. During excavations in Jankowo Dolne archaeologists identified a ridge tile among the fragments of tiles and it was dated to the 15th century[50]. A piece of a ridge tile was also discovered during exploration of the site in Mokrsko. Yet, we do not know whether this should be affiliated with the first wooden phase of the settlement or with the second, most likely unfinished, stone phase of the site building development[51]. Fragments of monk and nun tiles were discovered in Kościelna Wieś and Karmin. However, we need to be aware that in the majority of cases, reconstructions of the style of roof are merely suppositions.

It is relatively rare that excavations unveil traces of entrances to buildings, especially if they were built of wood. In Wola Piekarska archaeologists found a considerably large board on the south side of a log building, and it was interpreted as a threshold[52]. In this case, the entrance would be located on the southern side.

---

47 E. Prusicka-Kołcon, *Drugi sezon badań na tzw. gródku stożkowatym w Gozdowie, stan. 1, pow. Hrubieszów*, "Archeologia Polski Południowowschodniej", vol. 6, 2001, p. 142.

48 J. Kamińska, *Siedlątków...*, p. 37.

49 T. Łaszkiewicz, P. Wawrzyniak, *Popów – przyczynek do dyskusji nad funkcją niektórych gródków...*, p. 139.

50 C. Strzyżewski, *Jankowo Dolne gm. Gniezno, woj. poznańskie,* "Informator Archeologiczny". Badania 1991, p.119.

51 S. Kołodziejski, *Średniowieczne rezydencje...*, pp. 160–161.

52 W. Hensel, Z. Hilczer-Kurnatowska, A. Łosińska, *Studia i materiały do osadnictwa Wielkopolski wczesnohistorycznej*, vol. 7, Poznań 1995, pp. 271–274.

In one of the log houses in Gniazdków archaeologists excavated the bottom part of a door opening. However, in this case, several houses were situated around the courtyard and location of the entrance was dictated by the location of the house in the larger enclosure[53].

When exploring a building, the lower floor of which was recessed in the ground, one should assume in all likelihood that the entry was not below the ground level. Therefore it is hard to expect that the traces of a door opening are found at all. However, there were exceptions to this. A very interesting discovery was made in the building, referred to as the second building, during the exploration of the manor house on Ledniczka Island. The floor in this house was made of stones and it was recessed 1.1 m below the ground level. Close to a northern corner of the western wall archaeologists observed a gentle 1.8-meter long slope paved with stones. Based on stratigraphy it can be claimed in all likelihood that these are the remains of the entry steps[54]. The settlement in Nowe Miasto revealed a similar situation. When reconstructing a wooden keep the author of the research claimed that the entrance led through a narrow corridor in the eastern part of the basement[55]. It can be also assumed that the first floor recessed in the ground was accessed through trapdoors on the second floor that was most likely entered through external steps. The examples of such trapdoors are known from Pęczniew[56]. Analogical solution might have been used in the residence of Poznań bishops in Główna from the 13th century, where a trapdoor made of oakwood was preserved after it charred in a fire and collapsed into the cellar[57].

Now a few words about the closest surroundings of the buildings in discussion. Not much space was left for development around the main

53 Z. Lechowicz, *Gniazdków gm. Chotcza woj. radomskie*, "Informator Archeologiczny". Badania 1986, p. 180.

54 J. Górecki, M. Łastowiecki, J. Wrzesiński, *Gródek na Ledniczce…*, p. 209.

55 R. Grygiel, *Dzieje rezydencji*. In: Grygiel R., Jurek T., Doliwowie z Nowego Miasta nad Wartą, Dębna i Biechowa. Dzieje rezydencji i ich właścicieli, Łódź 1996, p. 27.

56 J. Kamińska, *Grodziska stożkowate śladem posiadłości rycerskich XIII–XIV w.*, "Prace i Materiały Muzeum Archeologicznego i Etnograficznego w Łodzi", vol. 13, 1966, p. 52.

57 P. Wawrzyniak, *Średniowieczna rezydencja biskupów poznańskich w Głównej w świetle badań archeologicznych w latach 2004–2005*. In: Nie tylko archeologia, E. Cnotliwy, A. Janowski, K. Kowalski, S. Słowiński (eds.), Szczecin 2006, pp. 322–323.

building located on a typical mound. Therefore, we hardly ever encounter any outbuildings or facilities. We have already mentioned residences, where archaeologists identified more than one building. It should be noted that most often these were usually relatively large settlements, although there are also discoveries of outbuildings located on small *plateaus* of typical mounds.

An interesting discovery made on the site in Gruszczyce may be used as an example. On a relatively small *plateau* (18×20 m) north-west to a log building archaeologists discovered the traces of a roofed hearth enclosed with a light construction. Around the hearth surrounded with glacial boulders there were the remains of five quadrilateral (20×20 cm) posts that most likely supported the roofing. The function of this structure has never been determined[58].

It is also hard to interpret the findings from the site in Dąbrówka. Exploration in the central part of the courtyard with a diameter of 13 m revealed the traces of a building built with the use of posts (7×7 m). Next to it towards the north archaeologists uncovered a furnace, the function of which remains unclear. The dimensions of the furnace were 0.8×1 m and its surface was covered with fragments of vessels dated to the 12th and 13th centuries. A hearth adjoined the furnace on the eastern side and it was slightly lower compared to the interior of the furnace. Three channels with a diameter of 25×30 cm led to the hearth and the longest channel measured 2.5 m[59].

We have no knowledge as regards the paving of the baileys. The settlements in Gruszczyce and Chłapowo revealed fragments of pavement built of erratic boulders. Traces of pavement were discovered in a few places in Wola Piekarska, including an area close to the entrance to the building[60]. In the case of three sites in Krępa, Jarocin and Pełczyska, the area in the direct vicinity of wooden buildings was paved with pebbles. Also the authors of the research in Dziankówek and Krępa speculate that pavement might have existed at these sites.

58 A. Marciniak-Kajzer, T. J., Horbacz, *Sprawozdanie z badań archeologicznych przeprowadzonych w roku 1995 w miejscowości Gruszczyce gm. Błaszki woj. sieradzkie*, "Sieradzki Rocznik Muzealny", vol. 10 (1995–96), p. 122.

59 E. Naumowicz-Śmigielska, *Wstępne sprawozdanie z badań wykopaliskowych na gródku średniowiecznym w Dąbrówce, pow. Poznań*, "Fontes Archaeologici Posnanienses", vol. 24, 1973, p. 251.

60 *Studia i materiały...*, vol. 7, p. 272.

Another issue for consideration is the functioning of enclosures around the buildings, which could have performed a defensive function as well as being used for order maintenance. According to oral reconstructions or drawings, buildings were usually protected with a palisade or fencing. Unfortunately, after a detailed examination of available research results, it can be stated that apart from embankments and moats, the discoveries of the remains of any defensive structures are relatively rare during excavations. One of the examples of such a structure comes from the settlement in Orłów, where during the first residential phase at the turn of the 13th and 14th centuries the area was encircled with a fence, the remains of which are poles dug in the ground every 50 cm. Most likely the gaps between the poles were originally filled with other wooden elements[61]. The enclosure built during the second residential phase was much better preserved. Archaeologists discovered 10 posts, the diameter of which measured between 15 and 20 cm[62]. The traces of a palisade were also uncovered in another trench, which allowed the conclusion that the size of the area closed with a stockade was probably about 35×48 m[63]. The remains of a surrounding palisade were also discovered during exploration of the manor house in Kunów[64]. The relics of a palisade were also identified in Zduny, which is at present a flat and oval elevation (40×46 m) rising 1.5 m above the ground level. It was determined, however, that initially the mound was slightly smaller and it was built on wooden padding directly on meadow humus. The edges were reinforced with stones and the palisade built of oakwood posts[65]. In their reports concerning the exploration of the settlements in Zawalów, Brzeziny-Trójnia and Szamotuły archaeologists also mention the discovery of traces of palisades.

An analysis of the existing research leads to the conclusion that traces of palisades are more often found on ramparts surrounding the settlements, than around *plateaus* of typical mounds. According to the analysed data

61 L. Kajzer, *Średniowieczny drewniany dwór obronny w Orłowie nad Bzurą*, "Slavia Antiqua", vol. 32, 1990, p. 257.

62 Ibid, p. 260.

63 Ibid.

64 T. Makiewicz, *Średniowieczne grodzisko stożkowate na stanowisk 5 w Kunowie, pow. Mogilno*, "Slavia Antiqua", vol. 19, 1972, p. 234.

65 R. Grygiel, *Wyniki badań archeologicznych rezydencji*. In: Grygiel R., Jurek T., Zduny. Późnośredniowieczne i nowożytne rezydencje właścicieli miasta, Łódź, 1999, pp. 28–29.

most frequently we expect to find traces of a palisade or fence directly around buildings. For this reason trenches are relatively rarely located outside the external line of the ramparts. Hence, we do not have sufficient information on any possible additional wooden defensive structures located outside the embankments built around the settlement. Quite frequently, however, we find mention of the strengthening of the slopes of moats, as for example in Kunów, Zawalów, Brzeziny-Trójnia, Popów and Zacharzew.

Summing up the above comments on the form of buildings and defensive palisades discovered within wooden settlements, leads us to the conclusion that the results of research seem to indicate that log buildings were definitely predominant. This conclusion seems to be confirmed by the fact that the few examples of buildings constructed using a different technique originated from ringfort settlements, for example, Bestwina, Dobrzyca and Krzykawka. Log buildings seem to be prevailing in typical motte-and-bailey settlements, which may confirm the widespread conviction that keeps were the most typical structures erected within such residences, as they were by far the most durable constructions. Among the buildings that are of interest to us, no similarity was found to a palisade construction discovered at the settlement in Plemięta, Chełmo Land[66].

The majority of buildings were embedded below the ground level of the time. Scholars have different interpretations of this fact. The bottom floor is attributed various functions and names, including a basement, an embedded ground floor, a dugout, or simply the foundation. The matter is further complicated by the fact that we are often not able to determine how deep the then ground level was in relation to the lowest usable level of the building. We can speculate that constructing a several-storey building on an artificial mound would be too risky. Hence, most frequently buildings were built on a more solid primary foundation that was graded or sometimes supported with padding or clay layer, which isolated it from moisture. Only at the stage of construction, the house was covered with soil, creating a typical motte. Unfortunately, there are not any remains of overground constructions, of course, in relation to the ground level from the time when the houses were occupied. Also we do not have any detailed historical descriptions of this type of buildings.

---

66 *Plemięta. Średniowieczny gródek w ziemi chełmińskiej*, A. Nadolski (ed.), Warszawa–Poznań–Toruń 1985.

Now let us examine the excavation results that led to the discovery of the relics of stone and brick manor houses.

The manor house in Wola Chełmska (Wola Justowska) is an atypical construction. As a result of archaeological and architectural research carried out in the present palace complex, it was found that the walls of the basement and ground floor are the relics of a medieval building. It was a several-storey building with a length of 26 m and with two rooms on both sides of the centrally located entrance hall attached to a tower built on the western side on a square plan with the side of 4.75 m. Walls were built of worked limestone and they might have been faced with brick above the ground level[67].

In Broniszewice archaeologists discovered the remains of a brick building (9.4×10.3 m) erected on a typical earth mound. The walls were preserved to the height of about 0.8 m. The width of stone foundations bonded with clay mortar was 1.15 m[68]. The building is dated to the 15th century.

In the 14th century the manor house in Chrostowa was a stone building on a square plan with a side of 7.5 m. Taking into consideration the large wall thickness (1.8–2 m) we can assume that most likely it was a keep. It was built of rough sandstone fitted with facing blocks laid directly on the rock with lime mortar. The keep was most likely accompanied by wooden outbuildings, the only remains of which is a burnt layer[69].

In Gorlice at the beginning of the 15th century, a long stone building was erected on a rectangular plan (5×21 m) on the edge of a river bank. Its bottom floor (basement?) most likely had a barrel vault. Probably still in the 15th century, a square building (7.5×7.5 m) was constructed next to it, with at least two-storeys. Both buildings were connected with a narrow corridor, which most likely housed stairs[70].

67 S. Kołodziejski, Średniowieczne rezydencje…, p. 196–7.

68 J. Tomala, *Budownictwo obronne…* pp. 62–63.

69 A. Jodłowski, *Gródek średniowieczny w Chrostowej, pow. Bochnia*, "Sprawozdania Archeologiczne", vol. 26, 1974, pp. 318, 325, 332.

70 J. Bogdanowski, *Obronna wieża mieszkalna dworu Karwacjanów w Gorlicach*. In: Architektura rezydencjonalna i obronna województwa rzeszowskiego w świetle badań naukowych prowadzonych w 25-leciu PRL, Łańcut 9–10 maja 1970, Materiały z sesji naukowej, Łańcut 1972, p. 160; S. Kołodziejski, Średniowieczne rezydencje…, p. 131.

Based on discovered foundation trenches in Iwno, researchers assume that they have found the remains of a brick building (8×8.5 m) dating back to the period between the 13th-15th centuries.

In the case of the settlement in Gozdowo, apart from a wooden log building, archaeologists encountered fragments of walls spaced 2.2 m apart[71]. However, it was not possible to reconstruct the plan of the building that was probably built between the close of the 14th and the beginning of the 15th century[72].

One of the largest brick or stone buildings erected on a mound was discovered in Potarzyca. The remains of a building were found in the northern part of the settlement. In the opinion of the author it might have been a keep (12×20 m). The thickness of walls reached 1.9 m, while their preserved height was 1.2 m. They were made of rough stones bonded with lime mortar. The corners that were not bound, were extended in the form of buttresses[73]. Thus, one of its longer walls, i.e. the northern wall was extended beyond the eastern and western walls, which in turn extended beyond the southern wall[74]. The manor house is dated to High Middle Ages[75] or to the 16th century[76]. Due to the lack of artefacts, a more precise chronological affiliation has not been possible so far.

The manor house in Siemkowice (9.8×10.2 m) was built on a mound surrounded with a moat. The walls thickness reached up to 2 m. They were built of rough or poorly worked limestone. Only the corners were made of slightly worked blocks. Most likely it was a three-storey keep. Its remains survived embedded in the north- western part of the subsequent manor house[77].

---

71 E. Prusicka-Kołcon, *Wyniki badań tzw. gródka stożkowatego w Gozdowie, stan. 1, pow. Hrubieszów*, "Archeologia Polski Środkowowschodniej", vol. 4, 1999, pp. 191–196.

72 E. Prusicka-Kołcon, *Drugi sezon badań na tzw. gródku stożkowatym w Gozdowie...*, p. 145.

73 J. Tomala *Późnośredniowieczne i nowożytne założenia obronne między Krotoszynem a Żerkowem*, "Archaeologia Historica Polona", vol. 15/1, 2005, pp. 250–251.

74 Cf. Ibid, fig. 8.

75 W. Hensel, Z. Hilczer-Kurnatowska, *Studia i materiały do osadnictwa Wielkopolski wczesnohistorycznej*, vol. V, Wrocław 1980, pp. 136–7.

76 J. Tomala *Późnośredniowieczne i nowożytne założenia obronne między Krotoszynem a Żerkowem...*, p. 251

77 M. Głosek, L. Kajzer, *Siemkowice, pow. Pajęczno*, "Informator Archeologiczny". Badania 1974, p. 260–261; M. Głosek, L. Kajzer, *Renesansowy dwór obronny*

As many as two medieval brick building phases were discovered during the exploration of the site in Strzyżewo Paczkowe. A brick building was erected here between the 14th and 15th centuries. The floor on the ground floor was also made of brick. Then at the end of the 15th century or at the beginning of the 16th century another brick house was built here with a clay dirt floor[78].

During the excavation works carried out within the existing Renaissance building in Wieruszyce, it was found that the oldest part of the manor house was located to the south of it. Archaeologists uncovered stone foundations (11×14 m), most likely dating to the second half of the 15th century. Part of that building was used in the 16th century as an extension to a new manor house erected around the year 1531[79].

Fragments of stone foundations were discovered within other sites, but it did not help to determine the plan of buildings or with more precise dating (Książ Wielki, Sienno, Biała Wielka and Zagórze (Mucharz Commune).

In the case of several settlements it was concluded that a wooden building was built on stone foundations, for example, in Petrykozy, where archaeologist discovered the remains of a building (8.5×8.5 m) dated to the second half of the 14th century and early 15th century. A thick layer of burnt clay was found above the foundation. Most likely it was pugging burnt in a fire and it covered the original wooden walls of the building[80]. In spite of the considerable size of the foundation, this led the author to the conclusion

w Siemkowicach (przyczynek do poznania przemian wiejskiej siedziby obronnej), "Kwartalnik Architektury i Urbanistyki", vol. 21, no. 2, 1976, pp. 153–166; L. Kajzer, *Pałace i dwory w dawnym województwie sieradzkim*, vol. 2, *Materiały do dziejów rezydencji w Polsce*, T. P. Jaroszewski (ed.), Warszawa 1994, p. 139–152.

78 C. Strzyżewski, *Strzyżewo Paczkowe, st. 37, gm. Gniezno woj. poznańskie*, "Informator Archeologiczny". Badania 1994, pp. 105–6.

79 J. Kozak, *Wieruszyce, pow. Bochnia*, "Informator Archeologiczny". Badania 1968, p. 407; "Informator Archeologiczny". Badania 1969, p. 405; "Informator Archeologiczny". Badania 1971, p. 299–300; "Informator Archeologiczny". Badania 1972, p. 289; "Informator Archeologiczny". Badania 1973, p. 297; "Informator Archeologiczny". Badania 1974, p. 291; T. Jakimowicz, *Dwór murowany w Polsce w wieku XVI (wieża-kamienica-kasztel)*, Warszawa-Poznań 1979, p. 122, przyp. 64; S. Kołodziejski, *Średniowieczne rezydencje…*, pp. 192–3.

80 W. Długoszewska, *Petrykozy gm. Białaczów, woj. piotrkowskie*, "Informator Archeologiczny". Badania 1990 p. 105; "Informator Archeologiczny". Badania 1991, p. 125–6; "Informator Archeologiczny". Badania 1992, p. 108–9.

that it was a wooden building. It seems, however, that the wattle and daub technique cannot be ruled out in this case. The manor house from the turn of the 15th and 16th centuries in Zameczek was also reconstructed as a wooden building on a stone foundation[81].

Relics that were discovered on several sites may not be interpreted as the remains of walled manor houses with absolute certainty. If only small fragments of walls were found, the difficulty lies in identification whether these are the actual remains of foundations, or perhaps only fragments of chimney draughts, or even underpinning for a furnace. This is how relics in Kłóbka were interpreted[82]. Unfortunately, authors do not very often specify their observations and write, for example, about "certain walled elements". In such a situation it is difficult to determine whether the term 'element' refers to a part of a building, a single wall, or perhaps only a chimney draught.

In the case of walled manor houses it is difficult to define a dominant, recurring model of building development. Both the size and shapes of the buildings here are very diverse. It should be presumed that the material used for construction depended mainly on the availability of raw materials, which is not revealed. Already in the Middle Ages there emerged a division in Poland between the southern zone with stone constructions and the northern using brick. Still in the case of manor houses in question we can observe a completely different phenomenon. Stone constructions prevailed on the whole area under consideration. Mentions concerning brick material were recorded only in the case of 6 sites, including Wola Justowska with a hypothetical brick facing of stone walls, as well as Książ Wielki and Żelazna, where stone and brick foundations were discovered. Only in the case of two sites in Iwno and Strzyżewo Paczkowe have archaeologists identified brick buildings. However, there might have been another possibility. Archaeologists usually manage to uncover only the lower parts of buildings, that is the foundations and these were rarely built of brick. If demolition was very thorough, the amount of brick fragments from a potential wall might

81 A. Nierychlewska, *Budownictwo obronne powiatu radomskiego w okresie od XIII do XVIII wieku*, Radom 2002, pp. 241–242.

82 T. J. Horbacz, *Dwór na kopcu w Kłóbce, gm. Lubień Kujawski, woj.* włocławskie. In: T. J. Horbacz, L. Kajzer, T. Nowak, L. Wojda, *Siedziby obronno-rezydencjonalne w powiecie kowalskim na Kujawach w XIII–XVIII wieku*, Łódź 1991, pp. 156–157.

be very small, which could be misleading. The issue of surrounding brick or stone manor houses with additional defensive elements is also difficult for a synthetic summary. We are dealing here with every possible location and the functioning of surrounding defensive structures which really do not differ from those discussed in the case of wooden manor houses.

The distribution of stone constructions on the map proves that they emerged not only in southern Poland, where the availability of building material was the easiest.

The vast majority of the manor houses in question, be they wooden, brick or stone, were either built on elevations, or were surrounded with various obstacles of different sizes, including ditches / excavations or water moats. This required the construction of additional facilities for relatively convenient communication. We can assume that different kinds of bridges and footbridges were most common.

Unfortunately, the remains of such structures are found rather rarely during archaeological exploration. Reports concerning such findings refer, inter alia, to the site in Krajkowo, where the remains of a 2–2.5-meter-wide bridge that led to the mound above the moat which was approximately 5–6 m wide[83]. In Kozłów communication between the manor house and outbuildings on the other side of a moat, was via a wooden bridge, fragments in the form of posts and boards were discovered during exploration of the moat[84]. A very similar situation was observed in Krzykawka, where the manor house also had two parts. The remains of a bridge, about 2 m wide, were discovered in the inner moat. The construction was supported on four posts in the corners. On the side of the mound, two posts had a stone lining at the bottom[85]. In the western part of the mound in Kunowo, archaeologists discovered an abutment of a bridge jutting 2 m into the moat. It was built of clay that was left after moat digging works[86].

83 P. Śniady, *Krajkowo, gm. Mosina, woj. poznański*, "Informator Archeologiczny". Badania 1991, p. 121.

84 S. Kołodziejski, *Średniowieczne rezydencje…*, p. 149.

85 J. Pierzak, D. Rozmus, *Średniowieczny gródek rycerski w Krzykawce, gm. Bukowno, woj. Katowice*, "Śląskie Prace Prahistoryczne", vol. 3, 1994, p. 125.

86 T. Makiewicz, *Średniowieczne grodzisko stożkowate na stanowisku 5 w Kunowie…*, p. 230.

Another area which should be given more consideration are the outbuildings of manor houses. Unfortunately, the current state of research is not impressive. Despite repeated appeals for not restricting the excavation area just to the location where archaeologists expect to find the manor house, but to also attempt to explore its closest vicinity, such actions are comparatively rare.

To begin our deliberations, let us consider the question about the possibility of distinguishing the remains of outbuildings from residential constructions *sensu stricto*. This question is most essential when we discover the remains of more than one building during excavations. It happens comparatively rarely during the exploration of motte-and-baileys. The small size of artificial mounds usually did not allow for the construction of a larger number of buildings.

In the case of mounds which have the remains of more than one building, sometimes archaeologists have managed to determine their potential function. In Mrówki, where three semi-recessed dugouts were discovered, the largest one was considered to be a residential construction, while two others were interpreted as pottery and blacksmith workshops[87]. Within the settlement in Orłów (phase 2) archaeologists discovered three wooden buildings, two of which were interpreted as outbuildings[88].

Only in a few cases, archaeological excavations of manor houses extended to neighbouring areas in search for accompanying villages or farms.

During the exploration of the manor house in Orenice, survey trenches were also located on two hills located within a 50-meter radius from the mound. Traces of accompanying settlements were identified on one of them[89]. Also in Kościelna Wieś several trenches were located in the place of the medieval settlement built in the immediate vicinity of the manor house[90]. A similar survey was carried out in Gruszczyce and Smogulec.

87 Ł. i A. Nowakowie, *Mrówki, pow. Konin,* "Informator Archeologiczny". Badania 1971 p. 254.

88 L. Kajzer, *Średniowieczny drewniany dwór obronny w Orłowie...*, p. 259.

89 L. Kajzer, *Orenice gm. Piątek, woj. płockie,* "Informator Archeologiczny". Badania 1987, pp. 201–2.

90 L. Kajzer, *Średniowieczna i nowożytna Kościelna Wieś w świetle archeologicznych badań terenowych*. In: Kościelna wieś na Kujawach. Studium osadnicze, L. Kajzer (ed.), Łódź 1994, pp. 107–158.

The excavations in Szamotuły were considerably more extensive. South of the settlement there is a hill 150 m long and 50–60 m wide, and the height of which reaches up to 5 m. Exploration revealed the remains of buildings that surrounded the manor house within a vicinity of 100 m. Archaeologists identified the remains of a wooden residential building without a basement (6×7 m) with a clay stove, a wooden outbuilding with a basement (4.5×6 m) and a semi-recessed dugout. Artefacts discovered within the site seem to be typical of the material found within manor houses, including, among other things, a fragment of a silver plated iron spur with balls at the end of the neck, a horseshoe and a fragment of the tip of a spear[91].

In Nowe Miasto, near the mound with remains of a wooden keep there is a clearly a visible external settlement. A detailed field survey revealed traces of a settlement contemporary to the keep. The author of the studies interpreted these traces as the remains of the actual manor house, claiming that the keep on the mound served only as the 'place of last defense'[92].

Excavation in Jankowo Dolne was expanded to a considerable extent, including the penetration of three hills in the vicinity of the elevation, where the remains of the medieval manor house were discovered. On one of the hills archaeologists discovered the remains of a church and cemetery, while on two others intensive residential traces dating back to the Middle Ages[93].

Around the settlement in Karsznice, field survey covered the area of around 6 km^2, which led to the discovery of 7 sites with settlement traces dating back to the Late Middle Ages, which could have been outbuildings[94]. Similarly, in Wola Piekarska, a field survey enabled archaeologists to locate settlements contemporary to the manor house to a distance of approximately 200 m to the west[95].

91 E. Krause, *Badania archeologiczne grodziszczka w Szamotułach w woj. poznańskim*. In: Średniowieczne siedziby rycerskie w ziemi chełmińskiej na tle podobnych obiektów na ziemiach polskich, Toruń 1987, pp. 131–135.

92 R. Grygiel, *Dzieje rezydencji…*, p. 245.

93 C. Strzyżewski, *Jankowo Dolne gm. Gniezno, woj. poznańskie*, "Informator Archeologiczny". Badania 1990, p. 98; "Informator Archeologiczny". Badania 1991, p. 119; "Informator Archeologiczny". Badania 1992, pp. 100–101.

94 P. Świątkiewicz, *Późnośredniowieczne grodzisko w Karsznicach, woj. płockie*, "Prace i Materiały Muzeum Archeologicznego i Etnograficznego w Łodzi", Seria Archeologiczna, vol. 35, 1988, pp. 153–4.

95 *Studia i materiały…*, vol. 7, p. 274.

3. Furnishings and Interior Fittings of Manor Houses

The equipment found in manor houses investigated by us can be discussed not only on the basis of discovered artefacts, but also in relation to stratigraphic systems observed at the site. Still, it is only a very small section of past reality that is potentially available in our perception. On the other hand, it is hard to consider some of the artefacts that have found their way into our hands as 'furnishings and interior fittings' of a manor house. A considerable number of the items were in general related to their residents. However, it is difficult to determine the precise criteria for categorization. Hence, this title should be considered as rather symbolic.

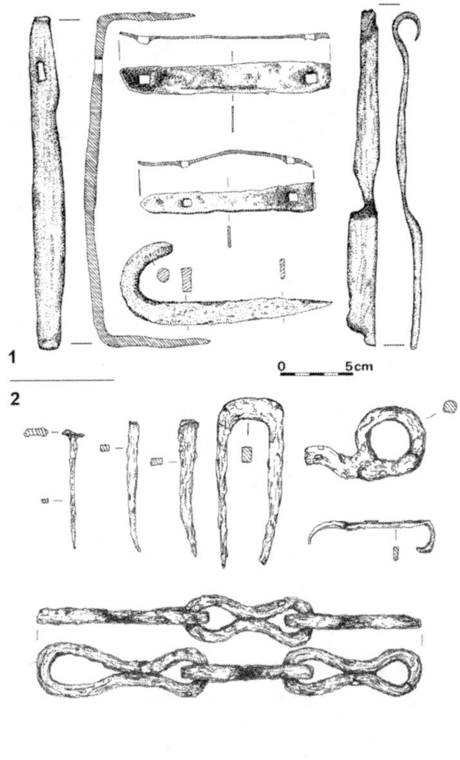

Fig. 7. Construction accessories. 1. Krzykawka. After: E. Szydłowska, *Średniowieczny gródek w Krzykawce…*, fig. 7, p. 153; 2. Trzemsze. After: M. Kociński, *Późnośredniowieczna siedziba obronna w Trzemszach…*, tab. XXIV, XXV.

In the above sections we have made an attempt to reconstruct manor houses based on the picture that we get from excavations. Now, let us focus on all kinds of elements that are fixed in buildings, such as windows, doors or floors. We have very limited data as regards windows. Based on written sources and iconography we know that during the time period under consideration the technique of making windows of crown glass mounted in lead cames was used[96]. It seems, however, that this 'technological innovation' had not reached the knight's manor houses in Poland of the time. There are no mentions of any crown glass findings or lead cames that supported small sections of glass, or even lumps of this metal that would have remained especially if a building was burnt down in fire, which happened quite frequently. The manor house on Ledniczka Island is an isolated example, in the case of which the authors have suggested that a piece of glass found by them might have been a fragment of a windowpane[97].

Membranes or animal hide as well as other organic material used for covering openings in the house decayed very quickly, and hence archaeologists hardly ever encounter such findings. For the time being archaeology has not contributed anything revealing on the subject. During excavation works in Radoszki, Chełmno Land, archaeologists encountered an interesting find dated back to the $14^{th}/15^{th}$ century and is worth mentioning here. This is an iron object identified as a window fitting[98].

Our knowledge as regards doors is not much better. Even to locate the entrance within the discovered remains of a house is most often impossible. The find in Chrostowa, where archaeologists discovered a fragment of a stone portal among the relics of a sandstone building[99], is of very special importance.

Most frequently iron fittings, locks, staples and keys are the only elements found during excavations that can be hypothetically affiliated with doors.

Fittings discovered during such excavations are usually heavily damaged and very often it is difficult to reconstruct their original form. Therefore we do not have

96 Cf comments – A. Wyrobisz, *Szkło w Polsce od XIV do XVII w.*, Wrocław 1968.

97 J. Górecki, M. Łastowiecki, J. Wrzesiński, *Gródek na Ledniczce...*, p. 233.

98 K. Grążawski, *Późnośredniowieczny gródek rycerski w Radoszkach gmina Grążawy w świetle badań archeologicznych.* In: Szkice brodnickie, vol. 1, S. Bilski (ed.), Brodnica–Toruń 1988, p. 58.

99 A. Jodłowski, *Gródek średniowieczny w Chrostowej...*, p. 325.

a good reason to suggest that they were fitted on the door, and not, for example, on a chest. The size of an artefact is usually the decisive factor in the case of such interpretation. We can assume that a large and massive object secured the door. Smaller and more delicate specimens more likely protected personal belongings collected in all kinds of trunks. Yet we cannot be certain that our speculations are correct. Such fittings were found in Borówek, Budzynek, Chłapowo, Orenice, Rozprza, Stare Skoszewy, Zduny and in many other manor houses.

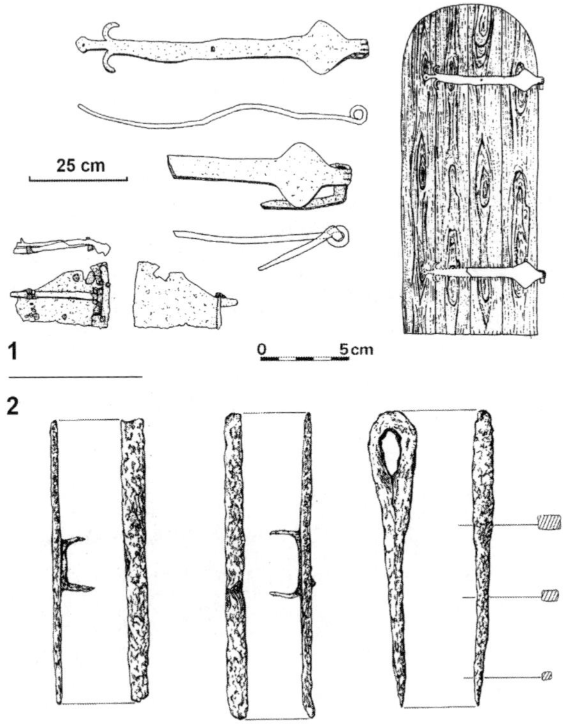

Fig. 8. 1. The iron door fittings and the reconstruction of a door based on the findings from Kozłowo gm. Sośniowice. After: J. Pierzak, D. Rozmus, *Gródek rycerski w Kozłowie...*, fig. 9, p. 31; 2. Bolts from Ledniczka. After: J. Górecki, M. Łastowiecki, J. Wrzesiński, *Gródek na Ledniczce...*, fig. 10, p. 208.

One of the most interesting findings of this type is described by the authors of studies of the settlement in Kozłów, however, it is located outside the area under consideration in this work. Archaeologists discovered there two forged metal fittings with a length of 80 cm. One of its ends was rolled up into a sleeve, in which a hinge was mounted. The other end was formed in the shape of a stylized lily and had a nail hole. In addition two iron hooks – the hinges - and almost the entire lock were found at this site. Such findings allow for a fairly reliable reconstruction of the door, probably the entrance to the manor house[100].

If the hinges and staples referred to above are preserved as fragments, which happens very often, they are difficult to identify. Most likely some of them are then described as 'unspecified iron objects'. Relatively frequently staples are identified. Such finds, sometimes even a few objects per site, were recorded, among others, in Chłapowo, Dąbrówka, Orenice, Orłów, Orszymowo, Wola Piekarska and Zduny. In Włoszczowa archaeologists discovered an extremely interesting find. One of four staples found on the site was made of a used horseshoe reshaped by thinning and sharpening its ends[101]. It seems that such a method was not an exception, and a similar practice involving the recycling of old horseshoes was already described in relation to the Early Middle Ages by J. Kaźmierczyk[102].

A hasp, which is a simple device for closing the door, has a very long history. It has been very common from the Middle Ages until contemporary times. Mainly due to the large variety of shapes, hasps are difficult to identify, especially oval specimens. It is likely that many iron links found during excavations were part of a hasp. Plate hasps are much easier for identification. Unfortunately, in their short reports, authors very often provide information limited to the fact of finding a hasp, without specifying its type. Therefore, it is impossible to determine which type of a hasp was more common.

Two oval hasps were found on the sites in Trzemsze and Jarocin and plate specimens were recorded in Smogulec and Kozłów. In Jarocin archaeologists also discovered bone objects, described by the author as plugs for hasps[103].

---

100 J. Pierzak, D. Rozmus, *Gródek rycerski w Kozłowie, gm. Sośnicowice*, "Rocznik Muzeum w Gliwicach", vol. 11/13, 1997, pp. 21–37.

101 Z. Pyzik, *Grodzisko średniowieczne we Włoszczowie*, "Rocznik Muzeum Narodowego w Kielcach", vol. 19, 1998, p. 162.

102 J. Kaźmierczyk, *Podkowy na Śląsku. Studia z dziejów kultury materialnej*, Wrocław 1978, p. 13.

103 R. Grygiel, *Zarembowie z Jarocina w świetle źródeł archeologicznych i historycznych*, Łódź 1992, pp. 27–28.

Perhaps a wedge-shaped object with a round cross-section is another peg for a hasp. Its base was drilled in order to fix a buckle through the perforation. The buckle consisted of two circular frames with a small hole at the juncture[104]. This artefact was discovered during excavations at the site in Orenice.

Keys are quite frequent artefacts found during exploration. However, usually we are not certain whether they were used to lock a door, or maybe trunks with precious belongings. Sometimes, as in the case of fittings, the size-criterion is applied, that is, the larger and more massive keys are considered to have been used in door locks, whereas smaller ones are affiliated with chests. Keys were found on the sites in Będkowice, Jarocin, Orłów, Petrykozy, Pęczniew, Trzemsze, Tyczyn, Sędziszów, Włoszczowa, Zduny and Żerniki-Jaryszki. A large 30–centimetre long key discovered in Kozłów was interpreted by the authors as the key to the gateway[105]. If keys are found, it is obvious that locks must have been used too. Unfortunately such findings are extremely rare. Again, the state of preservation of iron objects is to blame. It is extremely difficult to recognize any lock elements from centuries ago among corroded metal lumps. As mentioned above, locks preserved in their entirety are unique. The only example that we can quote is a fragment of a large lock found during excavations of the manor house in Orłów[106].

Another, much easier way of closing the premises was the use of bars and bolts, that is devices operating on the principle of inserting a longitudinal locking element in a prepared hole. In the case of a bar, there was an opening through which a hook-shaped key was inserted. The bar itself had a number of hollows to hook the key in order to move the bar. I managed to find only one mention concerning such a key discovered in Rozprza[107]. However, they must have been much more common, the evidence of which are specimens from the

104 M. Kołaczyk, Gródek stożkowaty w Orenicach gm. Piątek, woj. płockie w świetle bada z lat 1986–1987, Łódź 1990, (Master's dissertation in the archives of the Institute of Archaeology at the University of Łódź), tab. IX/2.

105 S. Kołodziejski, Sprawozdanie z badań przeprowadzonych w roku 1987 w Kozłowie, gm. loco, woj. kieleckie, Kielce 1988 (Typescript in ROBiDZ archives in Kielce), p. 6.

106 L. Kajzer, *Średniowieczny drewniany dwór obronny w Orłowie…*, p. 282.

107 A. Chmielowska, *Rozprza we wczesnym i późnym średniowieczu*, "Prace i Materiały Muzeum Archeologicznego i Etnograficznego w Łodzi", vol. 29, 1982 [1985], pp. 181, 204.

settlement in Plemięta, Chełmno Land[108]. Here again the seeming rarity of finds may result from problems with the interpretation of discovered artefacts. The same applies to bolts. Again, these items do not have any distinctive features and they may remain unidentified in a mass of corroded iron objects. Therefore any mention of them is very rare. As regards the materials under consideration in this book, one bolt was found in Kozłów, and another one in the manor house owned by the provost of the Płock Chapter in Proboszczewice. Such findings were also discovered in Plemięta[109] or Bachotek[110] on Chełmno Land, as well as at the site in Radzyń (Silesia)[111].

The findings of objects that performed the function of a handle are very rare. Such an artefact was discovered in the manor house in Zduny. This is a semi-circular curved tape-like iron holder with nail holes at the ends broadened into an oval shape[112]. However, we cannot be certain if it was used for opening a door and not a chest or cabinet.

Padlocks are another device among the various methods of locking that archaeologists encounter during excavations. Most likely, they were used more frequently for closing chests, in which precious items were kept, than for locking a door. Yet we shall discuss them here in order to get a full picture of the subject.

Padlocks were known on our territories from the Early Middle Ages. They are relatively often identified among archaeological artefacts. For example, padlocks together with keys were discovered in Trzemsze and Zduny. A padlock decorated with brass was found during the exploration of the settlement in Kępno. Another padlock with traces of bronze ornaments and

108 A. Kola, *Żelazny osprzęt średniowiecznej wieży mieszkalnej w Plemiętach i jej wyposażenia*. In: Plemięta. Średniowieczny gródek w ziemi chełmińskiej, A. Nadolski (ed.), Poznań 1985, p. 66.

109 A. Kola, *Żelazny osprzęt średniowiecznej wieży mieszkalnej w Plemiętach...*, pp. 66, 72–74.

110 K. Grążawski, *Średniowieczny gródek rycerski w Bachotku na ziemi chełmińskiej w świetle badań archeologicznych*, "Sprawozdania Archeologiczne", vol. 40, 1988, p. 330.

111 S. Kałagate, *Średniowieczny materiał zabytkowy z przypadkowego odkrycia na stacji meteorologicznej w Radzyniu gm. Sława, woj. zielonogórskie*, stan. 10 (AZP 63-*19/74*), "Wielkopolskie Sprawozdania Archeologiczne", vol. 3, 1995, p. 233–234.

112 R. Grygiel, *Wyniki badań archeologicznych rezydencji...*, pp. 113, 123.

a key was discovered in Orłów. There is also a specimen with copper elements from Włoszczowa as well as iron padlocks from the sites in Kozłów, Rozprza and Barłogi. In Jarocin archaeologists found a key to a cylindrical padlock.

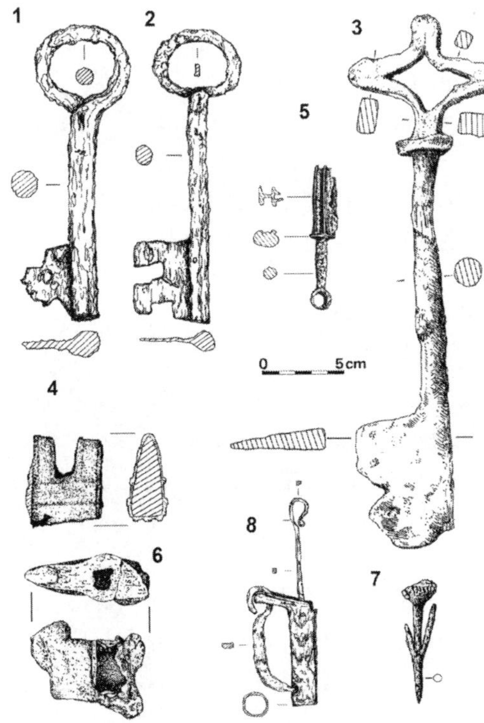

Fig. 9. Keys and padlocks: 1, 2, 8, Trzemsze. After: M. Kociński, *Późnośredniowieczna siedziba obronna w Trzemszach…*, fig. XXIV; 3. Kozłów woj. kieleckie. After: S. Kołodziejski; 4. Krzykawka. After: E. Szydłowska. *Średniowieczny gródek w Krzykawce…*, fig. 8, p.154; 5. Ledniczka. After: J. Górecki, M. Łastowiecki, J. Wrzesiński, *Gródek na Ledniczce…*, fig. 10, p. 208; 6, 7, Orłów. After: L. Kajzer, *Średniowieczny drewniany dwór obronny w Orłowie…*, fig. 17, p. 263.

The metal findings referred to above were usually made of iron, except for certain padlock elements, and they are the remains of devices used for locking a door or chest lids. However, we need to be aware that in most cases the door was probably closed with the use of various types of wooden mechanisms. The chances of finding them during excavations are essentially zero. We can only observe these types of mechanisms still functioning in some open-air ethnographic museums. The amazing simplicity and functionality of these devices convinces that they have not changed over the centuries.

The remains of floors are found during exploration of sites quite frequently. It seems that most often archaeologists encounter earthen or hard-packed clay floors, as for example in the manor house excavated in Krzykawka. In the case of the manor houses in Trzemsze and Jankowo Dolne, an earthen floor was identified only in one of the rooms in the building.

In many other studies, in which the authors recorded that they found a considerable amount of pugging, we can guess that it was the remains of the floor. However, as this opinion has not been expressed *explicite*, such cases cannot be taken into consideration. The remaining findings can be divided into two groups. The first category comprises of floors made of stones or bricks, whereas wooden floors belong to the second category.

The floor discovered in Chłapowo was made of cobble stones, whereas in Gruszczyce battens with a width between 28 and 45 cm and preserved thickness between 2 to 4 cm were used to build the floor. A similar discovery was made in Jeziorsko, where battens with a width of 0.10–0.15 m were laid on an insulating layer of clay.

Cobbled floor, most often made of pebbles, was discovered on a few sites, for example, in Wola Piekarska, Kościelna Wieś and on Ledniczka Island.

The occurrence of stone or brick floor seems to be much more natural in the brick or stone buildings. Unfortunately, there are only a few mentions on this subject. In Iwno archaeologists discovered the remains of a stone building with a cobbled surface in the basement[113]. In the manor house in Jankowo Dolne, one part of the ground floor was covered with a thick layer of clay forming an earthen floor, whereas remains of a floor made of poorly burnt 'Gothic' brick were discovered in the second part[114].

The presence of floor tiles was reported in Rozdrażew. However in this case some scholars put forward the construction of the manor house to the beginning of the 16th century. Therefore we do not know if the floor was built in the Middle Ages.

113 E. Naumowicz-Śmigielska, M. Grabska, *Iwno pow. Środa. Stanowisko 2 i 3*, "Informator Archeologiczny". Badania 1974, pp. 228–9.

114 C. Strzyżewski, *Jankowo Dolne gm. Gniezno, woj. poznańskie*, "Informator Archeologiczny". Badania 1990, p. 98; "Informator Archeologiczny". Badania 1991, p. 119; "Informator Archeologiczny". Badania 1992, pp. 100–101.

Another issue is how to identify iron structural elements of buildings found among artefacts, including all types of fittings, hooks and nails. Unfortunately, most often it is not possible to identify which building technique was used for the construction of a house discovered during excavations. Therefore, it is difficult even to presume what was the indented use of the items that are uncovered. For example, during the excavations of the court in Trzemsze archaeologists found 7 items defined as building cramps[115].

On the basis of archaeological studies we cannot say much about the appearance of interior walls, either in wooden or stone/brick manor houses. Pugging is the most frequent element found by archaeologists that may be associated with the finishing of walls. If pugging reveals any traces of wood, it is usually interpreted as evidence for the covering of walls with clay inside a wooden building. Such a situation was recorded in Dmosin, Jeziorsko, Stary Koniecpol and Szczekociny.

Archaeologists encountered extremely interesting finds in the case of two manor houses. Lumps of pugging with traces of incised ornament were found during exploration of the site in Jarocin. The small size of the discovered fragments did not allow for a reconstruction of the entire decorative motif. It is also hard to determine what surface was covered with the ornaments, and where they were placed. The author of the studies suggested that it might have been a decorative frieze on the internal wall in one of the rooms[116].

In Trzemsze archaeologists discovered a fragment of a ceramic tile decorated with a relief in the form of straight and arched lines. The preserved dimensions of the tile are 6.0×7.5 cm and it was only 0.8 cm thick. Therefore it was suggested that this element was used for facing the wall, as it was far too thin for a floor tile[117].

Clods and lumps of pugging are found very often during excavations. Pieces of more or less burnt clay, sometimes with imprints of wood, do not arouse any excessive interest from archaeologists, perhaps because the amount of information that they provide is actually modest. Most often we are not even able to determine whether they were a result of intentional human activity, or were created accidentally. The quantity and size of discovered fragments is

115 M. Kociński, Późnośredniowieczna siedziba obronna w Trzemszach..., p. 121.

116 R. Grygiel, *Zarębowie z Jarocina...*, pp. 12–13.

117 M. Kociński, Późnośredniowieczna siedziba obronna w Trzemszach..., pp. 70–71.

certainly of crucial importance in this case. If their quantity is significant and additionally there are clear imprints of wooden elements, it can be presumed with all likelihood that they were created intentionally, most often as a result of covering walls in a building.

Let us consider, however, whether the amount of lumps discovered is always large enough to be interpreted as residue 'plaster' that covered the entire walls. We need to take a closer look at a common reconstruction of a wooden keep. We assume that it was a small single-room two-storey building with the dimensions of 6×6 m and about 7 m high. If the average thickness of clay 'plaster' on the wall was 2 cm, taking into account uneven wooden material, the calculation shows that more than 2.5 m^3 of clay was needed for plastering walls. Of course, some of the clay that had not been burnt in fire, was washed out over the centuries as a result of atmospheric conditions and mixed up with humus. However, a large number of lumps was preserved in situ. They are small in size and their thickness does not exceed 2 cm. Sometimes we encounter mentions of large lumps of pugging. In such a situation, if they had been used for plastering walls, their total volume would have to amount to a few cubic meters. Such quantities are never found, though there are exceptions. We need to take into consideration another possibility as regards the formation of large pugging lumps. Probably in the vast majority, if not in all of the buildings in question, there was a hearth, used primarily for cooking, but also for heating and lighting of the interiors. As we know on the basis of iconography and ethnographic analogies, usually there was a hood over such a hearth to capture sparks, or sometimes also smoke extraction, although our knowledge on the functioning of flues is definitely very limited. Hoods, the framing of which was constructed mainly of wood, were pasted with clay on both sides. In such a case, the layer of clay had to be much thicker than on the wall to prevent ignition of the wooden structure[118]. Thus, if we find lumps of pugging of considerable thickness, but not in large quantities, presumably they can be affiliated with, among other things, the construction of various types of hoods protecting the hearth.

Archaeology can contribute definitely more data to the reconstruction of heating systems operating in medieval manor houses. Our chances to discover chimney drafts are very limited, and archaeologists in general cannot prove

118 K. Kwaśniewski, *Paleniska i piece w polskim budownictwie ludowym*, Warsaw 1963.

the presence of a fireplace. Sometimes, however, the remains of a hearth are found, usually in the form of burnt clay or a stone base. In such a situation, the difficulty lies in reconstructing the type of structure that was most likely built above the hearth. Stove tiles, better or worse preserved fragments of which are found quite often, usually carry the largest amount of information. There are also more spectacular discoveries, such as for example, the spot where a stove was originally located, or even more uniquely, fragments of constructions or objects that were a part of the hypocaust heating system.

The site is Jankowo Dolne is definitely one of the most interesting. During excavations archaeologists unveiled a building made of wood and stone (4.5×8.6 m). The floor was covered with a thick layer of clay. Here, along the north-eastern wall, over an area of about 5 m, archaeologists found *in situ* a 2.5-meter-wide heap of rubble that remained after a tiled stove, which yielded several hundred of tiles. In addition, archaeologists found a significant number of brick fragments and a clay ring that was a ventilating hole. Based on the analysis of coats of arms, the stove was dated to the first half of the 15th century. To the north of the above mentioned building, archaeologists encountered the remains of a brick hypocaust furnace. Further northwards, the remains of another tiled stove were discovered. Unfortunately, the extent of site destruction does not allow us to determine whether either of the two stoves operated simultaneously with the hypocaust furnace, possibly heating the same room or as an alternative source of heating, or whether the 'central heating system' was replaced with two tiled stoves[119]. So far the hypocaust furnace discovered in Jankowo Dolne has been the only such installation discovered during the excavation of knight's manor houses.

Furnace elements discovered during exploration of the site in Siedlątków were preserved quite well. Archaeologists reconstructed here two such heaters: one tiled stove located initially on the third floor, where visitors were entertained, and a dome-shaped one interpreted as a smith's furnace on the ground floor.

A similar, but even older heating system, dated back to the period between the 1430s and 1480s, is known from the settlement in Trzemsze. The local manor house was most likely heated with a stove made of vessel stove tiles with

119 T. Janiak, *Kafle gotyckie w zbiorach Muzeum Początków Państwa Polskiego w Gnieźnie*, Gniezno 2003, pp. 17–20.

round holes. A dome-shaped stove was used for housework of various type, and its traces were found in the north-western corner of the manor house[120].

Based on site excavations, we can conclude that most frequently furnaces were built of pot tiles. Tiles produced on potter's wheel were present on 25 out of 36 excavated sites, whereas plate tiles were discovered on 17 sites. There are also 10 sites where both plate and pot tiles were found. The latter group included both tiles in the shape of pots and bowls. Pot tiles had round, square, rectangular or clover-shaped openings, that was characteristic for almost all common types of tiles. The predominance of pot tiles should not be surprising, mainly due to earlier dating. They appeared on Polish territories in the second half of the 14th century.

To summarise the above information we must say that tiled stoves were quite rarely placed in medieval knight's manor houses. Therefore let us investigate other ways of heating residences.

Very often heaters discovered by archaeologists are referred to as hearths. Their descriptions are usually very laconic. Most likely these are the remains of fireplaces in the majority of cases. They must have been plastered with a large amount of clay if they were used in wooden buildings[121].

A fireplace was not only used as a heater, but also as a source of light. So how were the rooms illuminated if there was no fireplace?[122] Most likely residents used torches. However, such objects are very difficult to recognise in archaeological material, nevertheless we can find devices for fixing torches on the walls, as for example a specimen found at the site in Zduny[123].

Materials from the excavations also include objects having very similar shapes. However, they might have served other purposes, e.g. to extinguish the candle wicks or oil and tallow lamps without sinking them, i.e. lamp/candle extinguishers. In my opinion, an artefact that may be interpreted as a lamp/

120 M. Kociński, *Późnośredniowieczna siedziba obronna w Trzemszach...*, p. 17.

121 A. Marciniak-Kajzer, *Jak wyglądały późnośredniowieczne kuchnie?*, "Vox Patrum" vol. 59, 2013, pp. 449–161.

122 M. Dąbrowska, *Ogrzewanie i oświetlenie wnętrz mieszkalnych na ziemiach polskich w VI–XIII wieku*, "Kwartalnik Historii Kultury Materialnej", vol. 19, no. 3, pp. 370–398; M. Dąbrowska, *Oświetlenie i ogrzewanie średniowiecznych wnętrz zamkowych*, "Archaeologia Historica Polona", vol. 14, 2004, pp. 173–188.

123 R. Grygiel, *Wyniki badań archeologicznych...*, p. 194.

candle extinguisher comes from Włoszczowa, where it was described as an iron object ending with a sleeve[124]. Two slightly larger specimens of this type can be also found in the publication concerning the settlement in Plemięta[125].

I have not encountered any mentions concerning oil lamps found at the sites under consideration. Wax candles, were very expensive, and certainly were used much less frequently. It is extremely difficult to identify their traces in archaeological material.

Archaeologists rarely encounter objects made of organic materials during excavations, as a result of which our knowledge on furniture used in residences is limited. In fact, nothing can be said about tables / low tables or various types of seats or beds. We can guess that such furniture must have been used, because we know a few preserved specimens and iconographic presentations, as well as descriptions from a few inventories. However, there is one category of 'furniture', the use of which at manor houses is reflected in archaeological material. These are chests for storing precious items and these may be reconstructed on the basis of iron fittings, padlocks and keys, which are relatively frequent findings. Fittings may be easily interpreted as chest elements due to their semi-circular shape, for example, as found on Ledniczka Island, in Mymoń, Orszymowo, Smogulec, Trzemsze, or Włoszczowa.

On the basis of excavations we get quite a lot of information concerning kitchen utensils and tableware. During excavations archaeologists most frequently discover fragments of pottery. This source of information cannot be overrated. Unfortunately, due to its occurrence on a mass scale, pottery is often not treated with due attention and care. The accurate study, even sometimes of more than ten thousand pieces of pottery, requires not only a huge effort, but also the appropriate facilities (conservation laboratory, illustrator).

Attempts to introduce a classification of the fragments of ceramic vessels, which would simplify and facilitate their analysis, have already had a long history in Poland. These efforts have resulted in several regional typologies, which help in the comparative analyses of ceramic materials from different regions of the country. In this work, however, we will not focus on the theory

124 Z. W. Pyzik, *Grodzisko średniowieczne we Włoszczowie...*, p. 163.

125 A. Kola, *Żelazny osprzęt średniowiecznej wieży mieszkalnej w Plemiętach...*, p. 69, tab. II/12 and II/29.

of pottery studies. We will learn, however, what kind of vessels were used in medieval knights' manor houses.

As expected, pots are most frequently mentioned by the authors of studies. The frequency of the remaining categories of vessels will be mentioned below. Taking into consideration 95 excavated sites and excluding field surveys, the statistical distribution of vessels is as follows: jugs were found on 40% of the sites, bowls and small bowls were identified on 33%, lids were discovered on 30%, three-legged cauldrons were found on 6.3% of the sites, whereas mugs and cups were present on 3% of the sites. However, in the case of some sites, the descriptions of ceramic vessel forms in excavation reports are very laconic and I do not know whether the above percentages reflect the actual state of affairs. Descriptions of artefacts found on several sites prove that a really wide range of vessels was used in manor houses. All of the above mentioned vessel forms were discovered in Gruszczyce, Kępno, Kłóbka, Kościelna Wieś, Nowe Miasto and Siemkowice.

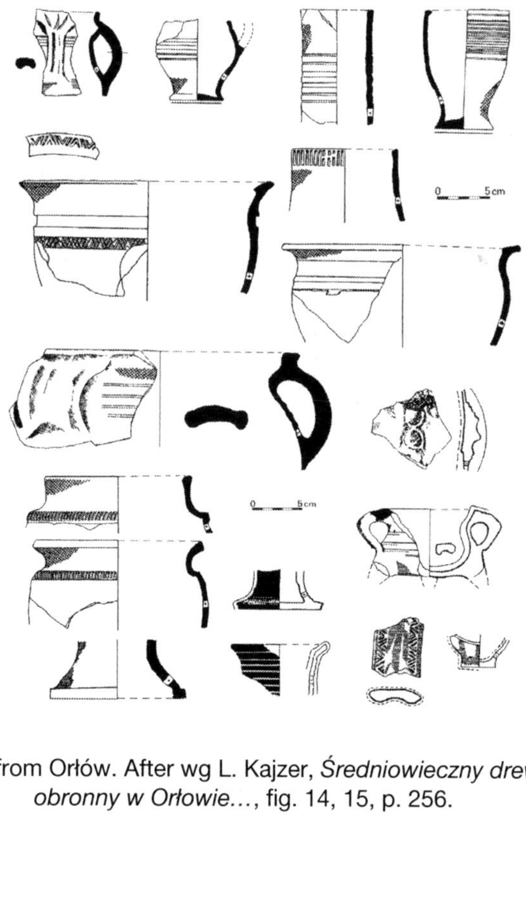

Fig. 10. Pottery from Orłów. After wg L. Kajzer, *Średniowieczny drewniany dwór obronny w Orłowie...*, fig. 14, 15, p. 256.

The excavations in Nowe Miasto yielded a large collection of at least 10 small bowls, undoubtedly for individual use at the table (tableware). Archaeologists also identified two 'goblets'. A very interesting set of dishes was found in Orłów, namely fragments of at least four tankards (mugs), a two-eared pot on three legs resembling a dish known as pipkin that occurred more frequently in the north-west of the territory under consideration. Another interesting discovery is a tubular vessel spout, the form of which was not possible to reconstruct. Vessels with such spouts occurred very rarely in our lands. It seems that they occurred more often in the north-western parts of our country. Do these last two vessels imply that there were any contacts with Western Pomerania, Neumark and Brandenburg? Another example of an interesting vessel is known from the excavations of the manor house in Zduny. It is a small pot with a tubular snout.

Other unique forms worth mentioning include a fragment of a zoomorphic dish found in Barłogi with the head of an unidentified animal and traces of broken ears and horns. It may be a fragment of an aquamanile. We know only several artefacts of this type from the present territories of Poland and they are dated back to the Late Middle Ages. Such objects are made of bronze or clay. Clay aquamaniles were found at the castle in Bobrowniki (a fragment of a horse or dog head?)[126], and in the vault of St. John's church in Mogilno (in the shape of a horse)[127]. The remaining two items come from Silesian cities. A fragment found in Wrocław seems to be a part of a horse figurine[128], whereas another specimen from Racibórz was in the shape of a horned animal, most likely of a cow[129]. As we can see on the basis of the above information, no aquamaniles have been found in manor houses or even private castles. Therefore the vessel from Barłogi should be considered as unique.

---

126 T. J. Horbacz, *Fragment późnośredniowiecznej akwamanili z Bobrownik, woj. włocławskie*, "Acta Universitatis Lodziensis". Folia Archaeologica, 1983, vol. 4, pp. 123–129.

127 J. Chudziakowa, *Akwamanila z Mogilna*, "Archaeologia Polski", vol. 22, 1977, Book 1, pp. 171–178; L. Kajzer, *Czy akwamanila mogileńska pochodzi z XII wieku?*, "Kwartalnik Historii Kultury Materialnej", vol. 29, 1981, no. 1, pp. 79–81.

128 J. Piekalski, A. Wiśniewski, *Akwamanila z mieszczańskiej parceli przy ul. Nożowniczej 13 we Wrocławiu*, "Śląskie Sprawozdania Archeologiczne", vol. 33, 1992, pp. 175–182.

129 The vessel was published only in local press. I would like to thank Mr Arkadiusz Przybyłok for the information.

Another extremely rare object is a piece of a lid with the handle in the form of a female figure, found during excavations in Jeziorsko. This decorated lid was meant for insertion inside the vessel inlet. A flange that prevented the lid from falling inside the vessel was partially preserved. A nodular protrusion that prevented the lid from falling when tipping a pot is an even more exceptional find. Archaeologists also discovered fragments of a vessel that might have been covered with a lid. It was identified not only on the basis of the corresponding diameter, but also a notch for the protrusion. The pot and its lid are dated to the first half of 14th century.

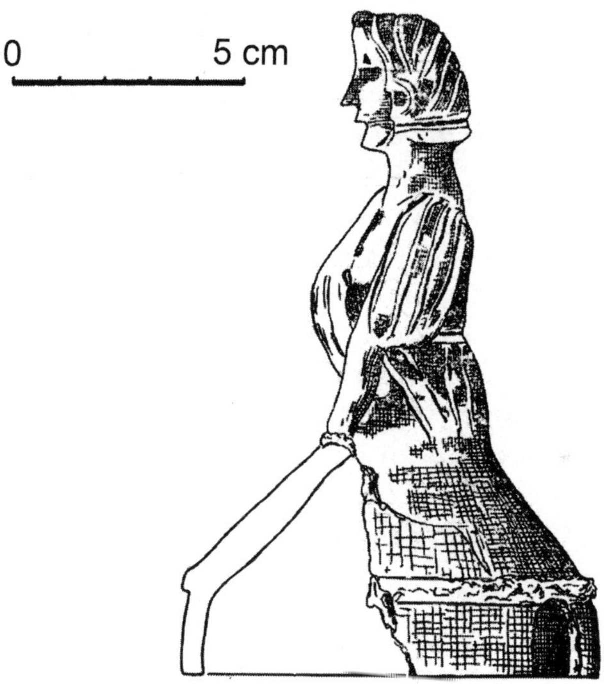

Fig. 11. Ceramic lid from Jeziorsko. After: E. Krause, *Średniowieczny gródek rycerski w Jeziorsku*..., fig. VIII, p. 318.

It is regrettable that only in few cases have the authors made an effort to determine whether the vessels that they discovered could be hypothetically grouped into those used in the kitchen or those used as tableware.

The above information concerning pottery found during the excavation of medieval knights' manor houses needs to be considered only as a superficial attempt at presenting this subject matter. I think every archaeologist realizes that the issue needs a separate detailed treatise that requires more insight than the quotation of published results from excavations.

The analysis of excavation results from approximately 200 sites provokes the following reflection. While the search for analogies between tiled stoves or elements of weaponry in the archaeological material found at other sites with manor houses is fully justified, it is difficult to provide a convincing argument for the comparison of particular vessels between each other. After all, they were not manufactured in manor houses. Dishes came either from the local, rural makers or might have been purchased or supplied on the basis of duty, or they were bought in a nearby town as handicraft deeply set in the urban (and often small-town) tradition of the region. Therefore if we want to study the technology and morphology of vessels affiliated with manor houses, I think we should compare them with the material from the surrounding villages and nearby towns. On the other hand, the range of dishes needs to be compared in a completely different manner. In this case, it seems justified to search for similarities between the elements of tableware or kitchenware from different manor houses. The similar cultural development and financial status of knights residing in the above mentioned residences (including, of course, the evolution in time) led most likely to the peculiar unification of needs and habits as regards both elements of kitchenware and tableware.

At the current stage of research the image of medieval pottery is shaped by the excavations of towns. The extremely spectacular results of research in Elbląg, Kołobrzeg and Wrocław were diligently elaborated, and more importantly, the results were published[130].

There is a lack of research, however, on the rural production of pottery. There are no publications available of materials discovered during the few excavations of rural sites, carried out mainly within rescue projects prior to

130 M. Rębkowski, *Średniowieczna ceramika miasta lokacyjnego w Kołobrzegu*, *Kołobrzeg* 1995; P. Rzeźnik, *Przemiany wytwórczości garncarskiej średniowiecznego Wrocławia w czasie wielkiej reformy miejskiej*. In: Kultura średniowiecznego Śląska i Czech „Rewolucja" XIII wieku, K. Wachowski (ed.), Wrocław 1998, pp. 121–153; J. Niegoda, *Naczynia ceramiczne*. In: Wratislavia Antiqua, vol. 1, Ze studiów nad życiem codziennym w średniowiecznym mieście. Parcele przy ulicy więziennej 10–11, we Wrocławiu, C. Buśko, J. Piekalski (ed.), Wrocław 1999, p. 157–182.

large investments. No wonder that in practice it is not even possible to make an attempt at developing a model of a rural potter's workshop, one that does not conform to the rules of the guild, separated from technical innovations, and cultivating (or not) the local traditions[131].

Fig. 12. Proto–stoneware jug from Gruszczyce. Fot. J. Błaszczyk

Metal vessels are much less frequently found during excavations. They have been discovered only at 5 sites. In Stary Kiełbów archaeologists discovered a small triangular vessel made of a single piece of copper sheet. It was shallow and of primitive workmanship. One of the three corners was elongated and pointed to mount a handle. Fragments of bronze vessels were discovered in Nowe Miasto and Orszymowo. In Włoszczowa archaeologists found an object made of copper or bronze and suggested that it was a stemmed pot. Two fragments of a small iron bowl come from Smogulec.

131 The study of excavations in Rusko village should be considered as unique: P. Rzeźnik, M. Trzciński, *Późnośredniowieczna ceramika ze wsi Rusko, gm. Strzegom, z badań w 1994 roku,* "Śląskie Sprawozdania Archeologiczne", vol. 37, 1996, pp. 301–314.

A slightly different finding was discovered in the manor house on Ledniczka Island. In the remains of a hearth archaeologists found two fragments of bronze hoops, most likely parts of vessels[132]. Compared to the above mentioned artefacts, the find from the bishop's manor house in Góra is really unique. It is an iron pan with a long handle dated very early to the second half of the 13th century and the first half of the 14th century.[133].

Based on the above listed artefacts, metal vessels seem to be really unique. Almost all of the above discussed fragments are characteristic elements, however, they are so small that reconstruction of the entire form of the object is not possible.

Fragments of glass products are also very scarce. Such vessels are not durable and usually very fragmented, as a result of which they are difficult to find and identify. Nevertheless, fragments of glassware were discovered at several sites, and archaeologists have even managed to determine the type of some original vessels. For example, fragments of glass vessels were found in Kozłów and Kościelna Wieś, however they were not very characteristic and it was not possible to reconstruct the original form. In Orłów and Popów archaeologists discovered fragments of flute glasses. A fragment of a stem from Będzieszyn most likely formed the base for a glass. The reconstruction of a vessel form was possible only in the case of findings from Jarocin. It was a bowl with ribs stuck on the surface. As regards other sites, we know a fragment of a glass vessel with nodules discovered during excavations of the remains of the duke's castle in Ryczeń (Silesia)[134].

The very small number of finds does not allow us to answer when glassware and metal vessels appeared in knight's manor houses. We need to wait until our knowledge is increased with the help of new artefacts, and especially their precise dating.

Apart from dishes, other items were also needed in the kitchen and at the table, above all cutlery. Besides knives, that will be discussed later, among materials discovered as a result of excavations spoons were found.

132 J. Górecki, M. Łastowiecki, J. Wrzesiński, *Gródek na Ledniczce…*, p. 225.

133 H. Kočka-Krenz, A. Sikorski, *Góra, gm. Pobiedziska, woj. poznańskie, stan. 1. Wstępne wyniki badań z lat 1985–1991*, "Wielkopolskie Sprawozdania Archeologiczne", vol. 1, 1992, p. 146.

134 J. Lodowski, *Ryczeń, gm. Góra, woj. leszczyńskie, stanowisko 1*, "Informator Archeologiczny". Badania 1981, p. 250.

Unfortunately, they were identified only at 3 of the sites in question, in Gruszczyce, Zduny and Podłężyce. All of them were made of iron. The specimen found in Podłężyce had a considerably long handle (36 cm) bent into a hook-shape for hanging[135].

Other kitchen utensils found during excavations include a fragment of a funnel made of iron sheet (Kiełbów Stary) as well as an iron spit (Rybojady). Preparation of food, especially spit-roasted meat, must have been very common. However, with a simple and not very characteristic form, such objects are not frequently recognized among artefacts discovered during excavations. At the sites under consideration archaeologists did not discover any supporting structure for spits, examples of which are known from Pomerania[136]. Undoubtedly, a pestle found in Borówek is another interesting artefact[137].

Many of the kitchen utensils were made of organic material, usually wood. For obvious reasons they are relatively rare in archaeological collections. A very interesting specimen comes from Orłów, where a wooden pounder was discovered. It was found inside a fully preserved utensil, hence the suggestion that is might have been used for pounding ingredients for cooking.

4. Other Artefacts

Let us take a closer look at tools and everyday articles used by the residents of knight's manor houses in order to make an attempt to reconstruct their activities. Were these objects related only to everyday life and housework or also tools for the manufacture of a larger number of articles? Contrary to appearances, this is an essential question, which also has impact on the function of the buildings under discussion, especially as regards keeps built on mottes.

In this context, an important question that we should ask at this point, is whether buildings or outbuildings of manor houses accommodated any craftsman's workshops and whether any products were manufactured therein.

135 J. Kamińska, L. Kajzer, *Grodzisko z XIII–XIV w Podłężycach, pow. Sieradz*, "Sprawozdania Archeologiczne", vol. 21, 1969, p. 204.

136 C. Buśko, *Archaeolog w kuchni*, In: Civitas et villa. Miasto i wieś w średniowiecznej Europie środkowej, Wrocław–Praha 2002, pp. 309–315.

137 A. Kosiorek, *„Dwór na kopcu" w Borówku...*, p. 231.

The studies in Siedlątków referred to in this work on numerous occasions, and especially the smithy reconstructed on their basis, exerted a great influence on interpretations of subsequent excavation results related to other motte-and-baileys. The conviction that such workshops existed was confirmed by the excavations carried out in Plemięta. These discoveries sensitized researchers to similar findings. Hence, when listing tools found at the site, the authors most frequently interpret them as objects that can be associated with a smithy. In several cases it was suggested that the outbuildings housed a blacksmith's forge.

At the site in the already mentioned Siedlątków archaeologists found the relics of a dome-shaped furnace and an interesting set of smith's tools: a nail making device, an anvil, 2 spades, 2 hammers, 12 setts, 1 burin, 1 chopper, 12 bars of iron, 2 plungers, 1 melting pot, and 1 casting mould made of sandstone. However, compared to the standard equipment of a blacksmith's shop, this set of tools is definitely incomplete and seems to be adjusted to treatment of semi-finished products and repairs. First and foremost the set does not include any large anvil or files that are indispensable in smithery[138]. They might have been removed during a fire, however we are not able to verify this version of events.

Now let us take a look at other discoveries, on the basis of which the authors suggested that blacksmiths' forges existed in the outbuildings of manor houses. In Borówek, apart from the building considered to be a manor house, archaeologists discovered the remains of a wooden building with a stone foundation of a furnace, which was interpreted as the remains of the blacksmith's forge. The artefacts discovered on site included a fragment of a file, two iron hand shanks and setts. There were also semi-finished products for the manufacture of bolt heads. Unfortunately, in the case of this discovery, we do not have a precise chronology of the above mentioned findings, because this site is dated from the beginning of the 15th century to the mid-17th century.

Traces of smithery were also identified at the site in Krzykawka. Archaeologists discovered here a semi-finished horseshoe and blacksmith's hammer - punch used for making holes in metal objects (horseshoes?). Other interesting finds include also three fragments of vessels made of a ceramic mass with a graphite admixture. The authors suggest that these were melting pots for

138 E. Nosek, *Czternastowieczna kuźnia w Siedlątkowie*, "Prace i Materiały Muzeum Archeologicznego i Etnograficznego w Łodzi", no. 15, 1968, pp. 95–131.

casting lead or silver. Pieces of lead ore found on the site might have implied such an interpretation[139]. Vessels with graphite admixture are often considered as melting pots due to their larger resistance to high temperatures. Of course, if we are not able to reconstruct the shape of the vessel or identify any other specific traces of use, such interpretation is only hypothetical[140]. At the same site archaeologists also discovered a triangular digger, which was considered to be a mining tool for the extraction of ores. Krzykawka is located in the region of Olkusz and Siewierz, where the deposits of galena, rich in lead and silver occur at relatively shallow depths. As suggested by the author of the studies, the blacksmith's workshop might have been located in the second part of the site, referred to as the bailey, where archaeologists found the relics of a building, perhaps built with the use of the post in ground technique[141].

Let us return to the subject of extraction and treatment of iron ores. So far no traces of smelting ores, such as bloomeries, have been found within manor houses or in the immediate vicinity of them, which is in line with our expectations. Therefore, we need to ponder over the relatively frequent findings of lumps of slag and ores on excavated sites. A discovery from Stary Kiełbów throws an interesting light on the issue. It was "slag in the form of a round cap with a concave and deeply porous top surface and partially icicle-like bottom. It is the surface part of the waste product formed during the process of iron smelting, presumably in a small pot" (a diameter of about 5 cm). In addition to the above mentioned fragment, archaeologists also found a few smaller pieces of a similar structure. The author of the study suggests that these are the traces of smelting a small amount of ore[142]. There is evidence of smelting ores in clay pots in rural areas as late as the 18th and 19th centuries[143]. A similar find, that is a lower part of a ceramic pot filled with a lump of melted iron comes from the manor house situated on a mound in Proboszczewice. This residence belonged

139 E. Szydłowska, *Średniowieczny gródek w Krzykawce...*, pp. 143, 148; J. Pierzak, D. Rozmus, *Średniowieczny gródek rycerski w Krzykawce...*, pp. 127, 131 fig. 8: e.

140 P. Rzeźnik, H. Stosik, *Ceramika grafitowa z Raciborza...*, pp. 171–185.

141 E. Szydłowska *Średniowieczny gródek w Krzykawce*, woj. Katowice, "Śląskie Prace Prahistoryczne", vol. 1, 1989, pp. 147–148.

142 Z. W. Pyzik, *Grodzisko stożkowate w Kiełbowie Starym, pow. Białobrzegi*, "Rocznik Muzeum Świętokrzyskiego", vol. 6, 1970, pp. 468, 475–476.

143 K. Moszyński, *Kultura ludowa Słowian*, vol. 1, *Kultura materialna*, Warszawa 1967, pp. 373–4.

to the bishopric in Płock[144]. Lumps of slag were also found in Golice, Kopytów, Mokrsko Dolne, Orłów, Rozprza, Smogulec, Szczekociny and Zduny.

A small anvil found in Mymoń is absolutely unique. Several interesting objects were found in Smogulec, five of which are bars defined as a blacksmith's semi-finished products, whereas other destroyed artefacts were interpreted with all likelihood as nail making devices. In Trzemsze archaeologists discovered punches and one hammer, whereas in Będkowice and Pęczniew a pair of pliers. One of three semi-recessed dugouts, traces of which were found in Mrówki, was interpreted as a blacksmith's shop, because archaeologists found 'smith's tool' there[145]. A large number of items interpreted as blacksmith's and locksmith's tools, as well as semi-finished products, were found at the settlement on Ledniczka Island, where archaeologists discovered 21 artefacts of this type, including: 16 punchers, a wedge, a stamp and 3 bars/semi-finished products. As no remains were found that might have been the traces of a workshop, the authors of the studies suggested that such outbuildings were located somewhere in the vicinity of the manor house[146].

The discovery of several tools should not determine the presence of a blacksmith's shop in the outbuildings of the manor house. The situation is slightly different in the case of a few sites, where the authors also identified, for example, a furnace. However, none of the above discoveries can be interpreted as a blacksmith's shop in the modern sense of the word, where large quantities of products are manufactured for sale. These smithies were rather backyard workshops of a local 'handyman' – blacksmith – locksmith, who dealt mainly with repairs and the manufacture of small uncomplicated items such as nails or even arrowheads or horseshoes, only for the needs of the manor house.

Now let us focus on other tools. During excavations in Zduny archaeologists discovered a tool for root wood, with which a lumberjack dug around the tree and cut most of its roots prior to eradication. Then, a rope was attached to the highest growing branches and with the help of a team of animals, the tree was pulled down together with the roots. Such practice was common, when

144 A. Marciniak-Kajzer, *Dwór obronny w Proboszczewicach*, "Acta Universitatis Lodziensis". Folia Archaeologica, vol. 18, 1994, p. 54.

145 Ł. i A. Nowakowie, *Mrówki, pow. Konin*, "Informator Archeologiczny". Badania 1971, p. 254.

146 J. Górecki, M. Łastowiecki, J. Wrzesiński, *Gródek na Ledniczce...*, pp. 219, 221.

farmers wanted to obtain land for cultivation, avoiding the difficult and time-consuming clearing of stubs and roots. As in the case of an axe, the blade of this tool is parallel to the handle, but still it asymmetrical, as it is arched and closer to one side of the opening, in which the handle is fixed. In the publication the object was mistakenly referred to as an adze.

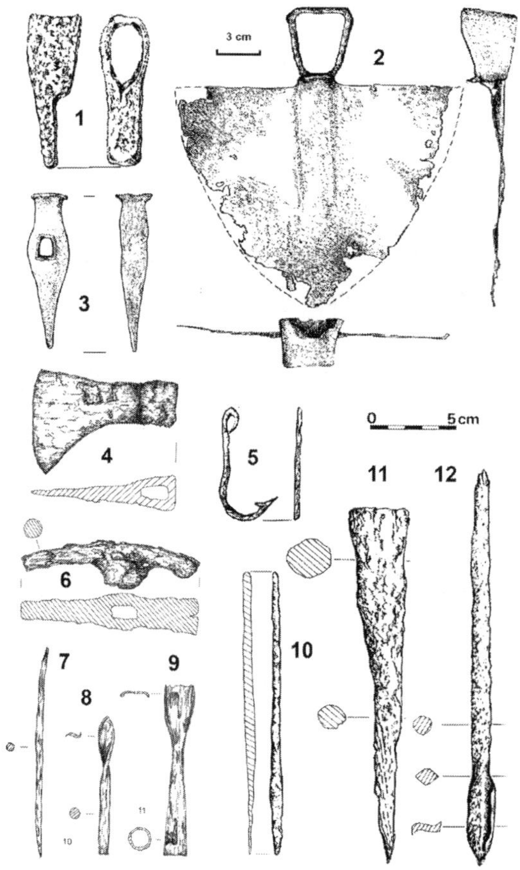

Fig. 13. Tools: 1, 5, 10–12, Ledniczka. After: J. Górecki, M. Łastowiecki, J. Wrzesiński, *Gródek na Ledniczce*..., fig. 23, p. 232; 2, 3, Krzykawka. After: E. Szydłowska *Średniowieczny gródek w Krzykawce*..., fig. 3–4, p. 144–145; 4, 6–9. Trzemsze. After: M. Kociński, *Późnośredniowieczna siedziba obronna w Trzemszach*..., fig. XXVI.

Manor houses drew their prosperity largely from land cultivation and hence a knight needed a significant number of agricultural tools. Although most likely such tools were stored in the outbuildings, and not in residential houses, archaeologists encounter this type of findings also in the remains of mansions. Sickles are definitely predominant. The largest number of sickles, i.e. over 20 items, was found during exploration of the manor house in Żerniki-Jaryszki. It was also recorded that at least one of the sickles had the traces of blacksmith's marks[147]. Numerous finds of sickles are known from the settlements in Trzemsze (7), Barłogi (4), Siedlątków (5), and Jarocin (4). On twenty other sites archaeologists discovered a single specimen. Some of the sickles had a serrated blade. The sickles from Jarocin had blacksmith's marks at the base of the handle. Numerous findings of agricultural tools are known from Jeziorsko. Apart from two sickles, including one with a serrated blade, archaeologists discovered a ploughshare. The plough had been most likely known in Poland much earlier, but it became common in the mid-13th-century. A large fragment of the iron colter of the plough as well as ploughshare were discovered in Chrostowa. The ploughshare in the settlement in Gruszczyce was found in an interesting stratigraphic context; it was resting on the wooden floor in the corner of a log building discovered at the site. In Koniecpol archaeologists found a fragment of the colter.

Another tool reported by archaeologists is a crude sickle, the blade of which is less curved than in the case of the sickle. However, any mentions of it are very rare. One specimen was discovered in Barłogi. A fragment of a tool, that I have seen only as a drawing, is referred to as a sickle and was found in Kozłów. As this is relatively large and lightly curved, it suggests that it may also be part of a crude sickle.

In addition to tools related to farming, in manor houses we also find tools for the processing of cereal crops. Such finds are not frequent, which is not surprising as watermills and windmills were widespread during the times in question. All kinds of grain crushing mills made of wood really had little chance to survive in archaeological material in such a form as to make correct interpretation possible. In the case of quern stones the situation was different and, for example, a fragment of one was found in Kłocko. Unfortunately, information about the discovery of two quern-stones in Strzemkowo is known only from the archival materials. In Kowala-Stępocina archaeologists discovered a stone grinder.

147 T. Stępnik, A. Dębski, *Sprawozdanie z badań archeologicznych późnośredniowiecznej osady rycerskiej w Żernikach–Jaryszkach, gm. Kórnik, woj. wielkopolskie*, "Wielkopolskie Sprawozdania Archeologiczne", vol. 10, 2009, p. 213.

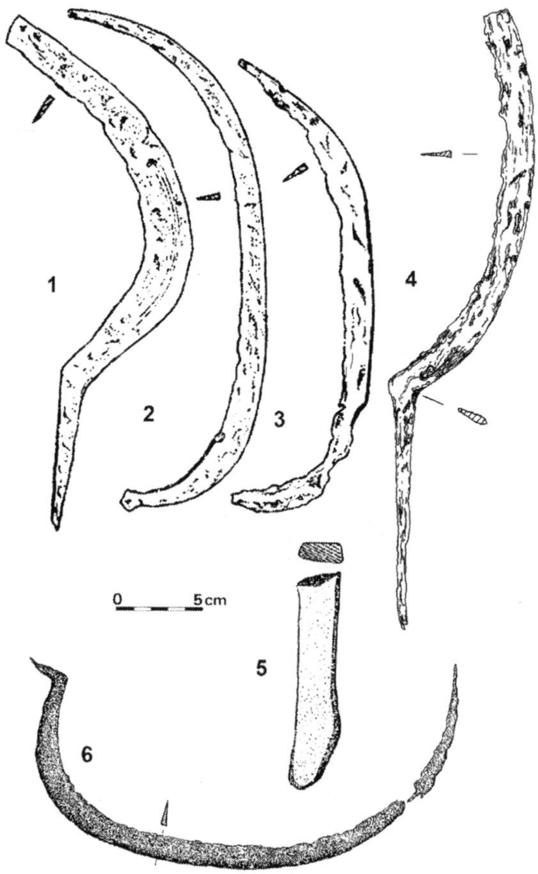

Fig. 14. Sickles and whetstone. 1–2, Rozprza. After: A. Chmielowska, *Rozprza we wczesnym i późnym średniowieczu…*, tab. VII, p. 206; 4, M. Kociński, *Późnośredniowieczna siedziba obronna w Trzemszach…*, fig. XXVI; 5, Orłów. After: L. Kajzer, *Średniowieczny drewniany dwór obronny w Orłowie…*, fig. 17, p. 263; 6, Krzykawka. After: E. Szydłowska, *Średniowieczny gródek w Krzykawce…*, fig. 3, p. 144.

To summarize the above mentioned findings of iron farming tools, it should be noted that archaeologists encountered a relatively large number of objects of this type, given the fragmentary form of discovered artefacts. Strangely enough, they were discovered in the manor houses, although one would rather expect them in the accompanying farmsteads. What was the reason for that? Was it dictated by the high price of such articles?

The shovel is another artefact associated with farming. It was more useful in gardening or orchard cultivation than in arable farming. Besides it is a universal tool used, for example, in building. It seems that wooden tools were more often used for horticulture and they did not survive until the present day. A wooden spade discovered during exploration of the bishop's residence in Dębno is a unique finding[148].

Shovel fittings are relatively rare among the artefacts. Three such items were found within the settlement in Kozłów, one in Kępno, Siedlątków and Włoszczowa. The hoe from Krzykawka has already been mentioned, but it was interpreted as a mining tool.

Extensively corroded objects are sometimes difficult for interpretation with any certainty. An example of such a situation comes from Orenice, where the finding was described as an adze or hoe. On the other hand, sometimes it may be very difficult to distinguish between an adze or a hoe, taking into consideration similarities in their form. A hoe was found at the residence in Rybojady. Another type of tool is the pickaxe, the only mention of discovering one comes from Siedlątków.

The manor houses in question were well equipped with tools for woodworking. It is hardly surprising, considering that the majority of everyday articles were made of this raw material. Axes and hatchets were basic tools. Unfortunately no precise criteria for differentiation have been determined. The common meaning of the term 'axe' refers to a household tool for chopping wood whereas hatchet refers to a carpenter's tool[149]. It is commonly thought that the difference between these objects often comes down to their size, namely an axe is larger than a hatchet, although this seems to be too simplistic[150]. These impressions seem to be confirmed in the studies of written sources conducted by J. Szymczak. According to his findings, the price of an axe as a weapon in the 13th and 14th century oscillated between 10–12 groschen, whereas a hatchet did not cost more than 3 groschen[151].

148 J. Kuczyński, *XIV-wieczny gródek w Dębnie, woj. kieleckie, gmina Nowa Słupia*, "Rocznik Muzeum Narodowego w Kielcach", vol. 12, 1982, pp. 211–233.

149 K. Moszyński, *Kultura…*, pp. 295–6.

150 Cf notes in: M. Głosek, *Broń drzewcowa i obuchowa*. In: *Uzbrojenie w Polsce średniowiecznej 1350–1450*, A. Nadolski (ed.), Łódź 1990, pp. 138–139.

151 J. Szymczak, *Produkcja i koszty uzbrojenia rycerskiego w Polsce XIII–XV w.*, Łódź 1989, p. 78.

Weapon experts have completely different problems with nomenclature, namely they wonder which axes should be considered as tools, and which should be interpreted as weapons, especially that written sources also mention the use of hatchets in battle[152]. However, let us leave semantic considerations and focus on objects that experts have interpreted as tools.

The most extensive collection of these tools was found in Siedlątków. Apart from the fragment of an axe and 4 hatchets, artefacts included 4 adzes, 2 chisels, 1 large wedge, 1 plane and 2 drills. Hatchets were found on several sites: in Pniewy, Rybojady, Siemkowice, and Trzemsze, whereas the object found on Ledniczka Island was referred to by the authors as a carpenter's axe.

If a discovered artefact is referred to as an axe it is usually listed with military items. However, it will do no harm to mention them at this point, especially that we often find only parts of axes and therefore it is more difficult to define their typology more precisely. Fragments of axes were found then in Gruszczyce, Kopaliny, Kozłów, Krzykawka and Zembrzyce.

Drills are relatively frequent artefacts. Two of them were found in Rozprza, and one at the sites in Jarocin, Kościelna Wieś, Kiełbów, Ledniczka, Mrówki and Trzemsze. At the site in Trzemsze, as well as in Wola Piekarska archaeologists also discovered one chisel.

When analysing archaeological materials, we rarely find any mention of cooper's chisels, planes or draw knives. One specimen of the tool referred to as a draw knife was found during exploration of the manor house in Siemkowice. An item from Siedlątków is referred to as a plane. One of the artefacts from Bachotek, Chełmno Land, was interpreted as a cooper's chisel[153].

As regards tools that were used not only for woodworking, knives are the largest group of artefacts. They were found at more than half of the excavated sites, if we do not include field surveys in these statistics. It should be noted that in the case of over 70% sites archaeologists found more than one specimen. Unfortunately, sometimes the authors report the findings of knives, but fail to specify their quantity. It seems that the largest collection of knives

152 Cf notes in: M. Głosek, *Broń drzewcowa i obuchowa...*; P. A. Nowakowski, *Arsenały domowe rycerstwa polskiego w średniowieczu*, Toruń 2006, pp. 77–78.

153 K. Grążawski, *Średniowieczny gródek rycerski w Bachotku na ziemi chełmińskiej w świetle badań archeologicznych*, "Sprawozdania Archeologiczne", vol. 40, 1988, pp. 332–333.

was discovered in the manor house in Żerniki-Jaryszki, where over thirty specimens were found. Large quantities of knives were also reported in Nowe Miasto (12), Siedlątków (8) Kiełbów Stary (7), Gruszczyce (6), Ledniczka (6), and Zduny (6). The large number of these artefacts should not be surprising, especially when we consider that a knife was a specialized tool in the Middle Ages. Different types of blades were used for specific purposes, even within a single branch of trade, e.g. woodworking or hide treatment. Other knives are interpreted as intended for the quartering and processing of meat or fish, and others for cutting bread, etc.[154]

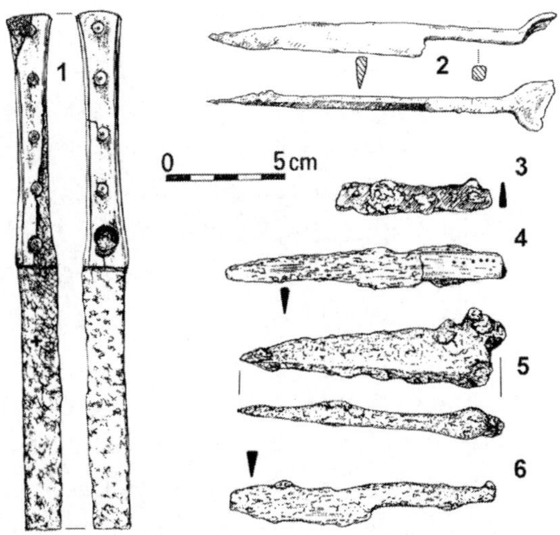

Fig. 15. Knives. 1. Ledniczka. After: J. Górecki, M. Łastowiecki, J. Wrzesiński, *Gródek na Ledniczce...*, fig. 12, p. 212; 2. Kozłów. After: S. Kołodziejski; 3–6, Orłów. After: L. Kajzer, *Średniowieczny drewniany dwór obronny w Orłowie...*, fig. 16, p. 262.

The forged iron parts of knives are preserved in the ground relatively well because of the material they were made of and their large mass, but handle pieces, most often made of organic material, are much less frequently found during excavations. Handle pieces were identified at four sites. We cannot be always one hundred percent certain that the items we discover are handle

154 P. Michalik, *Późnośredniowieczne i wczesnonowożytne noże z zamku w Pucku*, Warsaw 2000.

pieces of a knife and not of a different tool. However, it seems to be most likely. The author of studies concerning the site in Nowe Miasto reported the findings of two bone handle pieces, however he did not insist that they were intended for a knife. Additionally, one of the handle pieces was decorated with a geometrical ornament made of circles and lines. A richly decorated bone handle piece was found in Kozłów, whereas in Pęczniew archaeologists discovered a knife with a fragment of an antler handle piece. In archival materials we can find a mention concerning a knife handle piece found at the settlement in Smogulec. Two fragments of handle pieces were found in Barłogi, one of them with a bone peg/rivet. A similar peg/rivet was also identified in one of the handle pieces found in Jarocin. In Jarocin archaeologists also found at least three other bone handle pieces, including one that was richly ornamented, however, we cannot be sure that they were parts of knives[155].

Bone and antler objects are found relatively frequently during excavations. Unfortunately, it happens sometimes that these terms are used interchangeably. For example in one of the publications, the same artefact is referred to as a bone item, whereas in another as an object made of horn or antler. The difference between horn and antler material is often completely blurred. Such artefacts do not always become the subject of specialized studies, hence our modest knowledge about the use of such raw materials. However, in this chapter on tools, we need to say a few words about the production of objects made of bone or antler. We do not know any specific tools that might have been used for such production. However, we have found semi-finished products, which proves their local origin. In Orłów archaeologists discovered a semi-finished object from antler with traces of incised circles. Unfortunately, we do not know what objects were made from it (beads or buttons)? Some objects made of bone or antler/horn we are simply not able to identify. A bone polished tube is found quite frequently in archaeological inventories, for example, in Barłogi or Kiełbów. Usually the authors do not make any attempt at interpreting such objects.

Bone artefacts finds include several needles and awls. They were discovered in Kiełbów, Orłów, Petrykozy, Pniewy, Smogulec and Trzemsze. These are items that, for centuries, have been found in probably every household. Iron needles are much less frequent. In Orłów archaeologists discovered two needles,

155 R. Grygiel, *Zarembowie z Jarocina…*, pp. 27–28, 31.

one made of bone and one of iron, whereas an iron awl was found in Gruszczyce. Iron needles were also recorded at the site in Żerniki-Jaryszki, yet we do not know the exact number.

Whetstones are another object found in archaeological inventories. Although they are useful, even indispensable, in every household, they are not found as often as expected. Whetstones were discovered in Barłogi, Jankowo Dolne, Kowala Stępocina, Orłów, Popów, Siedlątków and Stare Skoszewy.

On traditional farmsteads scissors were used primarily for cutting the fleece of sheep. We do not know whether they were used for other purposes. Relatively few references to these objects come from excavated manor houses (only Podłężyce, Szczekociny or Żerniki - Jaryszki). However, contrary to appearances, such finds are not very rare. Apart from the above mentioned locations, scissors were discovered, for example, at the settlements in Radzynia[156] and Bachotek[157].

The presence of tools for catching fish should not be surprising. After all, water obstacles were one of the most common defensive systems protecting the residence. Fish ponds became popular already in the Middle Ages and with a large number of fasting days the demand for fish was growing. When discussing the manor houses in Lesser Poland, S. Kołodziejski drew attention that proximity to bodies of water was one of the most important factors as regards the choice of the spot for building the residence. Although most of the equipment used for fishing (nets, fish-pots, baskets) were made of organic materials that have not survived until the present day, nevertheless archaeological inventories include iron hooks for fishing rods. There are not many of them, possibly due to their small sizes, as a result of which they corroded faster and then were more difficult to spot. Moreover, we should also remember that even in the modern period wooden hooks were used in rural areas[158].

Iron hooks were found at several sites, including: Siedlątków (7), Zduny (1), Orłów (1), Petrykozy (2) and Ledniczka (2). More than one hook was found in Chłapowo (no data available), whereas in Pełczyska (in the Kielce Province) archaeologists found one double hook and one single hook. Hooks discovered

156 K. Ciuk, *Radzynia pow. Syców*, "Informator Archeologiczny". Badania 1968, pp. 362–263.

157 K. Grążawski, *Średniowieczny gródek rycerski w Bachotku…*, p. 330.

158 K. Moszyński, *Kultura…*, p. 84.

in Koniecpol and Witów are relatively large; the length of one of them exceeds 7 cm, whereas the length of the latter is almost 10 cm. Four large fish-hooks were also found in Gniazdków.

Apart from fish-hooks, other artefacts related to fishing include a sandstone weight for sinking nets found in Siemkowice. Three iron objects in the form of a fishing spear were found in Smogulec. As regards other motte-and-baileys, a very rich collection of fishing objects was found in Bachotek, in Chełmno Land. They were dated to the first half of the 13th century and the beginnings of the 14th century. Archaeologists identified 3 fishing weights, a four-pronged fishing spear, as well as an iron fishing lure[159].

Surprisingly elements of scales often appear among artefacts that are discovered. Of course, we need to pose the question as to what they were used for. I do not believe that the ingredient of meals were measured with great care. Most likely such scales were used for weighing more valuable items, for example, precious metals, coins or expensive spices. Were they used to verify the scales of wandering traders?

At the site in Stary Żmigród archaeologists discovered bronze scales. Elements of scales were also found in Trzemsze, these 13 fragments were identified on the basis of their similarity to the reconstructed scales from the site in Plemięta[160]. Weights were also found, for example, in Zembrzyce (2) or Orłów (1). In Witów archaeologists discovered two lead disks with a hole in the middle. Most likely they were used as weights. The only specimen of a scale pan comes from the manor house in Mrówki.

There are not so many objects among archaeological materials that can be associated with typical women's work. For example, we know only of one spindle whorl that was found in Witów. As regards the territories outside our area of our interest, one spindle whorl was discovered in Bachotek, Chełmno Land[161], and one in Jędrychowice, Silesia[162].

159 K. Grążawski, *Średniowieczny gródek rycerski w Bachotku…*, p. 330, fig. 16/1.

160 M. Kochanowski, *Elementy odzieży i sprzęt gospodarstwa domowego z grodziska w Plemiętach*, In: Plemięta. Średniowieczny gródek w ziemi chełmińskiej, A. Nadolski (ed.), Poznań 1985, p. 175.

161 K. Grążawski, *Średniowieczny gródek rycerski w Bachotku…*, p. 328.

162 M. Parczewski, *Jędrychowice, pow. Głubczyce*, "Informator Archeologiczny". Badania 1972, pp. 250–251.

Excavation studies also report on finding iron parts from carts. In Rozprza archaeologists discovered a wheel hub fitting, whereas in Siedlątków 8 cart and shaft fittings. Information regarding the discovery of iron parts from a cart also comes from Kozłów.

To continue the subject of horse-drawn carts we have to mention a reins separator found in Trzemsze. Horse combs were commonly used for horse care. Horses were definitely not kept in the buildings which we are referring here, mainly due to the small size of such residences. However, reports on finding such items are relatively frequent, for example, at the site in Barłogi (3), Gruszczyce (2), Trzemsze (2) or Żółków (1). Perhaps, the reason behind this situation is the value of such iron objects.

The vast majority of artefacts found during excavations are different types of iron fittings, clamps and iron rings. These rings are often interpreted as chain links. We can never be sure that a ring we have just discovered is, for example, a part of a bit or if a massive clamp was actually used as a shaft fitting. We will never know what was the intended purpose of a given fragment of the chain. Still, we should always try to consider how a particular object could have been used.

Sometimes among these indistinct iron objects we can identify fragments of various types of grips or handles. For example, at four sites in Kępno, Ledniczka, Siedlątków, and Wola Piekarska such objects were interpreted as bucket handles. Artefacts from Mymoń were referred to as bucket hoops. In Włoszczowa archaeologists discovered an object referred to as an iron handle from a chest, as well as a massive handle made of a metal rod with a rectangular cross-section.

Only in the case of one of the inventories, have I encountered mention of cleats for walking on ice found at the site in Siedlątków. An iron clamp with a hook mounted on a pole used for raising a bucket from a well and discovered in Kościelna Wieś is also an isolated case of finding such a device.

On the basis of the number of nails discovered at a site as well as their spatial distribution we can reach further conclusions, rather than just make the brief statement that they were present. For example, during excavations in Siedlątków a large number of nails was interpreted as the convincing evidence that the building was covered with a shingled roof. A similar situation was at the site in Popów.

I would like to draw attention to artefacts that contrary to our expectations were not found in great numbers, as in the case of fire steels. Archaeologists discovered many fire steels at the early medieval sites, whereas it is surprising that not many of them were identified among later artefacts. Is it possible that they fell into disuse? The answer to this question must be negative. Fire strikers were used even in the early 20th century[163]. How can we explain the scarce number of fire steels in late medieval materials? Maybe this common tool changed shape slightly and failed to be recognised as such by archaeologists. Drawings in the work of the ethnographer, K. Moszyński, present oval fire steels, classic C-shaped fire steels, C style with many minor variations (with open ends curved to inside or outside), D style and rectangular ones, from the modern period. Fire steels have a very simple form and can be easily confused with a staple or a simple bar of iron or a fragment of some fitting[164]. It seems that this issue requires a more comprehensive study. As regards the sites under consideration, 2 fire steels were found at the settlement in Majkowice - Surdęga (one in the drawings is of the oval type), 2 in Nowe Miasto, more than one in Pęczniew and single fire steels were discovered both in Tyczyn and Barłogi.

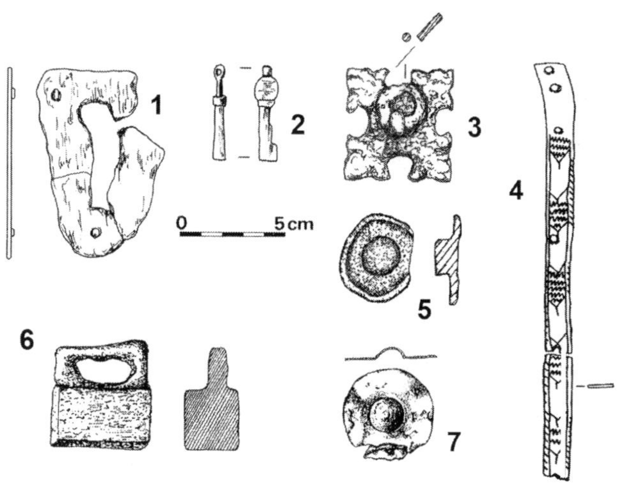

Fig. 16. Objects made of non-ferrous metals: 1, 2, Orenice. After: M. Kołaczyk, Gródek stożkowaty w Orenicach..., tab, VII, VIII; 3, Trzemsze. After: M. Kociński, *Późnośredniowieczna siedziba obronna w Trzemszach...*, tab. XXVI; 4, Jeziorsko. After: E. Krause, *Średniowieczny gródek rycerski w Jeziorsku...*, tab. X, p. 320; 6, Orłów. After: L. Kajzer, *Średniowieczny drewniany dwór obronny w Orłowie...*, fig. 17, p. 263; 7, Ledniczka. After: J. Górecki, M. Łastowiecki, J. Wrzesiński, *Gródek na Ledniczce...*, p. 208, fig. 10.

163 M. Gradowski, *To też są zabytki*, "Spotkania z Zabytkami", 1985, no. 2, pp. 34–35.

164 K. Moszyński, *Kultura...*, pp. 241–245.

Objects made of non-ferrous metals are rather rare among archaeological artefacts. They are quite often found in the form of bronze or tin rivets embedded in various objects. However, they are most frequently encountered as fragments, the identification of which is very difficult. In Siedlątków archaeologists discovered 46 fragments of bronze sheet, as well as one fragment in Stare Skoszewy. A lump of melted copper was found in Słupia and a copper rod in Włoszczowa. Two fragments of bronze fittings were found in Jeziorsko, whereas in Kościelna Wieś there was a 'patch' of lead and a bronze 'sheep' bell. The inventory of artefacts from Popów included fragments of unspecified bronze and lead objects, whereas in Gruszczyce there were bronze or brass pieces. The figures of artefacts found during excavations of the manor house in Majkowice-Surdęga include a drawing of two objects referred to as lead seals.

So far we have focused on the interiors of the house and its furnishing. The equipment of the household was most likely family property. Now let us proceed to the objects that might have been assigned to a particular person, although most likely such an interpretation may be influenced by our contemporary habits and views. For example, today a comb is a personal object, but was it the same in the Middle Ages?

Undoubtedly, apparel was personal. Unfortunately, based on archaeological excavations we cannot say much about the clothing worn by residents of manor houses. They were made of organic material and decomposed. Archaeologists encounter only rarely elements of clothes and shoes made of leather and hide.

The largest collection comes from the manor house in Orłów, that is 19 fragments of leather articles, including the remains of soles and the uppers of shoes. Archaeologists have identified between 6 and 8 shoes, such as: woman's footwear in the form of long toed poulaines or crakow shoes made of goatskin; a shoe with a low laced top and with a cut in the front part and made of calfskin; a fragment of the front part of a knee-boot also made of calfskin, fragments of two knee-boots, one of which was made of calfskin, and the other of cowhide; 3 sole pieces from women's shoes made of bovine hide. The discovered shoes were manufactured by a professional shoemaker, the evidence of which are regular seams. These shoes were reconstructed, and based their appearance they were affiliated with early Gothic style and dated back to the turn of the 13th and 14th centuries. Other findings come from the manor house in Gozdowo, where archaeologists discovered primitive home-made shoes made of calfskin as well as fragments of a belt and clothing. Elements of leather shoes were also discovered at the settlements in Bestwina and in Szamotuły. We do not know the precise dating of two leather objects discovered during excavations of the manor house in Rozprza. These are fragments of a leather glove and a child's shoe. Another interesting discovery is a bone button for clothes found in Nowe Miasto and dated to the 14th century.

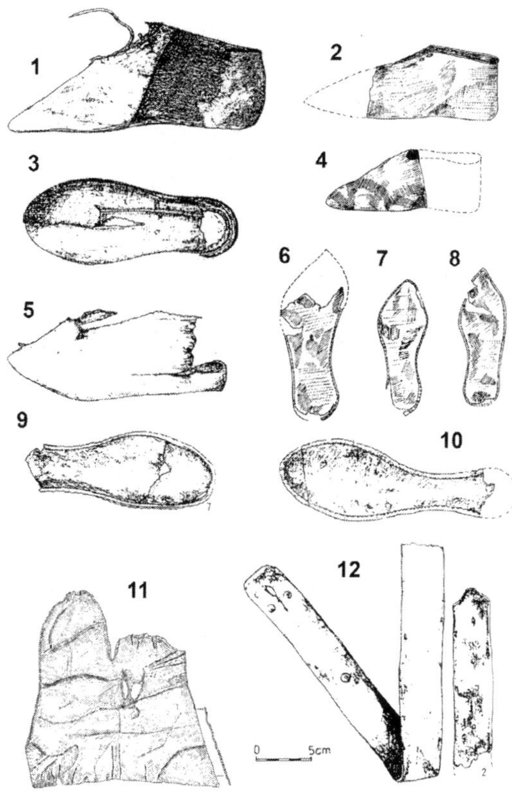

Fig. 17. Leather shoes, belt and glove: 1, 3, 5, 9, 10, 12, Gozdów. After: E. Prusicka--Kołcon, *Wyniki badań tzw. gródka stożkowatego w Gozdowie…*, p.195, fig. 4; 2, 4. 6. 8, Orłów. After: L. Kajzer, Średniowieczny drewniany dwór obronny w Orłowie…, fig. 19, p. 265; 11, A. Chmielowska, *Rozprza we wczesnym i późnym średniowieczu…*, tab. VII, p. 206.

Buckles are definitely most frequent apparel elements discovered during excavations. Of course not all of them were part of clothing, i.e. belts. Probably a large number of them was used for horse harnesses, and smaller specimens for the fastening of spurs. They were found at more than a ¼ of the excavated sites, when not including field surveys in this. Unfortunately, in the vast majority of the studies the authors did not provide more precise descriptions of the artefacts, including their size, and therefore we cannot even try to distinguish military items in this material and discuss them separately. For this reason you will find all mentions of these artefacts in this section, including their interpretation by the authors, if it exists.

The vast majority of buckles were made of iron, although there are specimens decorated with non-ferrous metals. For example, buckles plated with silver were discovered in Rozprza as well as in Trzemsze, where archaeologists found in total 7 items, including one with traces of silver plating. A fragment of a copper or bronze buckle was found in Włoszczowa, and fragments of two clasps were discovered in the manor house in Wola Piekarska, one of which was made of bronze with traces of silver plating and the other of iron.

In Stary Koniecpol archaeologists also found a very interesting specimen during exploration of the manor house. In the vast majority of late medieval buckles the prong is attached to one, usually the longer end of the frame. This specimen has a prong, which forms an integral part of a mobile axis / cross-piece fixed more or less in the centre of the rectangular frame, parallel to its longer sides. The specimen from Orłów is also very interesting. It has the shape similar to a figure eight and its prong is attached at the junction of the two rings. The whole buckle is bent in such a way that the central part is convex. In Barłogi, apart from the buckle, archaeologists also discovered fittings of a belt in the shape of a four-leaf clover. A rich discovery comes from the settlement in Gruszczyce, where they found 7 buckles. However, the largest number of clasps comes from the site in Siedlątków, where 13 buckles were discovered. One specimen here deserves special attention, namely a clasp made of two elements resembling rectangles of different sizes, with the prong mounted at the junction and closing the smaller of them.

Decorative items attached to garments are not very frequent artefacts. The few specimens include a round brooch found in Barłogi with a notch in the frame for fixing the pin. It was made of bronze and decorated with incised triangles. This object is relatively small and its diameter is only 2.1 cm. Unfortunately, in literature there are very few references related to jewellery from excavations. According to H. Kočka-Krenz round brooches started to appear on our territories already in the 12th century. Specimens decorated with triangle motives are known from the 1220/30s to the second half of the 14th century[165]. In this case the dating of the brooch corresponds fully with the dating of the manor house.

Another decorative item made of bronze was found in Kopytów. It is a pity that we do not have a precise description. In the report there is only mention of a fragment of a bronze pendant. In a similar stratigraphic context archaeologists also discovered a glass bead and a bronze bell. Unfortunately, these items are listed together and the dating of each stratum spreads widely between the 11th and 14th century. The remains of the manor house in Orłów also revealed a small glass bead with the diameter of just 0.6 cm. As regards neighbouring sites, a similar artefact was discovered in Witków. It was a glass opaque item[166].

Another pendant this time made of amber was found at the site in Nowe Miasto and it was dated to the 14th century. It was a small lump of unworked amber with a double-cone perforation. An amber ball with the diameter of 3 cm was found in the manor house in Siemkowice and it was dated between the mid-15th century to the end of the 16th century.

Another artefact that may be referred to as jewellery is a bronze ring found during exploration of the settlement in Rozprza[167].

Other interesting finds come from the settlement in Trzemsze. These are two bone plates. One of them has a circular shape with the diameter of about 3.5 cm and a perforation (0.4 cm) drilled in the middle and it is decorated with a concentric circle made of small marks. It might have been either a pendant or a counter from a game. The second object has a shape resembling a triangle with curved edges. The width of the base is circa 5 cm and its height is 5.2 cm. The shape of the plate suggests that it might have been a heraldic shield. However, we do not know its function.

165 H. Kočka-Krenz, *Biżuteria średniowieczna na ziemiach polskich jako wyznacznik chronologiczny*, "Archaeologia Historica Polona", vol. 6, 1997, fig. I, 22–23, p. 73; cf. also: R. Sachs, *Tak zwane „fibule w kształcie sowy" i ich znaczenie. Z badań nad treściami ideowymi ozdób w państwie krzyżackim*. In: Niemcy–Polska w średniowieczu, J. Strzelczyk (ed.), Poznań 1986, pp. 355–365.

166 R. Sachs, *Witków woj. zielonogórskie. Stanowisko 6*, "Informator Archeologiczny". Badania 1983, p. 222.

167 A. Chmielowska, *Rozprza we wczesnym i późnym średniowieczu…*, p. 182.

The number of findings does not allow any serious discussion as regards clothes and jewellery preferred by or just simply available to the residents of the manor houses. Our knowledge of jewellery worn by them is also not very rich. The situation in the case of other sites, where manor houses or castles were excavated, is not any better.

Objects associated with personal hygiene are found very rarely during excavation. Razors were found only in the case of four sites. Only the razor blade survived in the case of the specimen from Orłów, whereas in Włoszczowa archaeologists discovered a razor together with a movable sheath. Another specimen was found in Żerniki-Jaryszki.

Among other toiletries, combs seem to be much more frequent. While there are numerous studies of early medieval combs, late-medieval specimens are still waiting for a monograph[168].

Combs were found at 6 sites. The largest quantity was found at the settlement on Ledniczka Island, where archaeologists discovered double-sided three-piece antler combs. Two pieces of a double-sided antler comb with decorated lining were found in Dąbrówka, whereas a fragment of a double-sided three-part specimen made of bone was discovered in Jeziorsko. A similar artefact was discovered in Krzykawka. Decorated bone pieces from Jarocin initially might have been parts of a comb. Similar findings were also found in other manor houses, e.g. in Pełczyska.

Another object for individual use were iron cleats for walking on ice to prevent slipping. They were attached both to shoes or horse hoofs. Depending on their purpose, they varied in size and form. Cleats intended for people had 2 or 3 spikes, whereas the ones for horses had only one spike[169]. These artefacts are not frequent in the inventories analysed herein. We know only of two cleats intended for human use. One specimen comes from Siedlątków and the other from Borówek. Skates were used in a similar way. When wearing skates, people

168 Basic studies, including suggested typology, can be found in the works of: Z. Hilczerówna, *Rogownictwo gdańskie w X–XIV w.* In: *Gdańsk wczesnośredniowieczny*, vol. 4, p. 41–144, 301–328; A. Chmielowska, *Grzebienie starożytne i średniowieczne z ziem polskich*, Łódź 1971; E. Cnotliwy, *Rzemiosło rogownicze na Pomorzu wczesnośredniowiecznym*, Wrocław 1973.

169 K. Wachowski, *Militaria z grodu na Ostrówku w Opolu.* In: Studia nad kulturą wczesnopolskiego Opola, Wrocław 1984, p. 30.

were able to move faster and safer on frozen bodies of water. Skates were also used for entertainment. Two bone skates were found in Pniewy and a fragment of another specimen was discovered in Stary Kiełbów, whereas semi-finished skates were recorded in Rozdrażew.

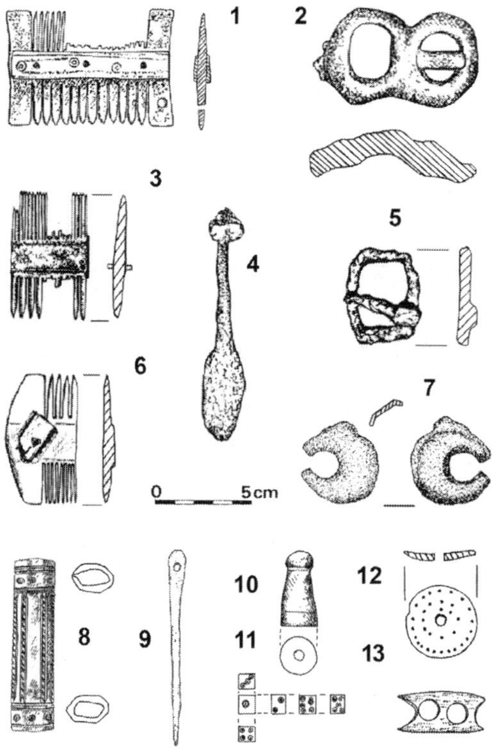

Fig. 18. Objects made of bone/ antler and other personal items: 1, 7, Krzykawka. After: E. Szydłowska, *Średniowieczny gródek w Krzykawce*..., p. 154, fig. 8; 2, 4, 9, 13, Orłów. After: L. Kajzer, *Średniowieczny drewniany dwór obronny w Orłowie*..., p. 263, fig. 17; 3, 5, 6, Ledniczka. After: J. Górecki, M. Łastowiecki, J. Wrzesiński, *Gródek na Ledniczce*..., p. 208, fig. 10; 8, 10, 11, Kozłów. After: S. Kołodziejski; 12, Barłogi. After: M. Troszczyńska, *Późnośredniowieczna siedziba obronna w Barłogach*..., tab. XXI.

While skates seemed to have been used more frequently by children, entertainment for adults is testified to by dice and counters for games. Dice were found at two sites in Budzynek and Kozłów. A bone object from Kozłów may be interpreted as a game counter. On the subject of entertainment we should also mention fragments of instrumental pipes discovered in Stary Kiełbów and Pełczyska. A wooden top from Orłów is another unique toy object.

Evidence of more noble activity undertaken by the residents of manor houses is given by the following group of artefacts. During excavation carried out on Ledniczka Island, archaeologists discovered a round fitting with the diameter of 4.5 cm made of a thin bronze sheet, convex in the central part. There are three rivet holes at the edges of that object. Perhaps we are dealing here with a 'hat-shaped' book fitting? Such metal ornaments were usually placed in the middle of the front cover.

In Zduny archaeologists encountered a bronze item in the shape of a pin or a burin with a hammer-shaped head. It seems that this object is a stilus. Such artefacts are seldom found during excavations of manor houses. Another stilus comes from the thirteenth-century residence of the bishops of Poznań in Główna[170].

A fragment of the knife handle made of ivory displays not only a sign of luxury, but also far-reaching contacts. The handle is carved with a motif of a lion/lioness hiding a small lion cub between her paws. Examinations revealed that this item was imported from the Mediterranean region. This artefact, so unique for Poland, was discovered in Orłów.

Now let us take a closer look at the findings of coins. These artefacts are not common, but crucial for more precise dating of sites.

Two coins were found among the relics of the manor house in Małków. Most likely one of them is a Cracow half-groschen coin (półgrosz) of Casimir III the Great dated back to the years 1333–1370. The latter one is a Cracow denar of Louis the Hungarian from the period between 1370–1382. In the course of the excavations in Żywiec, archaeologists discovered a button bracteate and denars of Władysław II Jagiełło. Archive reports concerning the discovery in Nabyszyce provide information about a silver coin of Wenceslaus II (1278–1305) and coins found during the transport of the earth from the mound in Trzciel. However, we do not even know their quantity. Coin findings are also not frequent at other similar sites. We can mention here though the Prague groschen (before 1305) found during excavations of the bishop's manor house in Dębno[171].

170 P. Wawrzyniak, *Średniowieczna rezydencja biskupów poznańskich w Głównej…*, pp. 322–323.

171 J. Kuczyński, *Dębno, pow. Kielce*, "Informator Archeologiczny". Badania 1972, p. 244; J. Kuczyński, *XIV-wieczny gródek w Dębnie…*, p. 226.

Military items have always aroused a great interest among archaeologists. Usually they are classified meticulously and described in detail. Fortunately, they are no longer considered as good indicators of chronology and old typologies are not used unquestioningly any more. Militaria were found at over 60 sites among those under analysed by us.

Definitely crossbow bolt heads are discovered most frequently by archaeologists. They were identified at 49 sites. The number of heads discovered during excavations is usually very different. The largest number was found in Nowe Miasto (93 specimens with a sleeve and 5 with a tang). Excavation reports concerning the site in Trzemsze describe 30 bolt heads (25 specimens with a sleeve and 5 with a tang). In Petrykozy archaeologists found 24 bolt heads (18 specimens with a sleeve and 6 with a tang) and the same quantity in Jarocin (20 specimens with a sleeve and 4 with a tang). In Jeziorsk there were 20 bolt heads (17 specimens with a sleeve and 3 with a tang). We know of 16 bolt heads from Smogulec (15 specimens with a sleeve and 1 with a tang), 14 bolt heads from Ledniczka Island (13 specimens with a sleeve and 1 with a tang), 14 bolt heads from Siedlątków (1 specimen with a tang and 13 with a sleeve), 11 bolt heads from Rozprza (1 specimen with a tang and 10 with a sleeve). Besides these, more than 10 bolt heads were discovered in Żmigród. Most frequently however, the number of artefacts of this type at particular sites does not exceed more than a few items.

Bow arrow tips were found at a much smaller number of sites. Usually these are single finds. Arrowheads were discovered in Będkowice (with a sleeve), Gruszczyce, Jankowo Dolne (2 pieces?), Kopaliny Pogwizdowskie, Kowala-Stępocina, Mymoń, Petrykozy (with a sleeve), Trzemsze (with a sleeve), Ziemin and Żerniki-Jaryszki. In Popów archaeologists discovered more than one arrowhead (?).

Such a significant discrepancy between the bolt heads and arrowheads is explained by a decreasing popularity of bows as weapon at that time. Its use was limited to hunting[172], although this is probably only one of many possible interpretations.

In several cases, the features of the head, or its poor condition of preservation, did not allow the possibility of determining whether we are dealing with tip of a projectile shot from a crossbow or a bow.

172 P. A. Nowakowski, *Arsenały domowe...*, p. 102.

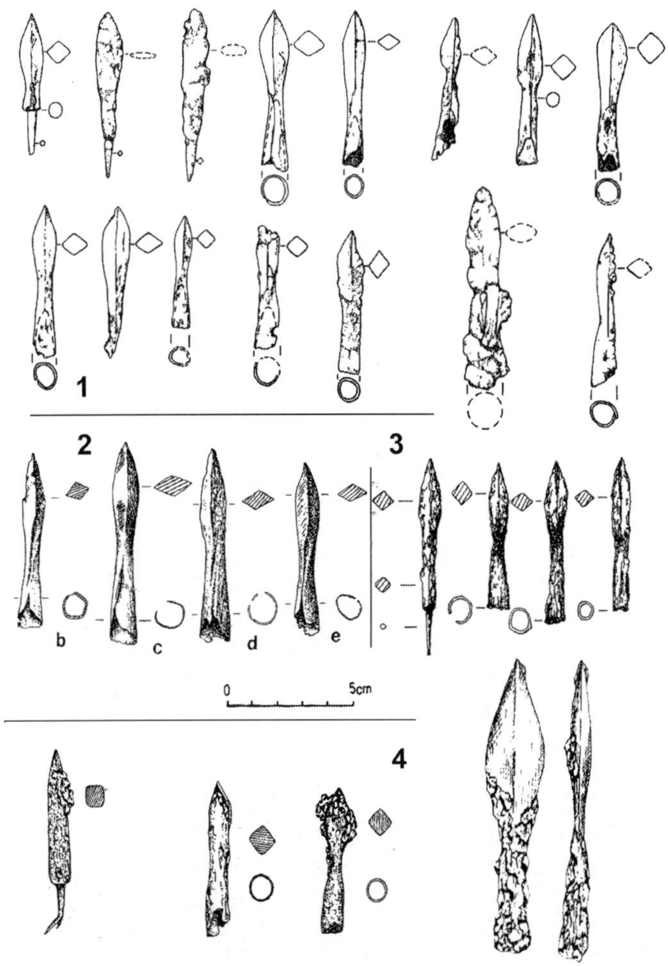

Fig. 19. Bolt heads: 1, Jeziorsko. After: E. Krause, *Średniowieczny gródek rycerski w Jeziorsku…*, tab. IX, p. 319; 2, Krzykawka. After: E. *Średniowieczny gródek w Krzykawce…*, ryp. 5, p. 149; 3, Trzemsze. After: M. Kociński, *Późnośredniowieczna siedziba obronna w Trzemszach…*, tab. XXI; 4, Orłów. After: L. Kajzer, *Średniowieczny drewniany dwór obronny w Orłowie…*, fig. 16, p. 262.

The tips of a spear are found during excavations in similar quantities to arrowheads. In this case however, it is difficult to distinguish between the tip of a spear or javelin. It is assumed that javelins were used in that period as hunting weapon and their heads were smaller compared to the tip of a spear. Moreover they should have spikes that made it more difficult to fall out when lodged in the target. They are less frequent in excavated archaeological material, as they were lost[173].

At the sites in question, archaeologists found approximately 13 specimens referred to as tips of a spear. The largest number of heads was found in Smogulec (3 pieces). Two specimens were discovered both in Trzemsze and Rozprza, and one at the sites in Gruszczyce, Jarocin, Małków and Orłów. At other sites archaeologists encountered only fragments of heads. Heads affiliated with javelins come only from 6 sites: two from Siedlątków and Żerniki-Jaryszki, and one from Będkowice, Kępno, Mymoń and Radzymin.

Apart from heads there are also elements of bows and crossbows. Unfortunately such findings are rare. The largest group of artefacts are nuts, that is, the elements of the release mechanism in the crossbow. They were found at the sites in Chłapowo, Kozłów, Nowe Miasto and Siedlątków.

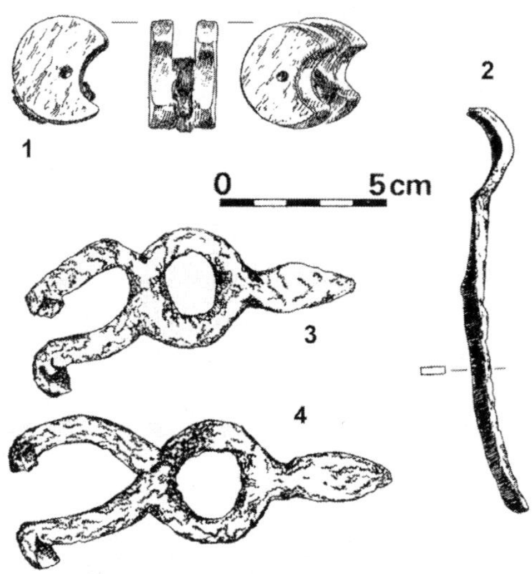

Fig. 20. Elements of the crossbow and accessories: 1, Kozłów. After: S. Kołodziejski; 2–4, Mrówki. After: P. A. Nowakowski, *Arsenały domowe…*, tab. 121–122, p. 363–364.

173 M. Głosek, *Broń drzewcowa i obuchowa*, In: Uzbrojenie w Polsce średniowiecznej 1350–1450, A. Nadolski (ed.), Toruń 1998, p. 134; M. Głosek, *Broń drzewcowa i obuchowa*. In: Uzbrojenie w Polsce średniowiecznej 1450–1500, p. 43; A. Nowakowski, *Uzbrojenie średniowieczne w Polsce (na tle środkowoeuropejskim)*, Toruń 1991, p. 69; P. A. Nowakowski, *Arsenały domowe…*, p. 93.

Other elements of the release mechanism in a crossbow can be also found among archaeological materials, for example, fragments of levers. Such artefacts were found during excavations in Siedlątków and Mrówki. In Janiszewo archaeologists found a crossbow stirrup.

However, the hook for drawing back a string is most frequent object found during exploration. It is not a part of a crossbow, but it is an indispensable element affiliated with that type of weapon. The largest number of hooks (three specimens) was discovered in Siedlątków and Mrówki. Two hooks are known from Nowe Miasto and one specimen from Chłapowo and Orenice. A slightly different type of lever used for drawing back a string was found in Jarocin, this one is referred to as a fragment of a goats foot lever. In Nowe Miasto archaeologists discovered four wide clamping rings and a massive link that might have been fragments of the crossbow bed and stirrup.

By far we have the smallest chance of finding fragments of a bow or crossbow made of organic materials. Such artefacts could have survived to our times only in exceptional conditions. Fragments of alder or hazel wood were found only at one site in Orszymowo and they might be relics of a bow. The remains of a bow from Brzeg are a very interesting analogy. They survived only owing to preservative properties of the environment in the former latrine[174].

Another interesting discovery was made during exploration of the manor house in Orłów, where archaeologists found a fragment of a sheepskin interpreted as a part of a sack, possibly a quiver or a bow case.

Now let us proceed to edged weapons. The common idea is that the sword was an indispensable attribute of the knight. Unfortunately, the number of swords found in archaeological material is inversely proportional to the number of words used with reference to swords in literature about medieval knighthood. The situation at the sites under consideration is similar.

The two best preserved swords were discovered during underwater excavation at the foot of the 13th-century settlement in Izdebno, on the peninsula of Wolskie Lake. One of them is XI,H,1 type, whereas the other is a XII, H, 2 type[175]. Two fragments of a sword or swords were discovered in Chłapowo. Unfortunately, the

174 M. Głosek, L. Kajzer, *Łuk średniowieczny znaleziony w Brzegu*, "Silesia Antiqua", vol. 19, 1977, pp. 243–252.

175 Typology – one of them is XI, H, 1 type, whereas the other is a XII, H, 2 type. M. Głosek, *Miecze środkowoeuropejskie z X–XV w.*, Warsaw 1984, p. 157.

state of preservation of these finds is very poor, which hinders not only typological analysis, but also makes it impossible to determine whether those two elements used to be one integral object or two different swords. These fragments were identified as a piece of a hilt with a pommel and part of a blade and a hilt. They are dated back to the 13th-14th century. A small piece of blade was also discovered during excavations in Mrówki. The only well-preserved specimen of a sword comes from Nowe Miasto and it is dated to the 15th-16th century. In Rybojady archaeologists discovered the hilt of a sword.

For obvious reasons the remains of scabbards for holding swords or other types of melee weapon are even less frequent; they were made of natural materials such as leather or wood. Additionally, metal fittings that reinforced sheaths might be difficult to identify, except for the chape protecting the tip of the scabbard. Iron fittings of a knife sheath discovered during excavations at the site in Mymoń deserve special attention among all the inventories of artefacts. Moreover, at the site on Ledniczka Island archaeologists discovered one piece of a scabbard fitting.

Other types of melee weapons represented among artefacts include combat knives, with reference to which archaeologists use different terms. Usually the term 'combat' is put in quotation marks, but this is not surprising as the division criteria are quite labile. M. Lewandowski defined combat knives as "daggers with a single-edged blade and with construction features and size peculiar to weapon". Lewandowski provided distinctive metric measures of the blade that should be longer than 15 cm but shorter than 40 cm[176]. Unfortunately metric criterion may be applicable only if we find a knife that is preserved well enough to reconstruct its initial dimensions, which is not always the case. Knives classified as daggers were found inter alia in Bąkowa Góra, Szczekociny and Żerniki-Jaryszki, whereas the specimen from Trzemsze had a hilt with disk-shaped pommel and guard. On Ledniczka Island archaeologists discovered two very interesting objects referred to as fragments of a dusack knife and combat knife, whereas a piece of a blade of a large combat knife comes from the site in Orłów. However, among the artefacts discovered in Orłów, there is another extremely unique object that deserves special attention, namely a fragment of the knife handle piece made of ivory and ending with a figure of a lion

176 M. Lewandowski, *Puginały średniowieczne z ziem polskich*. In: "Acta Archaeologica Lodziensia", no. 31, 1986, A. Nadolski (ed.), pp. 101–119.

hiding a lion cub or a puppy between its front paws. There are no analogies to this specimen among artefacts discovered at the sites excavated in Poland. Investigation for the provenance of the artefact shows that this specimen most likely originated from the Mediterranean region[177].

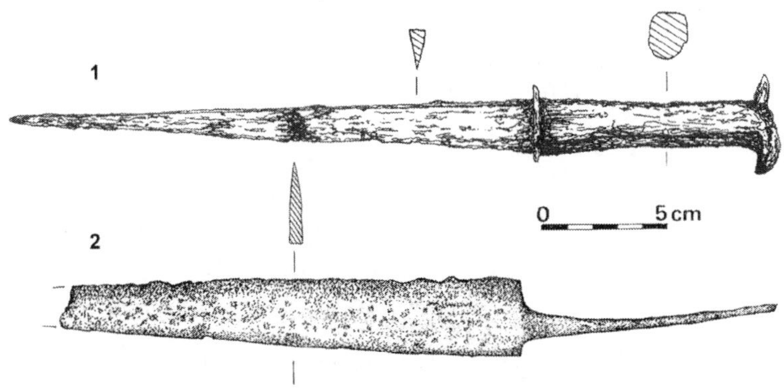

Fig. 21. Daggers: 1, Trzemsze. After: M. Kociński, Późnośredniowieczna siedziba obronna w Trzemszach..., fig. XXI; 2, Krzykawka. After: E. Szydłowska *Średniowieczny gródek w Krzykawce...*, fig. 5, p. 149.

Daggers were the only weapon worn with civilian clothes[178], and they were strapped to a belt by means of a sheath. As in the case of scabbards for holding swords, sheaths for daggers were made of organic material, as a result of which we have little chance to find entire specimens. Excavated materials sometimes include fittings, for example, at the site in Rybojady, whereas in Chłapowo archaeologists discovered the chape of a knife sheath.

Now let us take a look at blunt weapon found during excavations. I have already written about difficulties in differentiation between a battle axe, an adze or simple hatchet, especially that we find only corroded pieces of these objects. Single specimens that were classified as weapon were found at the sites in Gruszczyce, Kopaliny Pogwizdowskie, Kozłów, and Zembrzyce. Two specimens were discovered in Zduny, including one with a blacksmith's

177 J. Tomala, *Nowe odkrycia zabytków średniowiecznych z terenu Mazowsza*, "Kwartalnik Historii Kultury Materialnej", vol. 34, 1986, no. 2, pp. 286–288; L. Kajzer, *Średniowieczny drewniany dwór obronny w Orłowie...*, pp. 261–168.

178 Z. Wawrzonowska, *Uzbrojenie i ubiór Piastów Śląskich od XII do XIV w.*, Łódź 1976, p. 40.

mark. Two axes were found in Siedlątków. In Żerniki-Jaryszki archaeologists discovered one entire specimen and fragments of two others. Two other artefacts come from Rozprza; one of them is poorly preserved and referred to as a pickaxe and the other one as an axe. Similarly, a specimen from Mrówki survived only in fragments and it is difficult to classify; it might have been either an axe or a pickaxe. Basically there is no other kind of blunt weapons among the artefacts in question, such as clubs or maces. Only during excavations at the settlement in Popów archaeologists discovered a part of a combat flail.

Firearms appeared on a large scale on Polish territories in the second half of the 15th century. Written sources mention three types of firearm: hookguns, hand cannons and hand culverins. Based on these sources we may claim that Polish knights were in possession of such arms[179]. Unfortunately such findings are extremely rare. One of such discoveries was made in Nowe Miasto, namely a stone ball (bullet) with the diameter of 22 mm and an iron hook, perhaps a fragment of a hookgun. Balls, that most likely were used as bullets for firearms, were also found at other sites, for example, an iron ball from Bestwina and a stone ball from Jankowo Dolne, however we do know their diameters. Two other stone balls come from Żółków and the diameter of one of them is approximately 3 cm. Glass balls were found at the manor house in Borówek[180].

Now let us focus on protective body armour. Helmets represent the least frequent category of finds. Only one artefact of this type was found at the sites referred to in this book. It is a helmet with well-preserved skullcap and a visor from Siedlątków. It is the subject of an extensive monograph and numerous references in literature[181].

Fragments of body armour are represented in a greater number. By far most frequently archaeologists encounter pieces of plate armour, also referred to as a cuirass, i.e. iron plates and bands which formed breastplate and faulds[182]. The

179 J. Szymczak, *Początki broni palnej w Polsce (1383–1533)*, Łódź 2004, pp. 36–47; P. A. Nowakowski, *Arsenały domowe…*, pp. 104–105.

180 P. Strzyż, *Broń palna w Europie Środkowej w XIV–XV w.*, Warsaw 2014.

181 A.Nadolski, *Hełm i fragmenty zbroi z Siedlątkowa*, "Prace i Materiały Muzeum Archeologicznego i Etnograficznego w Łodzi", no. 15, 1963, p. 89–93; A. Nadolski, *Hełm i fragmenty zbroi z XIV wieku znalezione w Siedlątkowie nad Wartą*, "Studia do Dziejów Dawnego Uzbrojenia i Ubioru Wojskowego", vol. 4, 1969, pp. 5–23.

182 A. Nowakowski, *Uzbrojenie ochronne* In: Uzbrojenie w Polsce średniowiecznej 1350–1450, red. A. Nadolski, Łódź 1990, p. 64 et seq.

number of artefacts confirms the opinion of weapon experts that it was the most common type of torso protection. Rectangular iron bands with holes for rivets, or fragments thereof, with the use of which they were attached to a leather or textile doublet, were found on many sites. The largest quantity was found in Nowe Miasto, where archaeologists discovered 400 both entire and fragmented plates. An impressive collection of 145 pieces comes from Siedlątków. However, usually the number of finds is smaller, that is, a few or between ten and twenty pieces. Such collections were found in Borówek (several specimens), Chłapowo (7), Gruszczyce (7), Jarocin (2), Kępno (10), Kościelna Wieś (1), Orłów (2), Popów (15) Rozprza (1 plate and 1 fragment of sheet) and Zduny (8). In Borówek, apart from 6 small bands archaeologists also found a back-plate (plate cuirass). These artefacts might have belonged to one complete armour. Additionally there was also a fragment of a chainmail found at the same site.

Obviously only a larger number of plates, bands and other elements enables archaeologists to try to reconstruct a particular armour. Such an attempt was taken in relation to the finds from Siedlątków and Nowe Miasto. On the basis of the specimens from Siedlątków it was possible to determine that larger plates were most likely the remains of a breastplate, whereas smaller ones protected the sides of the knight. Some of the plates and bands are affiliated with faulds, and one of them was branded with the name of the armourer 'Nicchols'[183]. Moreover, the collection includes two couters, i.e. plates that guarded the elbow and a vambrace (forearm guard). The armour together with the above mentioned helmet were dated to the year 1370–1380 and it demonstrated a high technological advancement. Undoubtedly it was a very valuable item for its users[184].

Another attempt at reconstruction was made on the basis of artefacts from Nowe Miasto. Here, some of the plates were decorated with rivets in the shape of a stylized rose or plates with rosette ornaments. Apart from the plate armour, archaeologists also managed to reconstruct the faulds, as well as this they discovered fragments of a gauntlet and chainmail.

Fragments of chainmail are very rarely found by archaeologists. Apart from the above mentioned artefacts from Borówek and Nowe Miasto, the largest

183 A. Nadolski, *Hełm i fragmenty zbroi z Siedlątkowa…*, pp. 89–93; J. Szymczak, *Organizacja produkcji i ceny uzbrojenia*. In: Uzbrojenie w Polsce średniowiecznej 1350–1450, A. Nadolski (ed.), Łódź 1990, p. 223.

184 Ibid, pp. 89–93; A. Nowakowski, *Uzbrojenie ochronne…*. In: Ibid, p. 68.

find comes from Petrykozy, where archaeologists discovered 14 fragments of chainmail. Several lumps burnt in the fire were discovered in Smogulec as well as one fragment from both Zduny and Żerniki-Jaryszki.

In Nowe Miasto and Siedlątków archaeologists also discovered discs that knights fixed to the breastplate to attach a chain that secured the sword or dagger against loss if dropped from a hand. A similar find, but in the form of a plate with a perforation, is known from the manor house in Popów.

Horse tack and rider's equipment are discovered in the greatest numbers during excavations. Let us focus on spurs in the first place. Their distinctive shape makes them relatively easy to recognize, even if preserved in fragments. Usually they are described in detail. If not, the authors usually point out if the specimens that they found had attached rowels. I have never found any information concerning other types of spurs, so to avoid repetition, I will not dwell on the category to which the artefacts in question belong.

The largest collection of 11 well-preserved spurs with rowels at the end comes from the manor house in Mrówki. In the case of three spurs archaeologists also identified buckles for attaching them to the boots. Fragments of seven specimens were found both in Rozprza and Trzemsze. Spurs were also discovered in Zduny (6), Borówek (5), Siedlątków (5), Jarocin (4), Kozłów (4) Będkowice (3) Jeziorsko (3), Kępno (3), Kiełbów Stary (3), Żmigród (3) Barłogi (2) and Smogulec (2). In Żerniki-Jaryszki archaeologists discovered 9 fragments of spurs, but we do not know if these were the elements of nine different spurs. Sometimes the authors only list artefacts in plural, without providing information on the number of objects they discovered, as it was in Brzeziny – Trójnia, Dąbrówka, Szczekociny and Wola Piekarska. Archaeologists discovered only one spur at 7 sites and on Ledniczka Island they found one spur with a buckle.

Spurs were usually made of iron. Written sources provide us with information that they could be decorated in various ways, including with precious metals[185]. Unfortunately such findings are rarely found by archaeologists. One of four spurs

185 J. Szymczak, *Ostrogi żelazne i pozłociste*. In: Archaeologia i starożytnicy. Studia dedykowane Profesorowi Andrzejowi Abramowiczowi w 70 rocznicę urodzin, Łódź 1997, pp. 275–284; A. Marciniak-Kajzer, *Kilka słów o średniowiecznej złotej ostrodze z pogranicza krzyżacko-polskiego*, "Acta Militaria Mediaevalia", vol. 3, 2007, pp. 201–208.

found at the site in Jarocin had traces of silver ornamentation. Similar decorations were observed on spurs from Kępno and Tyczyn. Another specimen from the site in Zduny had traces of silver or tin ornamentation.

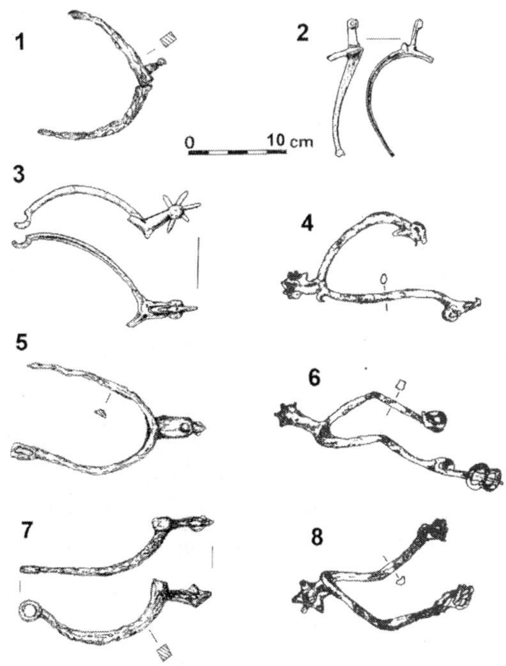

Fig. 22. Spurs: 1, 5, 7, Trzemsze. After: M. Kociński, Późnośredniowieczna siedziba obronna w Trzemszach..., tab. XXIII; 2, 3, Rozprza. After: A. Chmielowska A., *Rozprza we wczesnym i późnym średniowieczu...*, tab. VI, p. 205; 4, 6, 8, Mrówki. After: P. A. Nowakowski, *Arsenały domowe...*, tab. 121–122, p. 363–364

A slightly different way of decoration was observed on spurs found in Stary Kiełbów. In the case of two spurs, the heel bands were decorated with lined or herringbone patterns. It seems that a thin plate of precious metal, for example, silver, might have been impressed in the cuts by beating with a hammer, however such ornamentation did not survive until the present day.

In the outbuildings of the manor house in Szamotuły archaeologists found a silver-plated specimen with a ball at the end of the neck. These might have been rounded shanks for attaching a rowel.

Stirrups are very important element of the horse tack. They were popular, the evidence of which is a relatively large number of finds. The largest number of stirrups was found at the manor houses in Siedlątków (3) and Trzemsze (3). Two stirrups were found at the sites in Gruszczyce, Jarocin, Kępno, Kopaliny Pogwizdowskie and Rozprza. The specimens from Rozprza were extremely interesting, as they had traces of silver plating on iron. A single specimen was found on other 9 sites, including a unique fragment of stirrup made of bronze discovered in the manor house in Nowe Miasto.

Bits or their elements are identified relatively frequently among metal artefacts. Single finds are known from 14 settlements. The largest number of finds comes from the manor house in Trzemsze, where archaeologists discovered 3 well-preserved specimens and 4 fragments[186]. There is also a rich collection found in Jarocin with one entire bit and 6 fragments, including 3 rings[187]. Four other fragments were discovered at the site in Zduny, three in Kozłów and two in Będkowice and Nowe Miasto. Sometimes archaeologists encounter only single rings that are interpreted as fragment of bits, as in the case of artefacts from Orenice (1), Rozprza (3) and Smogulec.

In archaeological literature there are very few references to the horseshoes that are found quite frequently during excavations. Of the importance of the horseshoe to the condition of the horse it is not necessary to mention, but it is worth noting that in addition to those intended for horses, shoes were also used for other animals, for example, oxen, mules or donkeys. However, in their description of artefacts, the authors usually make do with reporting the fact that a shoe was found, without any additional information.

Single finds of horseshoes were made during excavations at 14 sites. 2 horseshoes were discovered in Gruszczyce, Mrówki and Orłów. Three specimens were found in Jarocin and Kępno and four in Chłapowo, Trzemsze and Zduny. In Krzykawka archaeologists found 3 fragments of horseshoes as well as a semi-finished horseshoe. Horseshoes were also found in the outbuildings of the manor house in Szamotuły, but we do not know their number. The largest collection of six specimens comes from the excavations of the residence in Siedlątków[188].

186 M. Kociński, *Późnośredniowieczna siedziba obronna w Trzemszach…*, pp. 44–45, tab. XXII.

187 R. Grygiel, *Zarembowie z Jarocina…*, pp. 35–36.

188 J. Kamińska, *Siedlątków…*, p. 37.

We have discussed the findings of elements of weaponry dividing them into particular categories of artefacts. It gives us an insight into the frequency of their occurrence in archaeological material. It is much more difficult, however, to create a picture of typical 'furnishings and equipment' characteristic of medieval manor houses only on the basis of artefacts from excavations. It is not really about the quantity of artefacts, but the number of categories of weapons, that is, grouping objects to show the versatility of the knight's equipment.

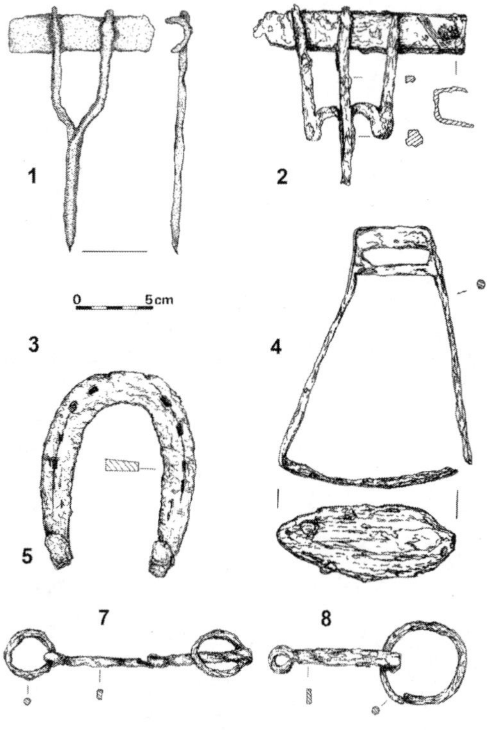

Fig. 23. Horse combs, horseshoe, stirrup and bits. 1. Barłogi. After: M. Troszczyńska, *Późnośredniowieczna siedziba obronna w Barłogach…*, tab. XVIII; 2–6 Trzemsze. After: M. Kociński, *Późnośredniowieczna siedziba obronna w Trzemszach…*, tab. XXI–XXIV

Based on such assumptions, the largest collection of findings definitely comes from Siedlątków, where archaeologists discovered a helmet and fragments of armour, axes, spearheads, bolt heads, fragments of a crossbow, spurs, a bit, stirrups and horseshoes. As you can see, the discovered artefacts allow the almost complete reconstruction of a knight's equipment. Another site abundant in finds is the manor house in Trzemsze. Excavations revealed such objects as: a dagger, arrowheads, bolt heads, spearheads, spurs, stirrups, bits and horseshoes. Also the discoveries made in Zduny are very interesting: that is, fragments of armour, spurs, bolt heads, axes, a stirrup, bits and horseshoes. In Nowe Miasto archaeologists discovered during the exploration of the site the following objects: a sword, fragments of armour, fragments of a crossbow, bolt heads, spurs and bits. Another collection of artefacts rich in military items is the manor house on Ledniczka Island: a fitting of a sword scabbard, a fragment of a dusack knife, a combat knife, bolt heads, a bit, a stirrup, a spur, a spur buckle and a horseshoe. The inventory from the site in Mrówki included spurs, bolt heads, a fragment of a stirrup, a fragment of a sword blade, part of a crossbow and an axet.

The above mentioned inventories included diversified military items, sometimes in almost ten different categories (fragments of armour, swords, axes, weapon heads, stirrups etc.) However, archaeologists are usually dealing with artefacts from two or three categories. Weapons were constantly evolving in the Late Middle Ages. Offensive weapons were developing which resulted in attempts at an improvement in protective armour. These changes occurred relatively quickly, too quickly, for the possibility of dating on the basis of excavations. In this situation, the picture that emerges from the analysis of the components of weaponry found during excavations is relatively static.

IV. AN ATTEMPT TO RECONSTRUCT THE IMAGE OF A MEDIEVAL KNIGHT'S MANOR HOUSE IN POLAND

Being aware of the currently popular post-modernist doubt about the possibility of reconstructing past reality, I will still make an attempt at describing the knightly manor house, as it appears to archaeologists. Even with the assumption that: *...one can study only what one has dreamed about*[1], I hope that it will be a useful attempt to summarize years of effort from many Polish researchers, as so far there has been no comprehensive compilation.

Concepts that connect motte-and-bailey residences with a country's defence policy are becoming less frequent in literature. Many authors have already written about the lack of actual military advantage of such facilities. Of course one cannot generalize here. A small mound surrounded by a shallow moat in the middle of a meadow had quite different possibilities of defence compared to a manor house located on the tip of a promontory in an upland region, where on the one hand, natural steep slopes were rising up above the height of ten meters, and on the other hand, access was prevented by a deep ditch and / or rampart. The defensive advantage of the former, surrounded by marshes and a moat that was probably drying up periodically, depended to a large extent on the season of the year. Access to the residence built on the mound was much easier in winter, when the swamp was frozen, or during a dry summer. Then, in addition to their own courage, the residents were defended by a palisade, or as is apparent from this study, more frequently by a solid fence. In the light of these remarks, one observation seems to be very interesting, namely the term 'manor house' or 'castle' is used most frequently in relation to residences located on elevations or high promontories, and quite sporadically when referring to typical lowland motte-and-bailey settlements.

1 H. White, *Metahistory. The Historical Imagination of Nineteenth Century Europe*, Baltimore 1973, p. 1; quoted by M. Bogucka, *Historia kultury materialnej a postmodernizm. Kilka uwag do modnego tematu*. In: O rzeczach minionych. Studia i Materiały z Historii Kultury Materialnej, vol. 71, Warsaw 2006, p. 32; D. Minta-Tworzowska, *Postmodernizm, myśl poststrukturalistyczna a archaeologia (zarys problematyki)*. In: Archeologia w teorii i praktyce, A. Buko, P. Urbańczyk (ed.), Warsaw 2000, pp. 87–95.

Some authors also pointed to the fact that the choice of location for the family hearth itself may indicate the different approach of individual founders to the issue of defence. Sometimes the seat is clearly visible from a distance - towering over the area, which demonstrates the aspirations of the owner. In other cases, the manor house seems to be almost hidden from unwanted visitors to avoid verification of its defensive potential. Examples of such a location are, among others, the manor houses in Kunów and Wilkanowo[2]. Such manor houses located in swampy areas or hidden in river valleys in fact might have been unnoticed for foreign enemies. The decision for such a residential location should be considered as right, because according to written sources, some turned out not to be fortified enough for the 'evil neighbour' who often forced the door, wounding defenders, carried away belongings, and even kidnapped people.

When studying the residences that belonged to the noble family of the Lis clan, S. Kołodziejski came to interesting conclusions. He realized that the representatives of this family, when choosing the location for their residence, preferred wet meadows, although elevated land features in the vicinity of watercourses were also available to them[3], which were more convenient for a settlement. Thus, the preferences of the founders, possibly associated with a family tradition, proved to be decisive in this case.

In the light of the military advantages under consideration, the small number of manor houses located on islands may be surprising. In the case of such settlements it was possible to provide security at a relatively low cost. According to written sources, the water surrounding the manor house, even in a moat, was a real obstacle and a boat was necessary to overcome it. During the raid on Zduny in 1499, armed invaders appeared "*cum navibus at aliis apparamentis hostiliter…*"[4]. Perhaps, the inconveniences of everyday life in a relatively small space, usually at some distance from farm outbuildings outweighed the safety aspects.

2 T. Makiewicz, *Średniowieczne grodzisko stożkowate na stanowisk 5 w Kunowie, pow. Mogilno*, "Slavia Antiqua", vol. 19, 1972, p. 240; W. Szymański, *Przyczynek do badań nad problematyką grodzisk stożkowatych (Orszymowo i Wilkanowo w pow. płockim)*, "Kwartalnik Historii Kultury Materialnej", vol. 16, 1968, no. 1, p. 69.

3 S. Kołodziejski, *Obronne rezydencje Lisów w północnej Małopolsce. Uwagi do problematyki badań*, "Acta Universitatis Lodziensis", Folia Archaeologica, vol. 18, 1994, p. 73.

4 T. Jurek, *Właściciele rezydencji*. In: R. Grygiel, T. Jurek, Zduny. Późnośredniowieczne i nowożytne rezydencje właścicieli miasta, Łódź 1999, p. 261.

We do not have any iconographic sources or descriptions of manor houses and their surroundings at the initial stage of their formation, i.e. from the end of the 13th century and 14th century. The illustrations usually presented larger buildings, usually built of stone or brick[5]. The earliest more elaborate written descriptions date back only to the 15th century.

As it may seem apparent the most 'risky' reconstruction is of the tower type of manor house. The determination of the number of storeys in the building, the remains of which are below ground level, is completely impossible for a layperson. However, archaeologists try to deal with the problem. Of course, well-preserved stratigraphy at the site as well as the way in which the building was destroyed are of essential importance. As long as the building was not burnt down and did not cave in, our chances to reconstruct the correct number of storeys are quite large, although such situations occur extremely rarely. So where does the conviction come from that mounds were built on with a tower and not with a one- or two-storey building with a basement? The idea did not emerge on the basis of archaeological discoveries. The decisive factor here was the similarity to brick or stone towers that have survived until the present day and are known even from Silesia or the borderlands (the Czech Republic, Germany) as well as more distant analogies from Western Europe. J. Kamińska wrote on this subject already back in 1966[6]. In later literature the thesis as regards the similarity of residences built on mounds to Western European motte-and-bailey manor houses was indisputably accepted and supported by historical sources.

In the case of the manor houses discussed herein, the authors quite often claim that the remains of buildings that they discovered during excavations should be reconstructed as towers. Unfortunately, they hardly ever quote any more convincing evidence based on stratigraphy in support of such an interpretation. Apart from Siedlątków, that has been referred to herein on numerous occasions, the site in Popów is another interesting example. Archaeologists discovered here the remains of a building (a tower keep?) constructed of oak and partially pine logs on a square plan with the sides of

5 P. Chotěbor, *Tvrze v ikonografických pramenech*, "Archaeologia Historica", vol. 17, 1992, pp. 177–187.

6 J. Kamińska, *Grodziska stożkowate śladem posiadłości rycerskich XIII–XIV w.*, "Prace i Materiały Muzeum Archeologicznego i Etnograficznego w Łodzi", no. 13, 1966, p. 43–78.

7.4 m. The first recessed floor was filled in with stones and clay up to the height of 2.4 m, so it was a kind of foundation stabilizing the entire construction, which may suggest that the actual height of the building was greater.

Much more often the authors are willing to reconstruct the houses in the shape of the tower if they discover during excavations the remains of buildings made of brick or stone, or at least constructions with stone underpinning. It seems that the width of the foundations is decisive here.

An important aspect of these deliberations is the symbolic meaning of the keep as the house of the master. In Polish literature, T. Jakimowicz reflected on this subject in his book published in 1979[7]. L. Kajzer suggested a much broader look at the problem, noting that keeps emerged at the time when other elements of knighthood symbolism were created, for example, all types of heraldic representations[8]. An extensive overview of European literature on the subject matter can be found in the work of M. Slivka, who considered this issue on the basis of tower buildings in Slovakia[9].

As I have already mentioned, the descriptions of manor houses dating back to the 13th and 14th centuries are rarely encountered in written sources. The bills from the royal court of Władysław II Jagiełło and Queen Jadwiga in relation to the construction of the wooden manor house in Jadowniki are valuable source of information. They were recorded in the year 1394. On their basis, T. Lalik attempted a reconstruction of the building process and appearance of the manor house[10]. "The manor house was not very large. The manor house consisted mainly of a chamber and room separated with the hallway. Interestingly, 3 padlocks and 3 iron fittings were purchased for the doors of the manor house. Hence, we can assume that there was the entrance door leading to the hallway and then the doors from the hallway to the room and the chamber. Only the room and the chamber had individual hearths,

7 T. Jakimowicz, *Dwór murowany w Polsce w wieku XVI (wieża-kamienica-kasztel)*, Warszawa–Poznań 1979.

8 L. Kajzer, *Grodziska średniowieczne i nowożytne*, "Prace i Materiały Muzeum Archeologicznego i Etnograficznego w Łodzi", no. 36, 1989–90, pp. 33–43.

9 M. Slivka, *Veže ako dominanty domínií (Symbolika a geneticko-typologický vývoj na Slovensku)*, "Archaeologia Historica Polona", vol. 12, 2002, pp. 9–29.

10 T. Lalik, *Budowa dworu drewnianego w Jadownikach w roku 1394*, "Kwartalnik Historii Kultury Materialnej", vol. 19, 1971, no. 3, pp. 463–468.

that is a stove and chimney. Perhaps there were other rooms without heating, just like in manor houses and castles erected in later times. These were mainly storage rooms, or alternatively a storage room and alcove, entered through the doors from the room or the main chamber"[11]. Unfortunately, the available sources are not sufficient to reconstruct the surrounding of these buildings. Other mentions are even more laconic, for example, a note from the year 1388 concerning dowry that included: the Górka village with the tower and other appurtenance (*et ipsam turiim cum villis adiacentibus*)[12].

There are a few more references in historical sources as regards manor houses dating to the 15th century. First, let us focus on those that mention tower buildings.

Indirect information about the appearance of the manor house from Błeszno village is dated to the year 1499 and relates to the division of property. Burneta is allotted the house within the landed estate and the grange, whereas her sister Dorota is granted the manor tower[13].

Information about the keep is also known from documents concerning Gruszów village, near Dobczyce. And so there are a few mentions from the years 1460 and 1479, in which the term *turris* is used. Let us quote two records from the year 1470: "*in turri et agros Mogilani*", and "*in Mogilani seu Gruschow, ubi turris est*"[14].

In those references where a tower keep is mentioned, it is usually only one of the elements among the manor buildings. However, we should remember that these references come from the second half of the 15th century. Therefore the question arises as to whether the absence of any descriptions of manor estates with a tower as one of residential buildings was merely due to the lack or terseness of any earlier sources? It is even more difficult to answer this question because on the basis of the above records it is not possible to guess how far away the keep was from the manor building. Was it in the direct vicinity within the area enclosed with a common fence or palisade or was the tower located

11 Ibid, p. 466.

12 *Słownik historyczno-geograficzny województwa krakowskiego w średniowieczu [Dictionary of History and Geography of Cracow Province]*, vol. I/3, s. 512 – entry: Dąbrowa, contributed by F. Sikora.

13 Ibid, I/1, p. 131 – entry: Błeszno, contributed by Z. Leszczyńska-Skrętowa.

14 Ibid, II/1, p. 90 – entry: Gruszów, contributed by F. Sikora.

in a different place as an individual defensive and residential building? The analysed references in historical sources quite often include descriptions of manor estates with several buildings. The widow of Peter of Jasienna who died in 1438 inherited three buildings with half of the landed estate, that is, the old house, the bath house, the new chamber with adjacent rooms and half of the mill etc.[15] The phrase *"three buildings with half of the landed estate"* may imply that *"the landed estate"* in this particular case referred to outbuildings and not residential *"buildings"*.

Another different and broad meaning of the term 'manor estate' emerges from another written source. A record dating to the year 1469 includes a description on the basis of which we can learn about the division of the landed estate in Chełm village between two brothers. Mikołaj received the house with the white chamber, rooms, the bath, malt house and stables, whereas Marcin was given: the house with the black chamber, rooms and stables ... Both brothers were to build a fence in the middle of the manor estate and border posts between the houses. The path to the garden should lead through the fence[16].

A fence is also mentioned in the record from the year 1488, in which Jakub of Gorlice made a bequest to his wife Barbara including the entire landed estate, as it is fenced[17]. Slightly later in 1496, Stanisław of Gorlice bequested to Jakub and his wife, Barbara, in perpetuity, his entire large manor, that had been fenced long ago, located within the manor estate in Gorlice[18]. Another record contains information about a moat. In 1498 Jan of Czulice leased the entire village, excluding the manor house encircled with a moat, the garden and an orchard, to Mikołaj Szalowski for four grzywnas *[an old Polish weight unit: 1 grzywna –about 200 g of silver]* per year[19]. As can be seen from another record, moats were considered useful even in the second half of the 15th century to increase the defence of the house. There is a record from the year 1466 with a description of the manor estate in Pałecznica village: "a new house surrounded by a moat, starting with the kitchen, then further through the central part of the manor estate to the barn"[20].

15 Ibid II/2, p. 248 – entry: Jasienna, contributed by: Z. Leszczyńska-Skrętowa.

16 Ibid I/2, p. 337 – entry: Chełm (dziś w Krakowie), contributed by: F. Sikora.

17 Ibid, I/4, p. 795–796 – entry: Gorlice, contributed by: J. Laberschek.

18 Ibid.

19 Ibid, I/3 p. 478 – entry: Czulice, contributed by: Z. Leszczyńska-Skrętowa.

20 Ibid, III/4, p. 851 – entry: Łaszów, contributed by: M. Wilamowski.

Unfortunately, usually the small extent of excavations, do not allow archaeologists to make comment about the appearance of the outbuildings that surrounded the manor house.

To resume the discussion about the defensive nature of the residences, it is necessary to state that written sources do not contain more precise descriptions that would enable the archaeologist to reconstruct them. Usually they provide an account of the effort put into capturing and plundering a particular manor house. However, taking into consideration the fact that this information is usually derived from court records, we need to be aware of its 'subjective' character. Such reports most often mentioned damaged doors, and hence we can guess that they had to be locked or barred if it was necessary to batter them down. Locking the door most likely secured the residence against assault and robbery, but not against burglary and theft in the modern sense of the words. We can quote a note about how in the year 1481 Michał of Zagórzany accused Mikołaj Kawecki that he and 50 companions intruded into his house in Zagórzany and having broken the gate and two doors, they took away clothes, shoes, doublets, axes and other items, the value of which amounted to 20 grzywnas *[1 grzywna –about 200 g of silver]*[21].

No detailed descriptions of those gates and doors exist, but the large number of people taking part in forcing them implies a substantial number of defenders and not that the residence guaranteed a defensive advantage. Sometimes a smaller number of attackers was sufficient. For example, in 1468 Peter of Książnice sued Piotr Goźdź of Łapczyca for an incident during which he and his four companions of equal rank as well six lower-class companions intruded into his house, smashed the gates and a pair of "*pallacii*" doors [to the hall?], four doors to chambers and took a sword decorated with silver and many other valuables[22]. As many as 12 doors and a gate were broken during a raid on the house of Halszka of Kwilina[23].

The remains of stone or brick buildings cause considerable difficulties with interpretation. As we usually find only a foundation, it is difficult to determine the construction and material used for erection of the walls. It seems that the lack of substantial quantities of stones or bricks at the site does not imply that the walls

21 Ibid, II/3, p. 460 – entry: Kawec, contributed by: Z. Leszczyńska-Skrętowa.

22 Ibid, III/2, p. 321 – entry: Książnice, contributed by: Z. Leszczyńska-Skrętowa.

23 Ibid, III/2, p. 414 – entry: Kwilina, contributed by: J. Laberschek.

of a building erected on stone foundations were made of wood. With the constant shortage of raw materials, we can have reasonable suspicions that the walls were demolished and the building material was used for the construction of another building. On the other hand, the presence of small quantities of stones or bricks at the site does not necessarily determine that the buildings were constructed of brick or stone. We could also presume with all likelihood that they were used only for the foundations, furnace underpinning or chimney draught.

Similar problems apply to the reconstruction of roofs in manor houses. Finds of roof tiles are few, and also it is difficult to date them precisely, especially at sites where the usage period extended beyond the Middle Ages. According to the information referred to above it seems however that their use was occasional. Also, there are few findings of shingles or tools for their production. It seems that the majority of roofs were covered with straw or with reeds in the case of houses situated on wetlands.

Historical sources do not contain much information as regards the covering of window openings. Apart from the above mentioned fittings that might have strengthened wooden shutters, there is no other essential data that can be used for reconstruction. One of the few pieces of information as regards their use is a note dated to the year 1455, from which we learn that Jadwiga, the wife of Piotr Leksicki sued Jura of Gruszów for intruding into her house and stealing iron window fittings that were worth 28 grzywnas *[1 grzywna – about 200 g of silver]*[24].

In fact, there are no such finds as, for example, glass or lead that might imply that glass panels appeared in knights' manor houses in the late Middle Ages. Only during research on Ledniczka Island archaeologists managed to discover one piece of glass, which may be interpreted as the fragment of a pane, although it is open to doubt[25]. Fragments of glass that might have been the part of a stained-glass window were reported by J. Kuczyński, when he discussed the results of excavations carried out at the bishop's manor house in Dębno[26]. I did not encounter any references in written sources as regards to glazed windows in knight's manor houses.

24 Ibid, II/1. p. 103 – entry: Gruszów–contributed by: F. Sikora.

25 J. Górecki, M. Łastowiecki, J. Wrzesiński, *Gródek na Ledniczce*. In Studia Lednickie, vol. 4, Poznań–Lednica 1996, p. 197–246, p. 233.

26 J. Kuczyński, *XIV-wieczny gródek w Dębnie, woj. kieleckie, gmina Nowa Słupia*, "Rocznik Muzeum Narodowego w Kielcach", vol. 12, 1982, p. 229.

We also do not know of any descriptions of floors in manor buildings. During excavations archaeologists documented the use of pugging, floors made of boards or those paved with erratic stones. The few discoveries of brick floors were made most frequently in residences that functioned until the modern period and probably it is not possible to date them back to the Late Middle Ages.

Carpets that are sometimes described in sources were rather used in medieval manor houses for the decoration of walls as well as for insulation purposes. Unfortunately, no findings in archaeological material may be considered to be their remains. The fact that they were used is known only from scarce written records.

Thus, according to a description dated to the year 1398, a chest from the manor house in Balice contained 36 pieces of silver and one carpet[27]. In another document dated to the year 1496 the inventory of belongings included 2 new and 1 partially used carpet[28].

Some evidence to reconstruct the appearance of walls is also found in archaeological material. We have already mentioned the suggestion given by authors that the walls were 'plastered' with clay. Clay applied on the external walls was used for fire protection and insulation, while covering the walls with clay inside the house might have had an aesthetic function. As confirmation of this thesis we can mention the site in Jarocin, where archaeologists found lumps of ornamented pugging[29]. Ceramic tiles on the wall might have been another method of decoration and we have already mentioned the artefact found in the manor house in Trzemsze[30].

Another interior element of the manor house that may be reconstructed on the basis of finds from the excavations is the heating system. We are dealing here with all types of heating systems available at that time, including the simplest hearths built of erratic stones and the 'central' hypocaust heating systems found

27 *Słownik historyczno-geograficzny...*, I/1, p. 17 – entry: Balice, contributed by: F. Sikora.

28 Ibid, III/3, p. 596 – entry: Libertów, contributed by: J. Kurtyka.

29 R. Grygiel, *Zarembowie z Jarocina w świetle źródeł archeologicznych i historycznych*, Łódź 1992, pp. 12–13.

30 M. Kociński, Późnośredniowieczna siedziba obronna w Trzemszach w woj. konińskim, Łódź 1995 (Master's dissertation in the archives of the Institute of Archaeology at the University of Łódź), pp. 70–71.

at the manor house in Jankowo Dolne. Untouched places where a fireplace or stove was originally located are found quite rarely. Therefore, most often we are forced to reconstruct these devices on the basis of such discoveries as fragments of blackened pugging and above all findings of stove tiles. Unfortunately we are not always able to determine how a given homestead was heated. The above-mentioned hypocaust heating system was undoubtedly very unique. As demonstrated in our previous deliberations, tiled stoves were not very frequent in manor houses under excavation. Most often they were built of vessel (pot) tiles. The sites where both vessel and plate tiles are discovered are problematic as regards interpretation. It seems that in the case of such discoveries it is most important to determine whether there were two different stoves in the building, or only one made of two types of tiles. Unfortunately, finding the answer to this question is usually not possible.

The presence of several heaters gives the researchers the potential for determining the purpose of the locations in which they operated. Tiled stoves, for obvious reasons, were built in chambers for entertaining visitors, whereas dome-shaped furnaces and open hearths operated in outbuildings or kitchens.

Unfortunately, we are not able to reconstruct the shape of open hearths that seemed to have prevailed in medieval manor houses. Due to the relatively small floor area of the premises that often served multiple purposes, that is, a bedroom, a dining room, a guest room, hearths seems to have been located by the wall, so they had the form of a fireplace. In addition, such location could facilitate in guiding the smoke away from the room. However, we do not have any clues available that would help us reconstruct such hearths.

Tiled stoves were certainly very expensive. However we need to consider whether it was the financial aspect that contributed to their low popularity in manor houses. We should take into account that a fireplace was much more functional; it heated the room quickly and was used for warming up or even cooking food. Above all, it was also the source of light[31], which was essential in the case of dark rooms, where the light came in mainly through a small window covered with membranes. And here we come to another important issue, namely the illumination of the chambers.

31 M. Dąbrowska, *Kominek – luksus czy konieczność?* In: Nędza czy dostatek na ziemiach polskich od średniowiecza po wiek XX, J. Sztetyłło (ed.), Warsaw 1992, pp. 177–181.

We know that in addition to fireplaces and open hearths, suet and wax were used for this purpose, however, the latter was quite expensive and wax candles were rather luxurious products[32]. During archaeological research no objects were found that could be interpreted as 'oil lamps' or candlesticks. In Zduny archaeologists discovered a device for fixing torches on the walls.

A very unique discovery was made during excavations at the side in Zgierz. It was a wooden building with a basement and with dimensions of 5×6 m. It was dated to the period between the end of the 14th century and the end of the 15th century. Unfortunately, we were not able to determine whether it was a manor house or a house associated with the presbytery that functioned in the vicinity (a school, the curate's house?). Archaeologists found an artefact there on the basis of which they suggested the reconstruction of an oil lamp. It was a circular object with the diameter of approximately 30 cm, made of a ceramic tube with a wall thickness between 0.3–0.5 cm and an internal diameter of circa 1.5 cm. The upper surface of the tube most likely had 12 openings radiating symmetrically and ended with circa 7 cm long sleeves with an internal diameter of 1.5–2.5 cm. The empty space in the tube was like an oil container, and wicks were placed through the sleeves, which served as burners. The author of the study provided convincing, though fairly remote, analogies to that lamp[33].

The possibilities of archaeology as regards to the reconstruction of other elements of interior decoration in medieval manor houses are limited. The vast majority of furniture was made of wood and other organic materials (leather, textiles, wicker) that very rarely survive in the ground, whereas their metal elements are not very characteristic, which makes it difficult to even try to reconstruct particular objects.

On the basis of iconography representing as a rule the interiors of castles or rooms in bourgeois houses, and most often from other European countries, we know that a diverse set of furniture was used in the late Middle Ages. Tables,

32 A. Rutkowska-Płachcińska, *Mieszkanie, higiena*. In: Historia kultury materialnej Polski w zarysie, red. W. Hensel, J. Pazdur, vol. 2, Od XIII do XV wieku, red. A. Rutkowska-Płachcińska, Wrocław 1978, pp. 339, 342; M. Dąbrowska, *Oświetlenie i ogrzewanie średniowiecznych wnętrz zamkowych*, "Archaeologia Historica Polona", vol. 14, pp. 178.

33 P. Świątkiewicz, *O średniowiecznej lampie ze Zgierza*. In: Od pradziejów do współczesności. Archeologiczne wędrówki. Studia dedykowane Pani Profesor Marii Magdalenie Blombergowej, Łódź 2007, pp. 59–61.

beds, small tables or all kinds of shelves, or more rarely cabinets, were most likely present in the majority of knight's manor houses in medieval Poland. Among the artefacts discovered during excavations, elements that can be considered as remains of furniture include, first of all, different kinds of fittings. However, it is difficult to determine whether they were fixed to doors, windows, furniture or maybe chests? It seems that the latter were one of the most important pieces of household equipment. This is where the most precious things were stored, and perhaps this is why they are often mentioned in historical records.

The list of contents of a chest from the year 1487 includes: a bonnet embroidered with gold, a silk bonnet, two kerchiefs (one made of silk and one Wrocław type), and a shirt with silver buttons[34]. An interesting record dated to the year 1447 can be found in relation to the manor house in Sobiesiernie, where the inventory included 2 cases (*ladule*) with documents and broken silver[35].

More equipment is listed in the record concerning the bequest to the children of the deceased Mikołaj Czarny of Podole and Jawczyce. They received among other things 2 large chests and 5 small boxes[36]. The same document also mentions a cabinet "*in stubalia nova*"[37]. It is difficult to prejudge whether it was a wardrobe as a stand-alone piece of furniture, or perhaps a lockable door in a wall recess (Almari), which are presented in iconography. We can further read about two tables of sound workmanship and four ordinary tables. On the basis of this record, we can perhaps draw conclusions not only as regards the quantity, but also various quality of furniture used in particular rooms[38].

However, according to written sources, chests were used not only to store valuables. Larger trunks with flat lids could also serve as beds. Probably this is

34 *Słownik historyczno-geograficzny województwa płockiego w średniowieczu [Dictionary of History and Geography of Płock]*, z. 4, oprac. A. Borkiewicz-Celińska, Warszawa 2000, z. 4, p. 314 – entry: Tyszki–Bregendy

35 *Słownik historycznogeograficzny województwa poznańskiego w średniowieczu [Dictionary of History and Geography of Poznań Province]*, cz. IV, z. 3 red. T. Jurek, oprac. P. Dembiński, K. Górska-Gołaska, T. Jurek, współpraca archeologiczna A. Łosińska, Poznań 2005, IV/3, p. 573 – entry: Sobiesiernie, contributed by: P. Dembiński.

36 *Słownik historyczno-geograficzny województwa krakowskiego...*, III/z. 3, p. 596 – entry: Libertów.

37 Ibid.

38 Ibid.

how we should interpret the mention about a chest with a silk head-rest listed among the objects attached in the village of Kobylepole that were the subject of litigation in 1491[39].

Most likely not only head-rests were used during a night's sleep. In written sources we find descriptions of various types of bedding. A record dated to 1451 in relation to the manor house in Brzączowice includes, among others: 3 feather quilts, 6 pillows, 9 pillow-cases, and 4 sheets[40]. In a record dated to the year 1466, we read that there was a family dispute concerning among other things: 3 silk quilts and 4 silk pillows[41].

Beds themselves are mentioned rarely. From a record dated to the year 1475 we can learn that Jakub of Trzeciesz sued his brothers for walking off with many belongings, including: beds, feather quilts, pillows and towels[42].

It seems that furniture used in the chambers of a manor house was not valuable. It is mentioned in written sources relatively rarely and if so, it is referred to as 'household equipment'. Let us quote a testament from 1485 with the followings bequest: two cups, household equipment, silver, gold, precious stones, colourful fur-lined overcoats, and silver spoons[43]. The little value of household equipment seems to be demonstrated by the fact that they were not listed in detail even in the case of disputes concerning the plundered property of another person. Such a situation is referred to in a record dated to the year 1476, in which we read about the appropriation of a red marten fur-lined overcoat, 3 new fox fur-lined overcoats, 8 silver spoons…, 18 florins in cash and all the household equipment[44]. A similar record was made in the year 1464, in which the inventory includes among other things: horses, vessels (*scutella*), silver spoons, pots and other household equipment, the value of which amounted to 100 grzywnas *[1 grzywna – about 200 g of silver]*[45].

39 *Słownik historycznogeograficzny województwa poznańskiego…*, IV/3, p. 475 – entry: Skórzewo, contributed by: P. Dembiński.

40 *Słownik historyczno-geograficzny województwa krakowskiego…*, I/2 p. 227 – entry: Brzączowice, contributed by: Z. Leszczyńska-Skrętowa.

41 Ibid, IV/1, p. 48 – entry: Maków, contributed by: A. Marzec.

42 Ibid, II/2, p. 204 – entry: Janczowa, contributed by: Z. Leszczyńska-Skrętowa.

43 Ibid, III/1, p. 169 – entry: Krużlowa contributed by: F. Sikora.

44 Ibid, II/4, p. 560 – entry: Kłaj, contributed by: F. Sikora.

45 *Słownik historyczno-geograficzny województwa* poznańskiego…, IV/3, p. 472 – entry: Skórzewo…

The term 'household equipment' is most often associated with kitchenware and household utensils. Let's take a look first at kitchenware and tableware, because a distinction between these two categories is not exactly possible.

During excavations archaeologists most often encounter pieces of vessels, the vast majority of which are fragments of ceramic pots. It seems that in the archaeological publications referred to herein much more attention is paid to the technology used in the vessels production, rather than to their potential function. For the purpose of our discussion, however, the latter issue seems to be of crucial importance. In addition to pots and bowls that had been popular in the previous periods, new types of vessels appeared in the late Middle Ages, for example jugs, three-legged cauldrons, lids, cups, etc. The wider range of vessels reflects both changed eating habits as well as table manners. Most likely for the first time in our lands there were 'individual' dishes, intended for one person to use, that is small bowls, cups or jugs. Metal vessels started to prevail in later periods, and these, as we know, are encountered very rarely by archaeologists. Reading the records in historical sources we become convinced that the small traces of these items found among archaeological artefacts is not tantamount to the absence of such items in manor houses. While ceramic and wooden vessels are usually not listed in written sources, mentions of metal pots appear quite often, which proves that they were very popular, and at same time seem to have been very expensive. There are descriptions not only of non-ferrous metal tableware, but also iron pots and vats.

Findings of cutlery are also exceptional, except for knives that were very universal tools used not only at the table and in the kitchen. The small number of spoons discovered by archaeologists does not mean that they were used occasionally. Probably the majority of them was made of wood, so they survive in the ground very rarely. Therefore in order to discuss table manners, archaeologists need to refer to written sources. First of all, it is necessary to determine whether the artefacts that we discover and consider to be unique, were such in reality. Let us look at a few descriptions.

In 1465 Dorota of Kalinowa was summoned to court having been accused by the brother of her husband of the appropriation of the following things: platters, bowls, cups and spoons to the total value of 2000 grzywnas *[1 grzywna – about*

200 g of silver][46]. Another record from the year 1460 includes the following list of objects owned by Elżbieta of Koniecpol: 2 fur coats, 5 shallow bowls, 6 plates and 4 silver cups plated with gold[47]. The testament of Andrzej of Krużlowa from the year 1485 includes the following bequests: 2 cups, household utensils, silver, gold, precious stones, colourful fur-lined overcoats, and silver spoons[48]. In addition to silver spoons, the dowry of Katarzyna of Radzanowo Stare written down in 1450 included tablecloths, but we do not know their quantity[49]. In 1451 Franciszek of Kunice was accused of stealing among other things 2 tablecloths and 2 tin platters[50]. In 1421 Katarzyna of Łapszowo accused Niemsta of Szczytniki and Skroniowo of intruding into the house of her mother in Szalowa and stealing among other things: 4 silver spoons valued at 2 grzywnas *[1 grzywna –about 200 g of silver]*, 2 silver-plated knives worth 2 grzywnas, 4 tin pots worth 2 grzywnas, a cauldron worth 2 grzywnas as well as a bowl valued at half a grzywna[51].

A rich collection of vessels is referred to in two other documents. The first one is a dowry written down in 1441 and it includes: 15 silver spoons made of 4 grzywnas of pure silver, 10 tin platters (*scutellas stanneas alias cenowich*), 10 tin plates, 10 iron pots...[52]. The record quoted below lists various kinds of utensils, which proves that there was not only a wide range of tableware. The range of kitchenware was also enriched to a considerable extent. A partial list of utensils in the manor house in Dąbrówka included: 20 cups (*scultella*) made of copper and tin-plated (*cuprea alias oczenowy*), 20 plates, 16 silver spoons, a boiler for brewing beer and other smaller pots for cooking fish, as well hearth iron elements (spits?). The total value of the equipment amounted to 50 grzywnas[53].

46 *Słownik historyczno-geograficzny województwa krakowskiego...*, II/2, p. 237 – entry: Januszowice, contributed by: Z. Leszczyńska-Skrętowa.

47 Ibid, II/1, p. 145 – entry: Hartmański Młyn, contributed by: J. Luciński.

48 Ibid, III/1, p. 169 – entry: Krużlowa.

49 *Słownik historyczno-geograficzny województwa płockiego...*, z. 3, p. 252 – entry: Radzanowo Stare.

50 *Słownik historyczno-geograficzny województwa krakowskiego...*, III/2 p. 346 – entry: Kunice; Ibid, I/2. p. 227 – entry: Brzączowice.

51 Ibid, III/4, p. 841 – entry: Łapszów

52 Ibid, III/2, p. 279 – entry: Książ Mały, contributed by: W. Bukowski.

53 *Słownik historyczno-geograficzny województwa poznańskiego...*, IV/3, p. 573 – entry: Sobiesiernie.

Let us note at this point that pots for cooking fish were listed in the plural, so there must have been several of them and they were probably made of metal, because ceramic vessels were usually not described.

Iron pots were listed in these records several times, but each time in small quantities. The fact that they were included in the inventory and that there was a small number of them implies that they were relatively expensive.

Staying on the subject of expensive dishes, I would like to draw attention to the fact that written sources in general do not mention glass vessels. In this case the situation is exactly the opposite compared to the artefacts referred to above. Fragments of cups, glasses or bowls are sometimes found during the excavations, but we do not encounter any mention of them in documentation. Unfortunately I do not know how to explain this situation.

In the historical records analysed herein there are no *explicite* mentions of stoneware or other refined ceramic products (eg. maiolica) that must have been valuable imported items. However we encounter the term "cup", without mentioning the raw material it was made of. Is it possible that these laconic expressions refer to these types of vessels?

It seems that the greatest number of objects, the remains of which are found during archaeological excavations, are kitchen utensils and household equipment. However, we should realize that on that basis of the excavations we are able to list only a small percentage of household items. This applies to the above comments on occasional discoveries of 'exclusive' objects. We also know that we have little chances of finding objects made of wood or other organic materials. We will not find any wooden jugs, kneading-troughs, barrels, small wooden pails, scoops and the whole range of so often used stave vessels or turned bowls and plates, as well as sieves or strainers made of bast. Our inventories also do not include any wooden spoons, pestles, or pounders / whisks. There are even no references concerning these utensils in historical sources. Hence, when reconstructing kitchenware, we are actually forced solely to resort to ethnographic analogies and our own imagination with the little help of a not very rich iconography, which relates rather to other countries and most often to a different social group of users.

Carts are quite often mentioned in written sources. As it could be observed on the basis of the examples referred to in the chapter on tools, correct identification of particular elements is extremely difficult. Different types of clamps, hooks, pins or links might have served various purposes and we have little chance to define their function correctly. Coming back to written sources, several types of wagons have been distinguished, e.g. wooden or iron carts. For example in the record made in 1430 Jakub of Iwanowice undertook to pay off the new cart with iron fittings and 2 horses[54]. The mention from the year 1492 includes information about a military wagon (currus falcatus)[55].

The previously mentioned sickles, axes and knives or scissors required sharpening from time to time. In theory it can be done with any stone, however, the high price of such tools must have resulted in more careful usage. Probably as such they were sharpened with whetstones, which is faster, better, and above all, saves on the metal. Therefore it can be assumed that whetstones were widely used, and because they were not too precious, we should often find them during exploration. For this reason, their relatively low frequency in archaeological inventories is surprising. Perhaps some of them went unnoticed or were treated as ordinary stones by less experienced archaeologists?

There is a similar situation with flint and steels. They must have been in common use and, although made of iron, probably not very expensive and easy to make due to their relatively simple form. Nevertheless, they are artefacts that are either rarely found or hardly ever identified by archaeologists.

The question arises, why tools were stored in manor buildings. The answer is that they may have been used frequently, perhaps for current repairs rather than for the manufacture of necessary equipment and utensils. Another reason was that these were valuable items. The limited state of research does not allow for a comparison with the set of tools stored in the outbuildings of manor houses. We have no knowledge as to whether there were more or fewer tools kept in the outbuildings compared to manor houses, or if there were any tools at all. Unfortunately, without more extensive sources we are not able to provide the answer to this question.

While the presence of sometimes specialized tools on the premises of the manor house may be surprising, yet the presence of elements of armour and horse tack does not seem to be extraordinary. This issue attracts the interest

54 *Słownik historyczno-geograficzny województwa krakowskiego...*, II/2, p. 182 – entry: Iwanowice, contributed by: Z. Leszczyńska-Skrętowa.

55 Ibid, III/4, p. 1036 – entry: Łukowica, contributed by: W. Bukowski.

of both archaeologists and historians and it often becomes a subject of shorter or longer dissertations[56]. As regards the sites referred to in this work, archaeologists found a significant number of artefacts that may be classified into every military category. This is also confirmed in written sources. A record dated to the year 1496 includes the inventory of equipment of two knightly sons: 12 elements of armour, 3 spears, 3 lances, 3 crossbows with 2 accessories, (cocking devices and quivers), a full set of armour for a heavy-armed rider and 2 sets of armour for a light-armed shooter, 4 saddles, 1 small gold-plated shield...[57]. Similar quantities are also listed in other records.

It is probably not necessary to specifically remind the reader that a knight, in addition to having his own weapons, had a duty to equip his retainers. Therefore each family should have been in possession of a larger quantity of military equipment, because even if an adult male heir was lacking, the remaining family was still obliged to send military expeditions. Weapon, apart from their purely military function, served also to emphasize the status of its owner. Therefore care was given not only to its functional qualities, but also to appearance.

Pieces of clothing are found rather rarely during archaeological excavation. We usually discover only those elements of clothing that were made of metal or bone. Sometimes, in favourable circumstances, we find preserved, sometimes in a vestigial state, fragments of objects made of leather or hide. Most frequently these are pieces of shoes and belts. There is also fragmented clothing or, less often, purses and other containers (pouches, quivers, etc.). The number of references in written sources describing rich attire is very high. However, we will not quoted them all here. Suffice it to say, however, that they were made of expensive, often imported materials, sometimes of fabrics interwoven with threads of gold or silver and trimmed with pearls.

A special part of the knight's attire was the belt. According to written sources a knight sometimes had several belts. As they were often given on pledge, there are many descriptions of belts in judicial records. By way of example, in 1431 Jan Strasz of Kościelniki pledged 3 silver belts, gilded on the surface[58]. We do

56 Cf: Footnotes in the chapter on military items.

57 *Słownik historyczno-geograficzny województwa krakowskiego...*, III/3, p. 596 – entry: Libertów.

58 Ibid, III/1 p. 45 – entry: Kościelniki, contributed by: Z. Leszczyńska-Skrętowa.

not know if these records should be treated verbatim. Were the belts made entirely of silver, that is of silver chain links combined together to make the belt flexible, or was the belt set with silver plates? Belts were also worn by women. In a record made in the year 1450 with a description of the dowry of Katarzyna of Radzanowo Stare, we can read about a belt with silver ornaments[59]. Apart from typical belts, women also wore decorated loincloths on the hip. One of them must have been very decorative or made of metal, as it was priced at 30 Hungarian florins. It was listed in a record dated to the year 1480 concerning the dowry of Elżbieta of Regulice[60].

As regards ornaments, although they were made of durable materials that would be able to survive in the ground, most likely they were well protected as valuable items and hence the chances of them being left in the ground were remote. So, once again we will have to support with written sources things relating to knightly possessions.

In 1468 the court ordered that Jan Nekanda return valuables worth 210 grzywnas *[1 grzywna -about 200 g of silver]*, including 12 gold rings and 50 pearls[61]. There are records in written sources made in the years 1432 and 1434 in relation to a bonnet with pearls that Mikołaj of Czech pledged for 10 grzywnas[62]. In the years 1468–1469 Anna of Grzegorzowice sued her guardian Jan Nekanda for 12 silver pendants, 2 silver tiaras and 12 rings made of gold and pearls[63]. Of course, not every knight's family could boast such wealth. On the other hand, the records do not refer to the most affluent families.

Let us proceed now to the issues related to personal hygiene. Archaeological finds include items that may be helpful in the reconstruction of this sphere of everyday life in the knight's manor house. I have already described the findings of combs and razors as well as aquamaniles, i.e. vessels used for washing hands prior to sitting at the table. Other vessels for washing are difficult to identify

59 *Słownik historyczno-geograficzny województwa płockiego...*, z. 3, p. 252 – entry: Radzanowo Stare.

60 *Słownik historyczno-geograficzny województwa krakowskiego...*, III/4, p. 906 – entry: Łękawa Marcinkowice, contributed by: M. Wilamowski.

61 Ibid, I/2, p. 212 – entry: Brodła, contributed by: Z. Leszczyńska-Skrętowa.

62 Ibid, I/3, p. 456 – entry: Czechy, contributed by: Z. Leszczyńska-Skrętowa.

63 Ibid, II/1, p. 120 – entry: Grzegorzowice, contributed by: F. Sikora.

among archaeological artefacts, which should not really be surprising. Larger utensils, i.e. jugs or wash-tubs were most often made of wood. Others, such as ceramic water containers, being versatile in form, may have been used for various purposes. We are not able to say much about the purpose they were intended for. Again, written sources might be of some help. In 1475, Jakub of Trzeciesz sued his brothers for taking away many belongings from home, including the towels[64]. Another record dated to the year 1487 is related to Jan Kożuszek of Tyszki who undertook to return to Barbara, his daughter-in-law, various items that belonged to her, including 3 towels and 1 basin[65].

Other issues for discussion are such areas of life as entertainment, social life or, in the widest of understanding, culture and science. Of course, the first question is about books, documents and writing instruments. I have already mentioned the artefacts found in Zduny (a stilus) and on Ledniczka Island (the fittings of a book), which prove that such objects were present, at least in some knight's manor houses. Listed below there is a mention from the year 1447 which includes 2 chests which contained documents. Another reference includes the list of books kept at the knight's manor house, although they belonged to a clergyman, as a result of which this record requires a different interpretation. In a record dated to the year 1395, Dorota and Tomek of Drwinia and Wyżyce were named as parties that sued Mikołaj of Knyszyn and his mother Krystyna and her other children for 33 stacks of cereal, cattle, pigs, horses, books, a hooded coat and 1000 grzywnas *[1 grzywna -about 200 g of silver]* that belonged to the canon of Cracow, Michał of Knyszyn[66].

Now let us focus on entertainment. Apart from the already mentioned skates, other items used for entertainment include different kinds of games. Artefacts that prove that games were used include mainly balls, counters and dice that were most often made of animal bones. During excavations archaeologists find objects defined as parts of musical instruments. We have already mentioned a fragment of a pipe.

64 Ibid, II/2, p. 204 – entry: Janczowa.

65 *Słownik historyczno-geograficzny województwa płockiego...*, z. 4, p. 314 – entry: Tyszki–Bregendy.

66 *Słownik historyczno-geograficzny województwa krakowskiego...*, II/4, 604 – entry: Knyszyn, contributed by: F. Sikora.

Fig. 24. Knife handle made of ivory, Orłów

A few words have been said with reference to issues related to the sphere of symbolism and in a broad sense spiritual culture when discussing the tower-form of manor buildings. However, this is not the end of the possibilities as regards our interpretations concerning this extremely difficult field of archaeological studies. As it seems, archaeologists have definitely underrated the subject of 'protective magic', to which the residents of manor houses resorted. And here another issue to be discussed in the context of the construction of knight's residences is that of a foundation sacrifice. During excavations we encountered findings at several sites that may be interpreted as such sacrifices.

In Gozdowo below the north-eastern corner of the stone house, archaeologists discovered a small pit containing a ceramic pot dated to 14th–15th centuries[67]. It prompted the author of the research to believe that these might have been the traces of the foundation sacrifice.

A discovery from Orszymowo is much more difficult to interpret. It is also the result of more complicated human activities. Under the wooden recessed building located on the mound, archaeologists found a thin burnt

67 E. Prusicka-Kołcon, *Wyniki badań tzw. gródka stożkowatego w Gozdowie, stan. 1, pow. Hrubieszów,* "Archeologia Polski Środkowowschodniej", vol. 4, 1999, p. 191.

layer containing numerous artefacts: fragments of pottery, iron handle, nails, possibly a fragment of a bow and burnt grains of various cereals etc. Only some of them had traces of burning. Other artefacts, for example, a bronze vessel, had traces of being deliberately broken into pieces. The author of the studies found no other logical explanation for this stratigraphic structure, and presumed the possibility that these are the traces of activities related to the making of a foundation sacrifice[68].

The alleged foundation sacrifice discovered during exploration of the manor house owned by the provost of the Płock Chapter in Proboszczewice had a slightly different form. Here, near the south-west corner of the building dating back to the second half of the 14th century, archaeologists found a cluster of erratic stones, between which there were fragments of pottery and a bone, i.e. a cow/ox shoulder blade, which was the most appreciated part of this animal for the consumer[69].

As can be seen from the above mentioned information, even an archaeologist who explores the fully Christian period of our history can find traces of activities that could be described as pagan, superstitious or magical. Of course, any attempt at explaining the function of such mysterious relics carries a significant risk of error. However, it depends mainly on us as to whether we take the risk and try to expand the boundaries of human activity, that we can infer on the basis of excavations[70].

The lack of large numbers of such items as amulets associated with pagan beliefs may be explained by the progress of Christianisation of the country. Unfortunately, any relevant evidence available in archaeological material is also scarce. In fact there are no reports concerning any discovery of devotional items. Only archaeologists who excavated the manor house in Mrówki mentioned a standing iron cross. Any reports in written sources are also very rare. There

68 W. Szymański, *Przyczynek do badań nad problematyką grodzisk stożkowatych (Orszymowo i Wilkanowo w pow. płockim)*, "Kwartalnik Historii Kultury Materialnej", vol. 16, 1968, no. 1, pp. 60–65.

69 A. Marciniak-Kajzer, *Dwór obronny w Proboszczewicach*, "Acta Universitatis Lodziensis". Folia Archaeologica, vol. 18, 1994, p. 30.

70 T. A. Kastek, A. Limisiewicz, R. Mruczek, *Domniemane ofiary zakładzinowe z terenu folwarku w Sobótce,* "Śląskie Sprawozdania Archeologiczne", vol. 43, 2001, pp. 461–472.

is a record dated to the year 1434 concerning an attack on the manor house and the seizure of, among other things, *"sanctuarium alias swanthoszcz"*[71]. This sanctuary was worth 100 grzywnas *[1 grzywna – about 200 g of silver]* but we have no idea what it might have looked like.

71 *Słownik historyczno-geograficzny województwa krakowskiego w średniowieczu [Dictionary of History and Geography of Cracow Province]*, cz. I, z. 2, (ed.) J. Wiśniewski, oprac. J. Laberschek, Z. Leszczyńska-Skrętowa, F. Sikora, J. Wiśniewski, Wrocław 1985, II/2 p. 244 – entry: Jaroszów, contributed by: Z. Leszczyńska-Skrętowa.

V. THE ENDING

It is finally time to spend a moment in reflection concerning the picture of a medieval knight's manor house that we can get on the basis of archaeological materials and that is presented in this work. I have already mentioned many times that the state of research is insufficient and we shall return to this subject in this chapter later on. First let us have a look at the situation in the neighbouring territories to the Kingdom of Poland, i.e. our conventional area for consideration.

The obvious question arises about the possibility of comparison of the knights' manor houses from the territory of medieval Poland to those in neighbouring countries, or to estates that were owned by the clergy or belonged to rulers. Even in the content of each chapter there were references to the excavation results of the remains of manor houses in Silesia or Chełmno Land. Admittedly, the reference material here is very rich. Such sites as Plemięta and Bachotek from Chełmno Land as well as Zbrojewsko and Ryczeń from Silesia are a valuable source of analogy. However, there is a formal problem. In principle such a comparison should be carried out on several levels. We should compare knights' manor houses from the territories of Poland to ones in the neighbouring countries. Similarly, knights' residences should be compared to those owned by clergymen, as well as owned by dukes, which shall be then multiplied by incorporating the sites from neighbouring countries. To trace the evolution of these settlements and see if they proceeded simultaneously, it would be necessary to present a picture of the dynamic changes, additionally supported by their precise dating. Unfortunately, the present state of research does not allow such an activity. Even in the introduction to this book a reservation was expressed concerning the failure to determine the owners of many of these settlements, which means that there are certainly houses owned by clergy or dukes even among those sites that were considered *a priori* as 'knights' residences. Given such a situation we could propose the thesis that these residences did not differ fundamentally as no important dissimilarities have been noted so far. In academic research, however, it is better to operate with facts rather than speculations and therefore this thesis is still waiting for verification.

Similar considerations apply to sites located outside the borders of the Kingdom of Poland, both in closer and more distant territories. Therefore, writing about the studies of defensive manor houses in Central Europe, I am not able to separate the knight's manor houses for the purpose of comparisons, especially that the residences of the motte-and-bailey type in the western region emerged much earlier in slightly different socio–economic conditions and they were related to a slightly different model of the feudal system.

Let us look briefly at the situation in the neighbouring territories. In 1984 A. Pawłowski presented the following estimations concerning relevant sites from Silesia. Among the sites that were well-known at that time, 377 were defined by A. Pawłowski as motte-and-bailey settlements, whereas 40 as residential keeps[1]. These settlements were predominantly single-unit buildings (85%), and the vast majority of them were located within the strip of river valleys and on flood-lands[2]. D. Nowakowski has recently published a work and in one of the chapters he recapitulated the current state of knowledge concerning motte-and-bailey residences in Silesia[3]. Unfortunately, as in the case of other regions of Poland, only a field survey was carried out at the majority of the sites. More extensive excavation works were carried out inter alia in: Bełcz Mały, Ostrawa, Ryczeń, Wrocław - Sołtysowice[4] as well as in Zbrojewsko[5] situated on the border

1 Stone or brick towers emerged in Silesia already at the begining of the 13th century. These were mainly the seats of dukes which are not the subject of our consideration. Exhaustive study of this category of residences can be found in the work of M. Chorowska, *Rezydencje średniowieczne na Śląsku. Zamki, pałace, wieże mieszkalne*, Wrocław 2003.

2 A. Pawłowski, *Wiejskie siedziby obronne na tle podziału politycznego Śląska w 1 połowie XIV wieku*, "Silesia Antiqua", vol. 26, 1984, pp. 111–118; For Silesia there are also valuable studies from the period before WWII that descibe nonexisting sites: M. Hellmich, Schlesische Burghügel und Burgwalle, Der Oberschiesier, 1930 (non vidimus); G. Grundmann, *Burgen, Schlősser und Gutshäuser in Schlesien*. Bd. 1, Die mittelalterischen Burgruinen, Burgen und Wohntűrme, Breslau 1939 (reprint 1982).

3 D. Nowakowski, *Siedziby książęce i rycerskie księstwa głogowskiego w średniowieczu*, Wrocław 2008.

4 J. Lodowski, *Relikty późnośredniowiecznych rezydencji obronnych w Chróścinie i Żuchlowie, pow. Góra*, "Śląskie Sprawozdania Archeologiczne", vol. 43, 2001, p. 565; A. Boguszewicz, *Architektura siedziby możnowładczo-rycerskiej w Wierzbnej koło Świdnicyw świetle badań archeologicznych*, "Archaeologia Historica Polona", vol. 15/1, 2005, pp. 279–305.

5 M. Gedl, *Pozostałości drewnianej budowli średniowiecznym gródku w Zbrojewsku*, "Archaeologia Historica Polona", vol. 12, 2003, pp. 73–80.

with Lesser Poland. The sites from Silesia are essential for understanding the phenomenon of the transformation of residences owned both by knights as well as the nobility. Owing to the faster progress of civilization in these areas, as well as strong Czech and German influences, the local culture, including material culture, was richer and at the same time more diverse, which can be observed mainly on the basis of excavations carried out in the cities. Unfortunately not much attention has been given so far to the material culture of manor houses.

The situation in Gdańsk Pomerania is slightly different. Here motte-and-bailey manor houses escaped the notice of researchers for a long time as they were more interested in the fortified monumental buildings of the Teutonic Knights. Only a few years ago, D. Piasek in his work summarising the hitherto research concerning this area, collected information on 41 sites with the remains of fortified seats of knights. On the basis of this data, he came to the conclusion that the numbers of this type of residence seem to be smaller than in other parts of our country. This claim is consistent with the common view that the Teutonic Knights were exceptionally strict about the enforcement of the castle building privilege (regalia). However, further observations made in his work seem to modify the existing 'intuitive' beliefs. The author draws attention to the fact that compared to neighbouring territories, natural land features were used more frequently in Gdańsk Pomerania for the construction of residences, as a result of which typical motte-and-bailey manor houses were less popular. Therefore such sites might have been identified less frequently[6].

In the regions to the west and south of Poland, the fortified seats of knights were often built of stone, as a result of which there were only references to such sites in all sorts of compilations of publications concerning mainly castles, but also taking into account information about smaller constructions. As a consequence such sites were better studied and also better protected. As a result of these measures, the amount of preserved residences is impressive and is an excellent material for the study of fortified as well as fortified residential buildings from the Middle Ages. Due to a large number of publications, I will present below only a subjective choice of works, those which seem to be the most essential as regards the issues discussed herein.

6 D. Piasek, *Rycerskie i szlacheckie siedziby obronne na Pomorzu Gdańskim w XIII–poł. XVII w.*, Gdańsk 2006, (typescript of PhD dissertation in the archives of the Institute of History at Gdańsk University).

When discussing the sites located in the region to the west of Poland, first of all we need to pay attention to a certain chronological incompatibility of the studied residences. The first defensive seats of knights were erected there much earlier in the 10th and 11th centuries. Another important difference is that most of the buildings, especially late medieval houses, were made of durable materials such as stone, and then also of brick. We need to bear in mind those two issues when carrying out any formal comparative studies. Thus, both in Austria and in Germany, and in most of the European countries, there is no division into castles and manor houses. Small residential and defensive residences, most often defined as Burghügel, Turmhügel or Hausberg are discussed together with larger castles in the same publications.

The earliest excavations carried out at the sites in Husterknupp[7], Hoverberg (wooden buildings)[8], or the slightly older manor house in Garsdorf[9] give us an idea of the medieval manor houses in the German-speaking countries of Central Europe. The above mentioned chronological difference causes further difficulties with interpretation, as exemplified by the site in Gommerstedt. The origins of this settlement date back to the turn of the 10th and 11th centuries, when a small wooden house (3.8x6 m) was built on a mound and encircled with a moat. The situation could be considered as analogical to that of many sites from Poland, though with later chronology, but for the fact that a wooden church was also built in the vicinity. At the end of the 13th or early 14th century, the building was extended with the use of stone, by adding outbuildings and a stone wall surrounding the whole estate[10]. So, in this case the formal analogy concerning the manor building itself is illusory. In Poland there are no similar sites, or at least their presence has not been confirmed in the course of field surveys. Founding of private churches by well-off families is dated back to the turn of the 11th and 12th centuries,

7 A. Herrnbrodt, *Der Husterknup. Eine niederrheinische Burganlage des frühen Mittelalters*, Beihefte Bonner Jahrbücher, 6 Köln–Graz 1958.

8 A. Herrnbrodt, *Die Ausgrabungen auf der Motte Hoverberg bei Birgelen, Kreis Geilenkirchen-Heinsberg*, "Bonner Jahrbücher" 155–56, 1955–1956, pp. 343–354.

9 W. Piepers, *Die Ausgrabungen auf Burg Garsdorf. Kreis Bergheim*, "Bonner Jahrbücher" 162, 1962, pp. 433–444.

10 W. Timpel, *Gommerstedt bei Bösleben, Kr. Arnstadt. Burghügel und Siedlung des Mittelalters*, "Ausgrabungen und Funde", Bd. 21, 1976, pp. 142–144.

however we have no knowledge of any fortified private settlements built by the nobility from that period[11]. A. Habovštiak writes about a similar situation in the territories of the present-day Slovakia[12].

One of the first basic studies that both provide an overview of the previous research as well as collect a considerable amount of literature are the works of M. Müller-Wille, *"Mittelalterliche Burghügel im nördlichen Rheinland"*[13] and H. Hinz *"Motte und Donjon"*[14]. Synthetic works discussing the history of knights' manor houses in Germany include the book by T. Biller *Die Adelsburg in Deutschland...*[15], whereas basic information concerning the history of the widely understood *militaris* architecture can be found in the textbook edition entitled *Burgen in Mitteleuropa. Ein Handbuch*[16]. An interesting overview of recent studies concerning residential towers can be found in the collective work entitled *Wohntürme* published in 2002[17]. Unfortunately, most of these works relate primarily to the study of the remains of fortified and residential residences, and little attention is given to artefacts. As the example of a model publication concerning excavation results, which not only discusses the transformation of settlement structures, but also pays a lot of attention to the analysis of explored artefacts, we should mention the work of I. Ericsson entitled *Vom slawischen Burgwall zum deutschen Gut* [18], concerning the site in Futterkamp, Holstein.

11 A. Tomaszewski, *Romańskie kościoły z emporami zachodnimi na obszarze Polski, Czech i Węgier,* Wrocław 1974.

12 A. Habovštiak, *Stredoveká dedina na Slovensku*, Bratislava 1985 p. 132.

13 M. Müller-Wille, *Mittelalterliche Burghügel im nördlichen Rheinland*, Köln/Gratz 1967.

14 H. Hinz, *Motte und Donjon. Zur Frühgeschichte der mittelalterlichen Aldesburg*, Köln 1981.

15 T. Biller *Die Adelsburg in Deutschland: Entstehung, Form und Bedeutung*, München 1993; *Burg und Schloss als Lebensorte in Mittelalter und Renaissance*, W. G. Busse (ed.), "Studia humaniora" 26, Düsseldorf 1995.

16 H. W. Böhme, B. von der Dollen, D. Kerber, C. Meckseper, B. Schock-Werner, J. Zeune, *Burgen in Mitteleuropa. Ein Handbuch*, vol. 1 and 2, Stuttgart 1999.

17 *Wohntürme, Veröffentlichungen der Deutschen Burgenvereinigun*, H. Müller (ed.), Langenweiβbach 2002.

18 I. Ericsson, *Vom slawischen Burgwall zum deutschen Gut. Studie zur mittelalterischen Siedlungsgenese im Raum Futterkamp, Holstein*, Lund 1984.

Researchers of fortified residential seats should not underestimate the news on both current research and recent literature, appearing periodically that has been published in Kiel since 1995, i.e. the materials of the Göttingen Academy of Sciences *Residenzen-Kommission*[19]. An excellent scholar, W. Paravicini, is in charge of the publication which presents the achievements of researchers from all over Europe.

As already mentioned, the certain social and economic backwardness of our country compared to western European monarchies in the Middle Ages, as well as a different political situation means that these territories are not really the most suitable for comparative analysis as regards the issues discussed in this work. Therefore I confined myself to listing the most important publications (in my opinion), in which you can find information about the excavations themselves, as well as studies of their results. In fact, in this case, the search for any possible analogies should be limited to specific categories of artefacts. The overall picture of the material culture of the knight's manor house cannot be taken into consideration here, because of a certain chronological incompatibility, for instance of the form of the residence itself.

Analogies that are much more compatible to our conditions can be found with our southern neighbours[20]. Particular attention in this case should be given to research in Slovakia as well as the Czech Republic and Moravia. Here, basic information can be found in a multi-volume publication, the first volumes of which were published already in the 19th century, namely in a monumental work of A. Sedlaček, "*Hrady, zámky a tvrze Království Českeho*"[21]. This researcher had many followers, and today there are up-to-date studies for each region. They differ in detail description, especially the extent of information that was taken into account as regards the artefacts obtained during excavations[22].

19 *Mitteilungen der Residenzen-Kommission der Akademie der Wissenschaften zu Göttingen*, Kiel since 1995.

20 T. Koppány, *A Középkori Magyarország kastélyai*, Budapest 1999, (*Manor-houses and Castles in Medieval Hungary*, pp. 261–267.

21 A. Sedlaček, *Hrady, zámky a tvrze království českeho*, vol. 1–15, Praha 1880–1927, (2nd edition, Praha 1927–1937).

22 A. Hejna, *České tvrze*, Praha 1961; D. Menclová, *České hrady*, vol. 1, 2, Praha 1972; Z. Měřínský, *Středověké hrádky a tvrze na jihozápadní Moravě*, "Archaeologia Historica", vol. 2, 1977, pp. 37–43; B. Polla, *Hrady a kaštiele na Východnom Slovensku*, Košice 1980; V. Nekuda, J. Unger, *Hrádky a tvrze na Moravé*, Brno 1981;

At this point I will not quote any descriptions of particular sites (cf.: footnotes). However, we should note that our southern neighbours have a slightly different approach to studies of feudal fortified settlements. We do not see there any aspirations for typological division between hillforts/mottes and castles. The function of a residence rather seems to be the criterion for distinction. According to Czech researchers, the castle was primarily the seat of a magnate who supported himself on a feudal rent. Another feature is the dominating defensive function over the residential and farming functions[23]. In this sense – the manor house / tvrz is the seat and centre of the knight's estate, from where the owner manages his smaller or larger farmstead. The term *tvrze*, used in the narrower sense: "sídla drobných feudálů", refers to smaller settlements. Sometimes, however, this term is used interchangeably with the term *hrad*, commonly reserved for castles, and a diminutive form of *hradek*.

Compared to Polish studies, the most significant difference is that the term *tvrze* sometimes also refers to considerably larger buildings that most likely in Poland would be considered castles. In consequence, all kinds of studies on the dynamics of the transformation of these residences are conducted together. The reason for this is probably the variety of forms and generally larger scale of residences that were predominantly built of stone. Anyway, the smallest of them, similar to typical motte-and-baileys do not arouse much of an interest among researchers[24]. When it comes to the dating of *tvrzí*, they emerged in the mid-13th century, and became popular in the first half of the 14th century. During the initial period, an upland location was predominant, without any water obstacles (Bezník, Bilantova Lhota, Dubenec, Vražba). The construction of water obstacles started only in the 14th century, when residences were located near water courses, to facilitate building a moat or pond. The earliest settlements varied in the size of the area surrounded by a defensive construction (300–1400 m^2), whereas buildings were centred around an inner courtyard. However,

T. Durdík, F. Kašička, B. Nechvátal, *Hrady, hrádky a tvrze na Písecku*, Písek 1995; J. Úlovec, *Hrady, zámky a tvrze na Chebsku*, Cheb 1998; L. Svoboda, J. Úlovec, P. Chotébor, Z. Procházka, Z. Fišera, J. Anderle, J. Slavík, M. Rykl, T. Durdík, V. Brych, *Encyklopedie českých tvrzí*, vol. 1, Praha 1998; vol. 2, 2000, vol. 3, 2005.

23 L. Svoboda, *Stavební vývoj českých tvrzí*, In: Encyklopedie českých tvrzí, vol. 1, Praha 1998, p. 11; T. Durdík, *Ilustrovaná encyklopedie českých hradů*, Praha 1999, pp. 8–9.

24 Cf. comments in A. Habovštiak, *Stredoveká dedina na Slovensku*... p. 127.

in the late 13th century, there were settlements where the most important building was an independent house, most often a tower (Kestřany, Cerekvice nad Bystřicí)[25]. Similarly to Poland, single-room buildings were predominant, but more often than in our country, the interior space was divided into two or three rooms, especially in houses built of stone.

In the second half of the 14th and early 15th century, until the Hussite Wars, i.e. in the heyday of the Czech state during the reign of Charles IV and Wenceslas IV, private fortified residences started to develop. Relatively flat areas were clearly preferred locations, and the seats were usually encircled by a water obstacle, often also used as a fishpond[26]. Usually more than one building was constructed inside the defensive enclosure, although there were still residences with one keep only (Dobrš)[27]. At that time they resembled rather the constructions that, according to Polish nomenclature, would be referred to as *small castles*. For obvious reasons, the time of the Hussite Wars was a period of investment stagnation. The subsequent period does not bring any radical changes in the layout of settlements, but it is associated with their adjustment to the use of firearms[28].

In the course of excavations, archaeologists very often were able to locate the remains of outbuildings in the vicinity of the *tvrzí*. And so the area of "hospodářský dvůr" was mainly between 600–1200 m^2 (Čimice: 600 m^2, Svrčovec: 800 m^2, Nepomyšl: 1200 m^2), though there were much larger facilities up to 3500 m^2 and such a hypothetical surface was defined for the residence in Slavkově[29].

In Czech and Slovak literature there are many publications on the material culture of the Middle Ages, of which particularly important is the monograph *Dějiny hmotně kultury*[30], as well as numerous articles published in the journal *Archaeologia Historica*[31].

25 L. Svoboda, *Stavební vývoj českých tvrzí...*, pp. 15–16.

26 P. Chotěbor, *Obranná zařízení*, In: Encyklopedie českých tvrzí, vol. 1, Praha 1998, p. 37.

27 L. Svoboda, *Stavební vývoj českých tvrzí...*, p. 18.

28 V. Nekuda, J. Unger, *Hrádky a tvrze na Moravé...*, p. 19.

29 L. Svoboda, *Stavební vývoj českých tvrzí...*, p. 15.

30 *Dějiny hmotně kultury*, vol. I (2) Kultura každodenního života od 13. do 15. století, J. Petráně (ed.), Praha 1985.

31 J. Unger, *Hmotná kultura středověké šlechty v archeologických pramenech na Moravě*, "Archaeologia Historica", vol. 10, 1985, pp. 323–329. This subject matter is also

Another interesting trend in Czech archaeology are the studies on everyday life in the Middle Ages, which are assumed to be interdisciplinary and perfectly fit into the trend of the studies of the past initiated by the *Annales school* and modern methodology of archaeology and history. We can mention here both popular studies on a narrow subject, an excellent example of which is the book by J. Unger Život na lelekovickém hradě...[32], as well as typical archaeological publications giving an extensive account of excavation results (with a broad description of artefacts)[33], and collections of articles[34].

Taking into account the much more advanced studies of castles and knights' manor houses carried out by our southern neighbours, as well as considerable similarities in the subject matter of research, we should seek inspiration for our deliberations in Slovak and Czech publications. A broader look at the material culture of the magnates and knights was presented there for the first time in the already mentioned monumental work *Encyklopedie českých tvrzí*. For the purpose of studying the artefacts discovered during excavations, the following divisions have been applied:

1) agricultural equipment
2) craftsman's tools
3) armour and weapons
4) horse tack elements, rider's equipment and wagon parts
5) household equipment
6) pieces of garment and jewellery
7) law related objects
8) evidence of spiritual culture
9) construction elements and furniture
10) miscellaneous, including coins etc.

---

present in British archaeology: P. Drewett, *Rich Man, Poor Man: An Archaeological Comparison of the Economy of a Castle and a Farm, in East Sussex, England, C. 1100–1500 A.D.*, In: Život v archeologii středověku, J. Kubková, J. Klápště, M. Ježek, P. Meduna (ed.), Praha 1997, pp. 160–168.

32 J. Unger, Život *na lelekovickém hradě ve 14. století. Antropologická sociokulturní studie*, Brno 1999.

33 J. Unger, *Kovál‍ov, šlechtické sídlo z 13. století na jižní Moravé,* Brno 1994.

34 Život v archeologii středověku, J. Kubková, J. Klápště, M. Ježek, P. Meduna (ed.), Praha 1997.

As it turns out, even seemingly insignificant differences in material culture, or rather in the extent of its diversity, combined with a different research tradition, do not allow for uncritical borrowings of, for example, classification systems. As can be seen at first glance, such a division does not take into account the Polish research tradition. Certainly, a slightly different division of military items is the most conspicuous. More important for me, however, is a certain duality of the criteria used, e.g. tiles with symbolic ornamentation are regarded as objects related to spiritual culture. We know that in the Middle Ages every decorative motif had a symbolic meaning. If we cannot recognize this, it is the evidence of our lack of knowledge. However, on the other hand undecorated tiles, for example pot tiles, will not be considered a manifestation of spiritual culture. As a result, one category of artefacts, i.e. tiles should be discussed in two separate units of classification. In fact, every attempt at determining the most important criterion for division causes similar problems.

A. Pałubicka suggested two types of description for artefacts: physicalistic (a description of the form) and mental (the way a particular item is used by a given community)[35]. The first one does not seem to provoke any questions. However, it is slightly different with the latter, i.e. the mental description of artefacts. A simple explanation of how an item, i.e. a tile, was used would come down to saying that it was part of a heating unit, that is a furnace. And perhaps here we have come to the cause of a certain inconsistency in the division proposed by V. Brych. In the context of classification, a simple description of the function of tiles is a prerequisite, yet insufficient condition. I would not like to become involved in any further epistemological deliberations, or discuss the possibility of archaeologists creating descriptions in the field of cultural studies[36]. For the purposes of these considerations, we only need to emphasize that in this case the mental description needs to be considerably widened and it should refer to the realm of symbols. Symbols must be also

35 A. Pałubicka, *Archeologia jako nauka historyczna o kulturze. O badaniach formy i funkcji znalezisk archeologicznych*, In: Archeologia w teorii i praktyce, A. Buko, P. Urbańczyk (ed.), pp. 76 et seq.

36 A. P. Kowalskiego, *Archeologia kulturoznawcza. Projekt dyskursu „negatywistycznego"*. In: Archeologia w teorii i praktyce, A. Buko, P. Urbańczyk (ed.), Warszawa 2000, pp. 115–136.

recognized on several levels, as they are crucial at least in several spheres of social life, including demonstration of religious and political beliefs, as well as a manifestation of material situation and social status, or even a certain aesthetic sensitivity.

Much has been written about the formal and political genesis of knights' fortified residences. The majority of publications were described in the initial chapters. Here, however, I would like to emphasize one difficulty, which seems to be of essential importance. A fortified private manor house emerged in the history of our country as an absolute innovation. In this case, political and economic conditions were an only prerequisite, but perhaps this is insufficient. It required also changes in mentality, which were associated with the growing strength of a new social hierarchy. To decide to leave the place of 'power', knights, or rather members of their elite, had to become independent not only economically, but also mentally. In fact it was a decision which resulted in the loss of a safe place of residence, protected not only by the embankments of the duke's castle, but also by the majesty of the ruler and his sergeants-at-arm. Farming one's own land also required a conscious choice of location for building a residence for the needs of the knight's family. We know, after all, that motte-and-bailey settlements referred to herein were the type of residences that required the construction of a farmstead and outbuildings in the immediate vicinity. This solution did not seem to be economically justified, especially as the accompanying buildings were outside the line of 'fortifications'. Why did they abandon the well-tried model of building with a bailey that could accommodate both the house and outbuildings surrounded by embankments, which ensured safety? It would have been a convenient solution that raised the rank of nobility and at the same time imitated the seats of dukes. In the light of the recent research on the functioning of regalia in the Piast monarchy[37], it is doubtful that a specific model of fortified residences might have been imposed by the ruler. So why were the tower keeps so popular? A slightly simplified view is prevailing in literature at present, namely that *motte* type residences were a borrowing from the territories of Western Europe. As a consequence, we should accept the thesis concerning a specific pursuit for fashionable innovations, resulting

37 M. R. Pauk, *Funkcjonowanie regale fortyfikacyjnego w Europie Środkowej w średniowieczu*, "Kwartalnik Historii Kultury Materialnej", vol. 51, 2003, no. 1, pp. 3–16.

in the 'crop' of motte-and-bailey residences in the late 13th century. Having analysed the studies conducted in Silesia, J. Kaźmierczyk already in 1965 came to the conclusion that there was no link between the "colonisation of the village by a foreign element, and the construction of residences typical of German building"[38]. It seems that subsequent studies confirm this thesis. Unfortunately, this conviction has still not been supported with any precise dating. However, we can exclude the overwhelming influence of foreign settlers on the adaptation of this type of residence in our territories.

It seems necessary to be reminded at this point of the almost forgotten remarks of L. Kajzer on local traditions that enabled the adaptation of such a form of architecture. This researcher pointed out that the early medieval ringforts had all the elements that later became part of motte-and-bailey residences, i.e. the elements of fortifications and the keep, which also had a symbolic meaning. We shall come back to this issue again. Maybe that is why the adaptation of a foreign model was possible, at first by the local dukes and then as magnates followed in their footsteps?[39]

It is equally important here to attempt at explanation of the reasons for resigning from the well-tried model of the ringfort. There are a few causes that may be named. First of all, castles began to take over the role of the main centres of power. In other places, where the construction of a brick fortress was not required, a house on a mound might have been sufficient. It was built at a considerably lower cost, but ensured relative security to people and their material goods which could be accommodated in a single building.

Another important question is whether the popularity of motte-and-bailey residences was increasing due to symbolic role of the tower? In the previous chapter we have already noted that the issue is more complicated. The choice of the form of a particular manor house could depend on environmental conditions, or even family tradition. Another issue that is

---

38 J. Kaźmierczyk, ., *Z badań nad grodami i miastami wczesnego średniowiecza na Śląsku*, "Archeologia Polski", vol. 10, 1966, z. 2, p. 682.

39 L. Kajzer, *Studia nad świeckim budownictwem obronnym województwa łęczyckiego w XIII–XVII wieku*, "Acta Universitatis Lodziensis", Folia Archaeologica, vol. 1, Łódź 1980, p. 137 et.seq.; L. Kajzer, *Z zagadnień genezy tzw. gródków stożkowatych (Uwagi na marginesie lektury VI tomu Początków Polski prof. Henryka Łowmiańskiego)*, "Kwartalnik Historii Kultury Materialnej", vol. 34, 1986, no. 2, p. 331–339.

still hotly debated in literature is the 'military' or 'shelter' function of towers built on mounds. Today, the view that they could fulfil the role of military watchtowers, has already been disappearing slowly. However, the issue as to whether they played the role of residential keeps, or 'last defence' is still under consideration[40].

The majority of researchers agree without reservation with the thesis that the tower forms were a borrowing from motte-and-bailey residences. However, those who attribute refugee or watchtower functions to keeps, usually do not ask themselves the question as to why the adaptation of the form did not go hand in hand with adaptation of the function? Why borrow the form of a keep (*donjon*) / residential tower and then make it a 'last defence'?

Another issue arises here, namely that no one disputes the residential function of stone or brick keeps built on mounds erected in Silesia or in the Czech Republic. After all genetically and formally these phenomena are identical; the difference consists only in scale.

It seems more reasonable to say that the wooden towers on mounds, or mottes, in the territories of Poland performed the same function as their stone or brick counterparts in other areas of Europe, where they were also initially built of wood on small embankments, except that it happened much earlier, e.g. in France even at the end of the 10th century. Ultimately, in the territories of the Czech Republic, where the towers appeared much later than in France, but earlier than in Poland, they were also initially built of wood, but then they were soon rebuilt into stone constructions. However, no one denies both their residential and fortified character.

Let us take a look at our closest analogies in Silesia. This is what M. Chorowska writes about stone or brick keeps erected by wealthy local knights: "They were designed equally to defend and to perform a residential and administrative function. So they were rather tower manor houses, which reflects the actual lifestyle of knights, who relied on farming"[41]. M. Chorowska also noted that only from the beginning of the 15th century tower manor

40 The differentiation between the *keep* (residential tower) and *bergfried* (last refuge) is generally accepted among archaeologists, however in historical or architectural publications this distinction is not always unambiguous.

41 M. Chorowska, *Rezydencje średniowieczne na Śląsku. Zamki, pałace, wieże mieszkalne*, Wrocław 2003, p. 136.

houses ceased to fulfil the requirements of enriching the founders and hence their expansion began, initially by the construction of additional outbuildings and residential buildings within the existing fortified enclosure, and then by transferring the residence outside the fortifications. This, however, was associated only with the Renaissance fashion for a comfortable and open house. However, as the author noted, the old keeps were still in use, as a sign of prestige and affiliation with a social group[42].

It has been written on numerous occasions about the illusory military advantage of wooden manor houses built on the mound or behind ramparts[43]. However, even these small defensive qualities were essential to ensure the safety of family and material goods, as evidenced in numerous records concerning the attacks and destruction of manor houses, that we know from written sources. Also D. Nowakowski wrote about a similar situation of life under the constant threat of raid and robbery in Silesia[44]. As opposed to the threats of war, the attack of a 'bad neighbour' was usually unexpected. Hence the speculation that the entire belongings were taken to the refuge tower only in times of danger, seem not to take into account the realities of the period.

This polemic recalls a slightly similar discussion about the evolutionary transformation of the *hall* defined as the proper residential premises, and the function of the tower in the medieval architecture of France[45]. The discussion on these views is summarized in the work of D. Barthélemy and he is also the author of the following conclusion: "Between the 11th and 15th centuries, the equipment, armour and games demonstrated the aristocratic character of the household, whereas the appearance and use of particular rooms still remained extremely primitive"[46].

42 M. Chorowska, *Rezydencje średniowieczne…*, pp. 166 et.seq.

43 L. Kajzer, *Zamki i społeczeństwo. Przemiany architektury i budownictwa obronnego w Polsce w X–XVIII wieku*, Łódź 1993, pp. 148, 156–158, 170–171, 176; S. Kołodziejski, *Średniowieczne rezydencje obronne możnowładztwa na terenie województwa krakowskiego*, Kraków 1994, pp. 67–68.

44 D. Nowakowski, *Siedziby książęce i rycerskie księstwa głogowskiego w średniowieczu*, Wrocław 2008, pp. 237–242.

45 D. Barthélemy, *Zagospodarowanie przestrzeni prywatnej XI–XIII w.* In: Historia życia prywatnego, vol. II, Od Europy feudalnej do renesansu, G. Duby (ed.), Wrocław 1998, p. 431–458.

46 Ibid, p. 449.

The contemporary vision is that the manor house was a homestead, the standard of which was much higher compared to peasant cottages. But the fact remains that even the separation of the owner's bedroom as a separate room has not been confirmed in the study of medieval dwellings, nor in Western European territories[47].

The small number of written sources, and in particular the less precise descriptions contained therein, are insufficient to make an attempt to reconstruct the appearance of manor houses, and especially of their equipment and furnishings at the end of the 13th century and in the 14th century. However, 15th-century sources often contain information about the "new" and "old" house. We also find mentions of the tower somewhere in the vicinity. Undoubtedly, this is proof that the residences underwent significant transformations. In this situation it is difficult to determine the original function of the houses or "old" towers, described therein. Therefore, to draw any conclusions on the basis of a comparison of size, morphology or function and referring them to the 'medieval manor house' in general is debatable.

The issue of the function of motte type residences is certainly one of the more widely discussed subjects, which perhaps has, unfairly, dominated the topic of 'manor houses'. Although in the light of the hitherto research this type of buildings seems to be prevalent at the time, we cannot forget that these are only our speculations. First of all, tower buildings did not necessarily function on every mound. In the case of large mounds, there was a possibility of a different building development. It should also be emphasized that a significant number of manor houses were not located on mounds. The choice of the location depended on the existing land features, giving improved defence by means of a system of ditches or embankments. In the case of such settlements, their residential function is not discussed.

And one more digression. The lasting popularity of tower houses, at least in the reconstructions of archaeologists is astounding. As the researchers argue, in European as well as Silesian and Pomeranian cities, such form ceased to be

47 Cf. interpretation of the manor house in Trzemsze and P. Ariès, *Historia dzieciństwa. Dziecko i rodzina w dawnych czasach*, Gdańsk 1995, pp. 20–21; P. Contamine, *Zagospodarowanie prywatnej przestrzeni* XIV–XV wiek. In: Historia życia prywatnego, vol. 2. Od Europy feudalnej do renesansu, G. Duby (ed.), Wrocław 1998, pp. 458–540.

attractive already at the turn of the 13th and 14th century[48]. It seems that this problem requires a greater interest from researchers.

As for the low comfort and small living area which follows both from the reconstructions proposed by researchers and by arithmetic calculations, I would like to draw attention here to the possibilities that so far have not been taken into account. First of all, in most cases it is assumed *a priori* that the surface of successive vertically arranged compartments was the same as the space demarcated by the foundations of the building. Also drawings with reconstructions most often present the building in the form of a simple 'tower', sometimes only with a small open porch for defenders on the top floor. These representations do not differ much from the ones illustrating e.g. Bronze Age fortified settlements.

We forget that in the case of timber constructions, especially log houses, the upper floors might have been much more spacious, going beyond the outline of the ground floor or basement.

Unfortunately, only a few wooden monuments have survived in Poland. Perhaps that is why we have forgotten how incredibly varied and technically complex wooden constructions may be. It seems to me that we should refer here to the Slavic tradition of carpentry, which lasted much longer than in Poland, and survived for instance in the folk culture in the territories of the former Russia.

To better realize the possibilities of creating the appearance, and to some extent also the size of a wooden building, let us take a look at the figures below. The first figure shows the Gothic tile found during archaeological excavations at the castle in Ujazd, near Tomaszów Mazowiecki. We can see a schematic representation of the *motte* type residence. Most likely a wooden building was erected on the steep slopes of a small mound. The entrance to the house was via ladder-like steps, or perhaps a primitive bridge (?). At the level of the first floor (it could be the second or third storey, if we take into account the existence of

48 Porównaj opinie G. Wilke, *Średniowieczne wieże w miastach Toskanii zasiedlane okresowo*, "Archaeologia Historica Polona", vol. 12, pp. 31–46; J. Piekalski, *Wczesne domy mieszczan w Europie Środkowej. Geneza-funkcja-forma*, Wrocław 2004; J. Piekalski, *Problem genezy budowli typu kemenate w miastach środkowoeuropejskiej strefy nadmorskiej*. In: Archaeologia et historia urbana, R. Czaja, G. Nawrolska, M. Rębkowski, J. Tandecki (ed.), Elbląg 2004, pp. 227–236; C. Buśko, *Budynki wieżowe w krajobrazie średniowiecznego miasta*. In: Dom w mieście średniowiecznym i nowożytnym, B. Gediga (ed.), Wrocław 2004, pp. 61–73.

a non-residential ground floor / basement) there are two large bays (possibly two-storey buildings), each covered with a separate roof[49]. The representation is quite realistic, and therefore we should presume that the author of the mould, in which the tile was made, must have seen other similar buildings. An interesting presentation was also observed on tiles found in Gniezno. It illustrates the Korab coat of arms, on which the tower also has two upper floors extending beyond the outline of the building[50].

Fig. 25. Gothic tile from Ujazd castle. Fot. J. Błaszczyk

Unfortunately, another illustration is merely a formal analogy. It is in fact a reconstruction of the 17th-century gate tower from the town of Ilimsk in Siberia (Russia)[51]. Here, we can see a three-storey building with the first floor extended by two large bays (approximately 2×4.5 m), which enlarged

49 A. Andrzejewski, L. Kajzer, *Z archeologiczno-architektonicznych badań weryfikacyjnych zespołu pałacowego w Ujeździe koło Tomaszowa Mazowieckiego w 2002 roku*, "Łódzkie Sprawozdania Archeologiczne", vol. 8, (2002/2003), p. 290; L. Kajzer, *Wstępna informacja o zbiorze późnogotyckich kafli z zamku w Ujeździe koło Tomaszowa Mazowieckiego*, Ibid, vol. 10, 2006–2007, pp. 267, 273, figure before p. 161.

50 T. Janiak, *Kafle gotyckie w zbiorach Muzeum Początków Państwa Polskiego w Gnieźnie*, Gniezno 2003, fig. 6 and 117.

51 Н. П. Крадин, Русское деревянное ебороное зодчество, Москва 1988, p. 111.

significantly the surface area of the tower. It is easy to calculate that if the size of the foundation was close to 7×7 m, which does not differ much from the remains of towers in our motte-and-bailey residences, the surface area of the floor was about 67 m^2. Assuming that the building had three floors, it gives 165 m^2 of usable surface, and with a possible basement we get 214 m^2, which can be compared to the surface of one floor in a small castle.

I should also quote here the opinions of historians of religious architecture, who suggested that the bell towers of wooden churches that were built in the 16th and 17th centuries, derived from earlier defensive construction. The similarity consisted in crowning the tower buildings with an overhanging floor – a large room. Its walls, which were extending beyond the face of the lower floors were to accommodate positions for defenders, similar in form to hoarding (a covered parapet for defenders)[52].

Looking for further analogies, we should remember about arcaded houses that survived in many open-air museums of folk architecture, with an upper floor extending in front of the elevation and supported by pillars. Apart from the larger living area, this type of construction provided roofed space protected both from rain and sun in the immediate vicinity of the house.

The examples discussed above show that the mounds did not have to be built upon with a simple, or even primitive cuboid[53]. It may well have been a much more spacious house not without individual stylistic features, or some decorative elements[54], but still remaining a 'fortified' residence.

52 C. Thullie, *Zabytkowe dzwonnice drewniane w Polsce*, "Teka Komisji Architektury i Urbanistyki", vol. III, 1969, pp. 119 et.seq.; M. Kornecki, *Gotyckie kościoły drewniane na Podhalu*, Cracow 1987, p. 23; M. Kornecki, *Kościoły drewniane w Małopolsce zagadnienia do uwarunkowań oraz systematyki typów i form architektury (od średniowiecza do XX wieku)*, Cracow 1999, p. 106.

53 It is possible that the knights towers debated in literature had impact on the form of reconstructed buildings; cf.: T. Kiersnowska, *„Słupy" rycerskie w Polsce średniowiecznej*, "Kwartalnik Historii Kultury Materialnej", vol. 20, 1972, no. 3, p. 437–450; E. Kowalczyk, *„Nazwy obronne" Słup, Samborza i Zawada a zagadnienie obrony stałej ziem polskich w średniowieczu*, Warszawa 1992.

54 Sometimes the authors of the research write that they found only several postholes at the *plateau of the mound*, which gave right to the claim that, e.g. there was only an observation tower. If the entire *plateau* was not excavated, we cannot exclude the possibility that the traces of posts are the remains of pillars supporting the protruding bay on the upper floor of the building.

The possibilities of reconstructing the functions of particular rooms in these wooden tower buildings have already been dealt with before. However, recapitulation might be useful. Most authors consider, probably rightly, that the basement (if any), and the ground floor housed utility rooms. Certainly it was not always a smithy. Probably there was a place for the storage of tools needed for home repairs or even small-scale production of every-day objects that were not too complicated and did not need to be manufactured by a specialized craftsman. Probably the so-called black chamber was also housed there. It was a room where food was cooked and where everyday life carried on. We must remember that the term 'kitchen' was not functioning yet at that time. The above mentioned floor with the living space (the so-called *white chamber*) of 40–70 square meters (possibly with additional bedrooms) should be regarded as sufficient space to reconcile both residential and entertainment functions. The space on the upper level (or upper floors) was probably used as granaries, and possibly also servants' rooms.

Again, our deliberations have been dominated by *motte* type residences. This is because for many people they are almost synonymous with medieval knights' manor houses. Other types of residences, especially those constructed on natural land forms, as a result of which there was larger space for building development, have not provoked any further discussions so far.

Another extremely interesting issue concerns not so much the buildings that have revealed several construction phases, but mansions that changed their place within one landed property. The route of such 'migration' is often repeated: a mound in the meadows – an island on the pond located at the edge of upland area – a manor house in the park.

The manor house in Kościerzyna near Sieradz is an excellent example. The first manor houses dating back to the 14th-century was located in the meadows, north-west of the present manor–park complex. The remains of another two manor houses – a late medieval and an early modern - are situated on a low embankment, which used to be surrounded by a moat and pond. An ice-house was built here in the 19th century. As early as at the beginning of the 18th century, a new residence was built next to the island, and then another one in the 19th century. The manor house that we can see there today was built in the 1930s[55].

55 L. Kajzer, *Pałace i dwory w dawnym województwie sieradzkim*, vol. 2, *Materiały do dziejów rezydencji w Polsce*, T. P. Jaroszewski (ed.), Warszawa 1994, pp. 57–71.

Many times I have mentioned that the state of research is unsatisfactory, which is a consequence of conducting verification surveys. As regards sites that were only 'explored' in theory, we cannot say anything more than that they were created as a result of human activity somewhere in the Late Middle Ages. Excavating only a small part of the site, we can confirm that it was inhabited and introduce to literature another wooden or stone/brick 'building' as well as we providing a broad chronology. Probably for fear of making an error in interpretation, researchers also happen not to include descriptions of the remains of burnt or decaying wood which they discovered during excavations, and they limit themselves only to a claim that the building was wooden, which narrows down considerably our possibilities of interpretation. As a result, we do not even know what the house looked like, or when it functioned, because dating between the 14th–15th or even 14th–17th centuries is definitely insufficient.

Now it is time to reflect on the state of research of the equipment and furnishings of the manor houses in question. The largest obstacle when you attempt a reconstruction of the appearance and equipment of premises is the way information about artefacts discovered during excavations is published. Too often the authors limit themselves to providing a summary list of artefacts. Another problem is related mainly to metal objects. Unfortunately, really too many items are described on those lists as 'unspecified'. The lack of money for X-rays and conservation is only a partial excuse. We are all aware of the fact that in the case of iron objects, and especially made of non-ferrous metals, metallurgical analysis may play an extremely important role. However, they are rarely conducted, also because of their high cost. Still it would be very important to perform such tests, especially for unique artefacts, which could be considered as imported. Then it would be easier to look for the way in which they were acquired and discuss them in more detail, including far-reaching influences and contacts that must have been not only commercial contacts.

It seems, that tiles are the most unevenly studied category of artefacts. If the collection found is abounding and interesting, archaeologists treat this topic monographically and attempt at the reconstruction of furnaces. However, if the collection of tiles is not too rich, information conveyed by researchers shall be described as at least modest. Tiled stoves made of pot tiles started to emerge in Polish territories in the second half of the 14th century. At that time they started to appear in the houses of the social and financial elites that still lived in defensive manor houses. Stoves became widespread as late as in the 15th century. Then the elites moved to brick or stone castles, whereas richer knights started to establish fortified manor houses. However, are they so rich as to fund the construction of a stove in addition to a defensive residence? Perhaps it was not always the most desirable expense. The difficulties with dating the residences do not allow for the moment for further discussion on this subject.

Of course fragments of clay vessels are discovered in the greatest numbers during excavations. It happens that the authors, while conducting comparative analyses of ceramic products, compare collections of artefacts from excavations of various medieval sites, sometimes very distant from each other. It seems to me that such a practice is not entirely justified by historical realities. There was no special way for the distribution of ceramic products intended for knights and there was no special 'store' in knights could purchase pots. Pottery was also not produced in manor houses to be exchanged. The type of dishes on the table and in the kitchen depended largely on the local market, tradition, modernity of pottery workshops manufacturing clay products in a nearby town, and possibly on the skills of the local rural potter. Therefore, we should look for similarities and differences in the immediate vicinity. As regards comparison with other manor houses, we can first of all collate the variety of forms of ceramic vessels, which is evidence of sophistication in food preparation and consumption. Vessels made of non-ferrous metals, glass and other imported dished (e.g. stoneware vessels) are excellent comparative material, but unfortunately they are rarely found.

Based on the information collected in this work, it seems that both kitchen equipment and tableware in manor houses can hardly be called a luxury. Much more expensive imported vessels are discovered by archaeologists during the excavations of medieval towns. Let us consider why? Was it for financial reasons? Such an answer is not satisfactory in the case of sites dating back to the 13th and 14th centuries. Then the residents of manor houses were definitely very wealthy people and in the next century many of their descendants moved to castles. May this difference be simply purely statistical: more unique artefacts are found in the larger amount of materials from the excavations in a city? Or maybe during this period tableware was not yet seen in terms of prestige? Unfortunately, our current state of knowledge does not allow the lending of credence to any of these hypotheses.

The problem in comparing the material culture of knights and nobility on the one hand, and townspeople on the other hand seems to be a particularly interesting subject. So far this issue has not been addressed by Polish scholars. A similar topic has already appeared in Czech literature, but it seems it did not trigger a broader discussion[56]. Also no attempts have been made on a larger scale to investigate the mutual relationship between manor houses and rural settlements, although such postulates have appeared in literature since the 1980s[57].

It seems that the most important issue is the need for a considerable increase in precision dating for the sites that have been explored. Medieval knights' manor houses have been investigated basically since the 1960s. Compared with the archaeologists of prehistory, we have relatively little experience. The 1960s and possibly 1970s should be considered as the 'period of infancy', when archaeologists learnt the unique character of not only the knight's manor house, but also late medieval sites in general. Only at that time were archaeologists learning about the production of pottery affiliated with that period and elaborated the typological sequences required for more precise attempts at dating excavated sites[58].

In the early period, i.e. 1960s and 1970s a total percentage of 41% manor houses were excavated[59]. The greatest popularity of excavations, however, fell within the 1980s, when 38% of sites of this type were explored. Since then, the amount of research has been declining steadily. In 1990s it was only 17% of the sites identified to date. The dynamics of these changes is illustrated by graph no. 1

56 Z. Měřínský, *Provoz a vybavení domácnosti ve vyšším sociálním prostředí (měšťanstvo a šlechta) na základě pramenů archeologických*, "Archaeologia Historica", vol. 15, 1990, pp. 19–42.

57 T. J. Horbacz, Z. Lechowicz *Przyczynek do problematyki osadnictwa późnośredniowiecznego i nowożytnego w rejonie Dmosina, województwo skierniewickie*, "Rocznik Łódzki", vol. 32, 1982, p. 275–303; J. Piekalski, A. Żurek, *Ze studiów nad siedzibami obronnymi północno-wschodniego pogranicza Śląska w XIII–XVII w.*, "Acta Universitatis Vratislaviensis", Studia Archeologiczne, vol. 24, 1993, p. 160; L. Kajzer, *Wstęp do archeologii historycznej w Polsce*, Łódź 1996, pp. 162 – et. seq.

58 The year 1980 may be considered as a symbolic end of that period, i.e. the date when J. Kruppé issued his book: *Garncarstwo późnośredniowieczne w Polsce*, Wrocław 1981.

59 It applies to regular excavations or field survey, during which at least one trench was explored.

below. I would not like to be accused of neglecting or underestimating the skills and knowledge of researchers, who first took the trouble to study sites connected to these times, and which had been outside the area of interest of archaeology for a long time. On the contrary, I fully appreciate their courage and determination. However, when analysing the dating provided by researchers, I noticed a certain regularity, which as it seems to me, cannot be explained unfortunately by the actual state of affairs or even by extraordinary coincidence. This regularity is statistical and it can be observed that as time goes by, the remains of manor houses are dated back to later and later phases of the Middle Ages. In particular it is visible when the manor house foundation dates are provided. Because they were used in different periods and random events (fires) were the most frequent causes of destruction, the end dates of the functioning of such manor houses are not suitable for such analysis. However, let us return to the dates specifying when individual manor houses were founded. It turns out that in the case of sites explored in the 1960s it was determined that 85% of them were erected in the 13th century. No manor houses was investigated, the beginnings of which would be dated to the 15th century. As time passed, the number of manor houses that were dated back to the 13th century gradually diminished and so by the 1970s it was 55%, in the 1980s it was 23%, and only 5% of manor houses in the 1990s. The curve that illustrates the number of sites originating in the 14th century is exactly the opposite. Only 5% of the sites were dated back to that period in the 1960s. In the consecutive decades it was 25%, 57% and 67%. The origins of manor houses were more frequently dated to the 15th century only in the second half of the 1970s. The number of sites with such chronology has been gradually increasing. Yet this is a difference of a few per cent only.

Unfortunately I find it difficult to factually substantiate this observed regularity. It is also hard to believe that such the status of our knowledge will be improved quickly. The number of planned and more extensive archaeological excavations has been constantly decreasing, and no one seems to be willing to carry out or to repeat studies of the artefacts filling the shelves of storehouses. However more and more is said about the need for repeated dating or even reinterpretation of the sites explored in the past[60]. We have to admit sadly that

60 L. Kajzer, *O budownictwie obronnym województwa łęczyckiego w późnym średniowieczu i czasach nowożytnych – w piętnaście lat później*, "Acta Universitatis Lodziensis", Folia Archaeologica 20, 1996, p. 111–122; T. J. Horbacz, *O niektórych*

an absolute date was obtained only for a few among the manor houses referred to herein.

We need to remember that excavation is a process of destruction and it depends on the skills and integrity of scholars as to how we manage to protect the picture of what the soil has protected and hidden from us, before archaeologists dug a spade into the ground. In one of his articles, Z. Kobyliński quoted the words of a Dutch researcher who seems to have formulated most explicitly the research stipulations of contemporary archaeology. F.R. Ankersmith said: "With faith in reason, the modernist historian's unquestioned task has been to dig into the past, to investigate it, to discover a past reality and reconstruct it scientifically, to find the 'one line running through history. We would do better to examine the result of a hundred and fifty years' digging more attentively and ask ourselves more often what all this adds up to. The time has come that we should think about the past, rather than investigate it"[61].

I hope that medieval knights' residences will occupy an important place in that process of thinking.

„kopcach historycznych" w Sieradzkiem w kilkadziesiąt lat później, "Archaeologia Historica Polona", vol. 5, 1997, p. 69–82; *A. Nierychlewska, Budownictwo obronne powiatu radomskiego w okresie od XIII do XVIII wieku*, Radom 2002, pp. 60–65.

61 F.R. Ankersmith, *Historiografia i postmodernizm*. In: Postmodernizm, R. Nycz (ed.), Cracow 1997, p. 170, quotation from Z. Kobyliński, *Antypozytywizm a ochrona dziedzictwa archeologicznego*, In: Archeologia w teorii i praktyce, (ed.) A. Buko, P. Urbańczyk, Warszawa 2000, p. 171.

VII. SHORT BIBLIOGRAPHY FOR CONCERNING ARCHAEOLOGICAL SITES

Barłogi gm. Grzegorzew, woj. wielkopolskie
K. Gorczyca, *Barłogi st. 2 gm. Rzgów...*; L. Kajzer, *Zamki i dwory obronne...*, p. 189–190.

Bebelno gm. Włoszczowa, woj. świętokrzyskie
C. Hadamik, *Bebelno koło Włoszczowy...*; C. Hadamik, *Średniowieczne dwory obronne w powiecie włoszczowskim...*, pp. 12–21.

Bestwina gm. Czechowice-Dziedzice, woj. śląskie
H. Malinowska-Łazarczyk, *Bestwina, pow. Bielsko-Biała...*; S. Kołodziejski, *Średniowieczne rezydencje obronne możnowładztwa na terenie województwa krakowskiego...*, p. 113.

Będkowice gm. Wielka Wieś, woj. małopolskie
S. Kołodziejski, *Średniowieczne rezydencje obronne możnowładztwa na terenie województwa krakowskiego...*, p. 114.

Będzieszyn gm. Ostrów Wielkopolski, woj. wielkopolskie
L. Kajzer, *Wstęp do badań nad siedzibami obronnymi Kaliskiego...*; J. Tomala, *Budownictwo obronne...*, pp. 61–62.

Biała Wielka (Kopiec) , gm. Kłobuck, woj. śląskie
W. Błaszczyk, T. Radkiewicz, *Wyniki badań powierzchniowych...*; S. Kołodziejski, *Średniowieczne rezydencje obronne możnowładztwa na terenie województwa krakowskiego...*, pp. 116–17.

Biskupice gm. Grodziec, woj. wielkopolskie
K. Gorczyca, *Biskupice, pow. Grodziec...*

Borówek gm. Bielawy, woj. łódzkie
A. Kosiorek, *„Dwór na kopcu" w Borówku...*
Broniszewice gm. Czermin woj. wielkopolskie
J. Tomala, *Budownictwo obronne...*, pp. 62–63.
Brzeziny–Trójnia gm. Lubartów, woj. lubelskie
A i R. Niedźwiadkowie, A. Rozwałka, *Wyniki badań gródka stożkowatego w Brzezinach–Trójni...*
Budzynek gm. Dalików, woj. łódzkie
A. Szymczak, *Budzynek gm. Dalików...*; L. Kajzer, *O budownictwie obronnym województwa łęczyckiego...*, pp. 111–122.
Chłapowo gm. Dominowo, woj. wielkopolskie
Studia i materiały..., vol. 1, p. 109; E. Naumowicz-Śmigielska, *Chłapowo, gm. Dominowo...*
Chrostowa gm. Łapanów, woj. małopolskie
A. Jodłowski, *Gródek średniowieczny w Chrostowej...*; S. Kołodziejski, *Średniowieczne rezydencje obronne Półkoziców...*, pp. 147–166.
Czarnuszka gm. Dobrzyca, woj. wielkopolskie.
Studia i materiały..., vol. 1 p. 137; J. Tomala, *Budownictwo obronne...*, p. 70.
Czułczyce gm. Sawin, woj. lubelskie
J. Cichomski, *Czułczyce gm...*
Dąbrówka gm. Dopiewo, woj. wielkopolskie
Studia i materiały..., vol. 1, p. 157; E. Naumowicz-Śmigielska, *Wstępne sprawozdanie z badań wykopaliskowych...*
Dmosin woj. łódzkie
T. Horbacz, Z. Lechowicz, *Przyczynek do problematyki osadnictwa...*
Dobrzyca woj. wielkopolskie
P. Wawrzyniak, *Dobrzyca...*; J. Tomala, *Budownictwo obronne...*, pp. 72–77.
Dziankówek, gm. Lubień Kujawski, woj. kujawsko-pomorskie
L. Wojda, *Weryfikacje siedzib mieszkalno-obronnych...*, pp. 160–166.
Głuszynek gm. Topólka, woj. kujawsko-pomorskie
L. Kajzer, *Głuszynek, gm. Topólka...*
Gniazdków gm. Chotcza, woj. woj. mazowieckie
Z. Lechowicz, *Wyniki badań na stanowisku 1 w Gniazdkowie...*; A. Nierychlewska, *Budownictwo obronne...*, pp. 120–124.

Golice gm. Poddębice, woj. łódzkie
L. Kajzer, *O budownictwie obronnym województwa...*, p. 114; L. Kajzer, *Zamki i dwory...*, p. 206.

Gorlice woj. małopolskie
J. Bogdanowski, *Obronna wieża mieszkalna...*, p. 131

Gozdów gm. Werbkowice, woj. lubelskie.
E. Prusicka-Kołcon, *Wyniki badań tzw. gródka stożkowatego w Gozdowie...*; E. Prusicka-Kołcon, *Drugi sezon badań...*

Gruszczyce gm. Błaszki, woj. łódzkie
A. Marciniak-Kajzer, T. J., Horbacz, *Z problematyki siedzib „pańskich"...*; A. Marciniak-Kajzer, T. J., Horbacz, *Sprawozdanie z badań archeologicznych...*

Horodysko pow. Chełm, woj. lubelskie
J. Ślusarski, *Horodysko, pow. Chełm...*

Iwno gm. Kostrzyn, woj. wielkopolskie
Studia i materiały..., vol. 2, p. 178; E. Naumowicz-Śmigielska, M. Grabska, *Iwno pow. Środa...*

Izdebno pow. Żnin, woj. kujawsko-pomorskie
O. Romanowska-Grabowska, *Izdebno pow. Żnin...*; *Studia i materiały...*, vol. 2, pp. 180–81.

Jankowo Dolne gm. Gniezno, woj. wielkopolskie
C. Strzyżewski, *Jankowo Dolne...*; C. Strzyżewski, *Kafle gotyckie...*

Jarocin woj. wielkopolskie
R. Grygiel, *Zarembowie z Jarocina...*

Jeziorsko gm. Warta woj. łódzkie
E. Krause, *Średniowieczny gródek rycerski w Jeziorsku...*

Kakawa Godziesze Wielkie, woj. wielkopolskie
J. Tomala, *Budownictwo obronne powiatu kaliskiego...*, pp. 102–103.

Kalinowa, gm. Błaszki, woj. łódzkie
L. Kajzer, *Zamki i dwory...*, p. 212.

Karmin gm. Dobrzyca, woj. wielkopolskie
J. Tomala, *Budownictwo obronne wschodniego pogranicza...*, p. 166.

Karsznice gm. Góra Św. Małgorzaty, woj. łódzkie
P. Świątkiewicz, *Późnośredniowieczne grodzisko w Karsznicach...*

Kępno woj. wielkopolskie
J. Augustyniak, *Wyniki badań wykopaliskowych na grodzisku...*,

Kiełbów Stary gm. Stara Błotnica, woj. mazowieckie
Z. W. Pyzik, *Grodzisko stożkowate w Kiełbowie Starym...*

Kleszczyn Stary gm. Brzuze, woj. kujawsko-pomorskie
L. Kajzer, A. Horonziak, *Budownictwo obronne Ziemi Dobrzyńskiej...*, pp. 148–151

Klwów, woj. mazowieckie
E. Ćwiertak, *Wyniki weryfikacji grodzisk...*, p. 190–191; E. Ćwiertak, *Ze studiów nad wiejską siedzibą obronną...*, p. 245.

Kłocko gm. Sieradz, woj. łódzkie
B. Głowacka-Fronckiewicz, T. J. Horbacz, *Późnośredniowieczne grodzisko...*

Kłóbka gm. Lubień Kujawski, woj. kujawsko-pomorskie
T. J. Horbacz, *Dwór na kopcu w Kłóbce...*

Koniecpol Stary gm. Koniecpol, woj. śląskie
Z.W. Pyzik, *Grodzisko średniowieczne w Starym Koniecpolu...*; W. Gliński, *Uwagi na temat siedziby możnowładczej...*

Kopaliny Pogwizdowskie gm. Nowy Wiśnicz, woj. małopolskie.
A. Jodłowski, *Badania grodziska w Kopalinach...*; S. Kołodziejski, *Średniowieczne rezydencje obronne możnowładztwa na terenie województwa krakowskiego...*, pp. 128–9.

Kopytów gm. Błonie, woj. mazowieckie
S. Suchodolski, *Kopytów, pow. Pruszków...*

Kościelna Wieś gm. Osięciny, woj. kujawsko-pomorskie
L. Kajzer, *Średniowieczna i nowożytna Kościelna Wieś...*

Kościerzyn gm. Sieradz, woj. łódzkie
L. Kajzer, *Pałace i dwory w dawnym województwie sieradzkim...*, pp. 57–71.

Kowala Stępocina gm. Kowala, woj. mazowieckie
E. Ćwiertak, *Ze studiów nad wiejską siedzibą obronną...*, p. 245; A. Nierychlewska, *Budownictwo obronne...*, pp. 161–2.

Kozłów woj. małopolskie
S. Kołodziejski, *Średniowieczne rezydencje obronne możnowładztwa na terenie województwa krakowskiego...*, pp. 149–150.

Krajkowo gm. Mosina, woj. wielkopolskie
P. Śniady, *Krajkowo, gm. Mosina...*; A. Łaszkiewicz, *Kafle i piece kaflowe...*
Krępa gm. Dobrzyń, woj. kujawsko-pomorskie
L. Kajzer, A. Horonziak, *Budownictwo obronne Ziemi Dobrzyńskiej...*, cz. IV, pp. 152–156.
Krzykawka gm. Bukowno woj. małopolskie
E. Szydłowska, *Średniowieczny gródek w Krzykawce...*; J. Pierzak, D. Rozmus, *Średniowieczny gródek rycerski w Krzykawce...*
Książ Wielki woj. małopolskie
S. Kołodziejski, *Średniowieczne rezydencje obronne możnowładztwa na terenie województwa krakowskiego...*, pp. 153–4; S. Kołodziejski, *Obronne rezydencje Lisów w północnej Małopolsce...*, pp. 59–76.
Ktery gm. Krzyżanów, woj. łódzkie
J. Tomala, *Ktery gm. Krzyżanów...*; L. Kajzer, *O budownictwie obronnym województwa łęczyckiego...*, p. 114.
Kunowo gm. Mogilno, woj. kujawsko-pomorskie
T. Makiewicz, *Średniowieczne grodzisko stożkowate...*
Ledniczka (Rybitwy) gm. Łubowa, woj. wielkopolskie
J. Górecki, M. Łastowiecki, J. Wrzesiński, *Gródek na Ledniczce...*
Lubień Kujawski woj. kujawsko-pomorskie.
L. Kajzer, *Dwór obronny w Lubieniu Kujawskim...*
Łączki Jagiellońskie gm. Wojaszówka, woj. podkarpackie
A. Żaki, *Sprawozdanie z prac badawczych prowadzonych w Wietrznie-Bóbrce...*, pp. 499–509; A. Żaki, *Starożytne i średniowieczne warownie...*, p. 5–55.
Majkowice-Surdęga gm. Ręczno, woj. łódzkie
A. Chmielowska, *Sprawozdanie z badań kompleksu osadniczego...*
Małków gm. Warta, woj. łódzkie
G. Leńczyk, *Kopce historyczne...*, pp. 229–231; L. Kajzer, *Zamki i dwory...*, p. 225.
Mokrsko Dolne gm. Sobków, woj. świętokrzyskie
S. Kołodziejski, *Średniowieczne budownictwo obronne na pograniczu Małopolski...*, pp. 153–4; S. Kołodziejski, *Średniowieczne rezydencje obronne możnowładztwa na terenie województwa krakowskiego...*, pp. 160–161.

Mrówki gm. Wilczyn woj. wielkopolskie
Ł. i A. Nowakowie, *Mrówki, pow. Konin*...; K. Gorczyca, *Skansen archeologiczny*...
Mrukowa gm. Nowy Żmigród, woj. podkarpackie
A. Żaki, *Mrukowa i Żmigród Stary*...; S. Kołodziejski, *Średniowieczne rezydencje obronne możnowładztwa na terenie województwa krakowskiego*..., p. 163.
Mymoń gm. Rymanów, woj. podkarpackie
M. Cabalska, *Grodzisko w Mymoniu*...; P. N. Kotowicz, *Problematyka „Zamczyska"*...
Nabyszyce gm. Odolanów, woj. wielkopolskie
J. Tomala, *Budownictwo obronne*..., pp. 117–118.
Nowe Miasto nad Wartą woj. wielkopolskie
R. Grygiel, T. Jurek, *Doliwowie z Nowego Miasta*...
Orenice gm. Piątek, woj. łódzkie
L. Kajzer, *Orenice gm. Piątek*...; L. Kajzer, *O budownictwie obronnym województwa łęczyckiego*..., p. 115.
Orłów gm. Bedlno, woj. łódzkie
L. Kajzer, *Średniowieczny drewniany dwór obronny w Orłowie*...
Orszymowo gm. Mała Wieś, woj. mazowieckie
W. Szymański, *Sprawozdanie z badań sondażowych*..., pp. 231–235; W. Szymański, *Przyczynek do badań*..., pp. 55–71.
Pełczyska gm. Wartkowice, woj. łódzkie
J. Kamińska, *Grodziska stożkowate*..., p. 48; L. Kajzer, *Pełczyska, st. 2, gm. Wartkowice*...
Petrykozy gm. Białaczów, woj. łódzkie
W. Długoszewska, *Petrykozy gm. Białaczów*...; *Archeologia w województwie piotrkowskim*..., pp. 20–21.
Pęczniew woj. łódzkie
J. Kamińska, A. Chmielowska, *Sprawozdanie z badań archeologicznych*..., pp. 216–219; L. Kajzer, *Uwagi o ewolucji*..., pp. 589–603.
Pniewy woj. wielkopolskie
7. *Studia i materiały*..., vol. 5, pp. 86–88.

Podłężyce gm. Sieradz, woj. łódzkie
J. Kamińska, L. Kajzer, *Grodzisko z XIII-XIV w Podłężycach…*; L. Kajzer *O budownictwie obronnym województwa łęczyckiego…*, pp. 111–122.
Popów gm. Pęczniew, woj. łódzkie
T. Łaszkiewicz, P. Wawrzyniak, *Popów - przyczynek do dyskusji…*
Potarzyca gm. Jarocin, woj. wielkopolskie
Tomala J. *Późnośredniowieczne i nowożytne założenia…*, pp. 250–251
Radzymin gm. Naruszewo, woj. mazowieckie
J. Pyrgała, *Badania sondażowe wczesnośredniowiecznych grodzisk…*, pp. 192–194
Rozdrażew woj. wielkopolskie
L. Wojda, *Rozdrażew, woj. kaliskie…*; J. Tomala, *Późnośredniowieczne i nowożytne założenia…*, pp. 247–8.
Rozprza - Łochyńsko, woj. łódzkie
A. Chmielowska, Z badań nad wczesnośredniowiecznym kompleksem osad*niczym…*; A. Chmielowska, *Rozprza…*
Rybojady gm. Trzciel, woj. lubuskie.
A. Kołodziejski, *Wstępne badania archeologiczne…*; *Studia i materiały…*, vol. 5, pp. 455–6.
Rzeczków gm. Skierniewice, woj. łódzkie
A. Kosiorek, *Z najnowszych badań archeologicznych…*, pp. 89–90.
Sędziszów gm. Sędziszów, woj. świętokrzyskie
S. Kołodziejski, *Średniowieczne rezydencje obronne możnowładztwa na terenie województwa krakowskiego…*, p. 173
Siedlątków gm. Poddębice, woj. łódzkie
J. Kamińska, *Siedlątków…*; E. Krause, *Nowe źródła archeologiczne…*
Siemkowice woj. łódzkie
M. Głosek, L. Kajzer, *Renesansowy dwór obronny w Siemkowicach…*
Skoszewy Stare gm. Nowosolna, woj. łódzkie
L. Kajzer, *O budownictwie obronnym województwa łęczyckiego…*, p. 117; M. Góra, *Wyniki badań wykopaliskowych…*
Słupia gm. Jodłownik, woj. nowosądeckie.
G. Leńczyk, *Katalog…*, p. 30, 99; S. Kołodziejski, *Średniowieczne rezydencje obronne możnowładztwa na terenie województwa krakowskiego…*, pp. 176–77.

Smogulec gm. Gołańcz, woj. wielkopolskie
E. Cnotliwy, R. Rogosz, E. Wilgocki, *Grodzisko stożkowate w Smogulcu...*

Sobolów (Sobolewo-Sieradze) gm. Łapanów, woj. małopolskie
K. Reguła, *Badania archeologiczne...*; S. Kołodziejski, *Średniowieczne rezydencje obronne możnowładztwa na terenie województwa krakowskiego...*, pp. 177–178.

Sromowce Wyżne, gm. Czorsztyn, woj. nowosądeckie.
A. Żaki, *Fortalicjum średniowieczne ...*; S. Kołodziejski, *Średniowieczne rezydencje obronne możnowładztwa na terenie województwa krakowskiego...*, p. 179.

Staw gm. Szczytniki, woj. wielkopolskie.
L. Kajzer, *Wstęp do badań nad siedzibami obronnymi kaliskiego...*, p. 399; J. Tomala, *Budownictwo obronne...*, 134–136.

Stryków woj. łódzkie
B. Muzolf, *Stryków, st. 5 - siedziba obronna ...*

Strzałków gm. Lisków, woj. wielkopolskie
J. Tomala, *Budownictwo obronne...*, pp. 139–140.

Strzemkowo gm. Inowrocław, woj. kujawsko-pomorskie
A. Cofta-Broniewska, *Strzemkowo gm. Inowrocław...*; *Studia i materiały...*, vol. 6, p. 284–5.

Strzyżewo Paczkowe gm. Gniezno, woj. wielkopolskie
C. Strzyżewski, *Strzyżewo Paczkowe...*

Szamotuły woj. wielkopolskie
E. Krause, *Badania archeologiczne grodziszczka w Szamotułach...*

Szczekociny woj. śląskie
Z. W. Pyzik, *Szczekociny, pow. Włoszczowa...*; S. Kołodziejski, *Średniowieczne rezydencje obronne możnowładztwa na terenie województwa krakowskiego...*, p. 181; S. Kołodziejski, *Średniowieczne budownictwo obronne na pograniczu...*, p. 154.

Taczów gm. Zakrzew, woj. mazowieckie
E. Ćwiertak, *Ze studiów...*, pp. 247–248; A. Nierychlewska, *Budownictwo...*, pp. 230–232.

Trzciel woj. wielkopolskie
A. Kołodziejski, *Trzciel pow. Międzyrzecz...*; Z. Kurnatowska, A. Łosińska, *Weryfikacja grodzisk wielkopolskich na półmetku...*, p. 43.

Trzemsze gm. Przykona, woj. wielkopolskie
M. Kociński, *Późnośredniowieczna siedziba obronna w Trzemszach…*

Tyczyn gm. Burzenin, woj. łódzkie
J. Kamińska, R. Gupieńcowa, *Sprawozdanie z badań archeologicznych…*; L. Kajzer, *Uwagi o ewolucji…*, p. 596.

Wilkanowo gm. Mała Wieś, woj. mazowieckie
W. Szymański, *Przyczynek do badań nad problematyką grodzisk…*, pp. 65–71.

Wistka (Krajów), gm. Przysucha, woj. mazowieckie
E. Ćwiertak, *Ze studiów nad wiejską siedzibą obronną…*, p. 248; A. Nierychlewska, *Budownictwo obronne…*, pp. 233–235.

Witów gm. Burzenin, woj. łódzkie
J. Kamińska, A. Golczyńska, *Kopiec w Witowie…*, pp. 162–165.

Włoszczowa woj. świętokrzyskie
Z.W. Pyzik, *Grodzisko średniowieczne we Włoszczowie…*; C. Hadamik, *Średniowieczne dwory obronne…*, pp. 31–37.

Wola Chełmska, (Wola Justowska - Kraków).
E. Zaitz, *Sprawozdanie z badań archeologicznych…*; W. Zin, K. Radwański, A. Kadłuczka, *Wstępne wyniki badań…*, pp. 163–166.

Wola Książęca gm. Kotlin, woj. wielkopolskie
Studia i materiały…, vol. VII, pp. 269–70; J. Tomala, *Budownictwo obronne wschodniego pogranicza…*, p. 166.

Wola Piekarska gm. Dobra, woj. wielkopolskie
Studia i materiały…, vol. 7, pp. 271–274; Z. Kurnatowska, A. Łosińska, *Weryfikacja grodzisk wielkopolskich na półmetku…*; L. Kajzer, *Zamki i dwory…*, p. 255.

Zacharzew gm. Ostrów Wielkopolski, woj. wielkopolskie
J. Tomala, *Budownictwo obronne…*, pp. 141–2.

Zagórze (Sosnowiec), woj. śląskie
T. Kosmala, *Sosnowiec–Zagórze…*; S. Kołodziejski, *Średniowieczne rezydencje obronne małopolskich Gryfitów…*, pp. 83, 86.

Zagórze gm. Mucharz, woj. małopolskie.
T. Kosmala, *Zagórze st. 13, gm. Mucharz…*

Zameczek gm. Przytyk, woj. mazowieckie
Z. Lechowicz, *Kasztelania skrzyńska...*, pp. 23–24; A. Nierychlewska, *Budownictwo obronne...*, pp. 241–2.
Zawalów gm. Miączyn, woj. lubelskie
A. Urbański, *Grodzisko stożkowate w Zawalowie...*
Zduny woj. wielkopolskie
R. Grygiel, T. Jurek, *Zduny...*
Zembrzyce woj. małopolskie
S. Kołodziejski, *Średniowieczne rezydencje obronne możnowładztwa na terenie województwa krakowskiego...*, pp. 203–204.
Żerniki-Jaryszki gm. Kórnik, woj. wielkopolskie
T. Stępnik, A. Dębski, *Sprawozdanie z badań...*
Żmigród Stary pow. Jasło, woj. podkarpackie
A. Żaki, *Mrukowa i Żmigród Stary...*; J. Marszałek, *Katalog grodzisk...*, p. 263.
Żółków gm. Żerków, woj. wielkopolskie
G. Teske, J. Tomala, *Archeologiczne badania domniemanego grodziska...*; J. Tomala, *Późnośredniowieczne i nowożytne założenia...*
Żywiec woj. śląskie
B. Gołąb, *Sprawozdanie z wykopalisk...*; S. Kołodziejski, *Średniowieczne rezydencje obronne możnowładztwa na terenie województwa krakowskiego...*, pp. 205–6.

VII. BIBLIOGRAPHY

Andrzejewski A., Kajzer L., *Z archeologiczno-architektonicznych badań weryfikacyjnych zespołu pałacowego w Ujeździe koło Tomaszowa Mazowieckiego w 2002 roku*, "Łódzkie Sprawozdania Archeologiczne", vol. 8, (2002/2003), p. 290.

Ankersmith F.R., *Historiografia i postmodernizm*. In: Postmodernizm, R. Nycz (ed.), Kraków 1997, pp. 145–172.

Archeologia w województwie piotrkowskim. Informator 1988–1994, M. Gąsior, M. Szukała (ed.), Piotrków 1995.

Ariès P., *Historia dzieciństwa. Dziecko i rodzina w dawnych czasach*, Gdańsk 1995, pp. 20–21.

Banasiewicz E., *Grodziska i zamczyska Zamojszczyzny*, Zamość 1990.

Barber R., *Rycerze i rycerskość*, Warszawa 2000.

Barthelemy D., *Zagospodarowanie przestrzeni prywatnej XI–XIII w.* In: Historia życia prywatnego, vol. 2, Od Europy feudalnej do renesansu, G. Duby (ed.), Wrocław 1998, pp. 431–458.

Bieniak J., *Elita ziemi dobrzyńskiej w późnym średniowieczu i jej majątki*. In: Stolica i region. Włocławek i jego dzieje na tle przemian Kujaw i ziemi dobrzyńskiej. Materiały z sesji naukowej (9–10 maja 1994 roku), O. Krut-Hozonziak, L. Kajzer (ed.), Włocławek 1995, pp. 23–60.

Bieniak J., *Tytuł rycerski jako kryterium identyfikacji osób w średniowieczu*. In: Personae–colligationes–facta, Toruń 1991, pp. 66–73.

Biller T., *Die Adelsburg in Deutschland: Entstehung, Form und Bedeutung*, München 1993.

Błaszczyk W., Radkiewicz T., *Wyniki badań powierzchniowych przeprowadzonych na terenie powiatu Częstochowa w roku 1963*, "Biuletyn Śląskiego Instytutu Naukowego", vol. 40, 1964, p. 116.

Bogdanowski J., *Obronna wieża mieszkalna dworu Karwacjanów w Gorlicach*. In: Architektura rezydencjonalna i obronna województwa rzeszowskiego w świetle badań naukowych prowadzonych w 25-leciu PRL, Łańcut 9–10 maja 1970, Materiały z sesji naukowej, Łańcut 1972, pp. 157–166.

Bogucka M., *Historia kultury materialnej a postmodernizm. Kilka uwag do modnego tematu*. In: O rzeczach minionych. Studia i Materiały z Historii Kultury Materialnej, vol. 71, Warszawa 2006, pp. 31–34.

Bogucki A., *„Strennus" jako tytuł rycerzy pasowanych (XIII-XV w.)*, "Przegląd Historyczny", vol. 77, 1986, no. 4 (1987), pp. 625–647.

Bogucki A., *Rycerz i panosza w źródłach polskich XIV i XV wieku*. In: Społeczeństwo Polski średniowiecznej, S. K. Kuczyński (ed.), vol. 7, Warszawa 1996, pp. 165–200.

Boguszewicz A., *Architektura siedziby możnowładczo-rycerskiej w Wierzbnej koło Świdnicyw świetle badań archeologicznych*, "Archaeologia Historica Polona", vol. 15/1, 2005, pp. 279–305.

Böhme H. W., Von der Dollen B., Kerber D., Meckseper C., Schock-Werner B., Zeune J., *Burgen in Mitteleuropa. Ein Handbuch*, vol. 1 and 2, Stuttgart 1999.

Braudel F., *Kultura materialna, gospodarka i kapitalizm, XV-XVIII wiek*, vol. 1, Struktury codzienności. Możliwe i niemożliwe, J. Kochanowicz (ed.), Warszawa 1992.

Brych V., *Hmotná kultura středověké tvrze v Čechách*. In: Encyklopedie českých tvrzí, vol. 1, Praha 1998, pp. 47–83.

Buczek K., *Prawo rycerskie i powstanie stanu szlacheckiego w Polsce*, "Przegląd Historyczny", vol. 69, 1978, no. 1, pp. 23–46.

Busse W. G., *Burg und Schloss als Lebensorte in Mittelalter und Renaissance*, "Studia Humaniora" 26, Düsseldorf 1995.

Buśko C., *Budynki wieżowe w krajobrazie średniowiecznego miasta*. In: Dom w mieście średniowiecznym i nowożytnym, B. Gediga (ed.), Wrocław 2004, pp. 61–73.

Buśko C., *Archeolog w kuchni*. In: Civitas et villa. Miasto i wieś w średniowiecznej Europie środkowej. Wrocław–Praha 2002, pp. 309–315.

Cabalska M., *Grodzisko w Mymoniu, pow. Krosno w świetle badań archeologicznych*, "Materiały Starożytne i Wczesnośredniowieczne", vol. 3, 1975, pp. 321–339.

Chmielowska A., *Grzebienie starożytne i średniowieczne z ziem polskich*, Łódź 1971.

Chmielowska A., *Rozprza we wczesnym i późnym średniowieczu*, "Prace i Materiały Muzeum Archeologicznego i Etnograficznego w Łodzi" , nr 29, 1982 [1985], pp. 181, 204.

Chmielowska A., *Sprawozdanie z badań kompleksu osadniczego w Majkowicach, woj. Piotrków Trybunalski*, "Sprawozdania Archeologiczne", vol. 28, 1976, pp. 235–242

Chmielowska A., *Z badań nad wczesnośredniowiecznym kompleksem osadniczym w Rozprzy, pow. Piotrków Trybunalski*, "Prace i Materiały Muzeum Archeologicznego i Etnograficznego w Łodzi", vol. 13, 1966, pp. 249–266.

Chorowska M., *Rezydencje średniowieczne na Śląsku. Zamki, pałace, wieże mieszkalne*, Wrocław 2003.

Chotěbor P., *Obranná zařízení*. In: Encyklopedie českých tvrzí, vol. 1, Praha 1998, pp. 37–39.

Chotěbor P., *Tvrze v ikonografických pramenech*, "Archaeologia Historica", vol. 17, 1992, pp. 177–187.

Chudziakowa J., *Akwamanila z Mogilna*, "Archeologia Polski", vol. 22, 1977, no. 1, pp. 171–178.

Cichomski J., *Czułczyce gm. Sawin woj. chełmskie*, "Informator Archeologiczny". Badania 1980, p. 191.

Ciuk K., *Radzynia pow. Syców*, "Informator Archeologiczny". Badania 1968, pp. 362–263.

Cnotliwy E., Rogosz R., Wilgocki E., *Grodzisko stożkowate w Smogulcu gm. Gołańcz, woj. Piła, w świetle badań weryfikacyjnych*, "Slavia. Antiqua", vol. 34, pp. 141–205.

Cnotliwy E., *Rzemiosło rogownicze na Pomorzu wczesnośredniowiecznym*, Wrocław 1973.

Cofta-Broniewska A., *Strzemkowo gm. Inowrocław, woj. bydgoskie. Stanowisko 3A*, "Informator Archeologiczny". Badania 1984, p. 176.

Contamine P., *Problemy XIV–XV wiek*. In: Historia życia prywatnego, vol. 2. Od Europy feudalnej do renesansu, G. Duby (ed.), Wrocław 1998, pp. 451–458.

Contamine P., *Zagospodarowanie prywatnej przestrzeni XIV–XV wiek*. In: Historia życia prywatnego, vol. 2. Od Europy feudalnej do renesansu, G. Duby (ed.), Wrocław 1998, pp. 458–540.

Cynarski S., *Dzieje rodu Lanckorońskich z Brzezia*, Warszawa–Kraków 1996.

Ćwiertak E., *Ze studiów nad wiejską siedzibą obronną w ziemi radomskiej w XIII–XVIII w.*, "Prace i Materiały Muzeum Archeologicznego i Etnograficznego w Łodzi" , Seria Archeologiczna, no. 34, 1987, pp. 241–249.

Ćwiertak E., *Wyniki weryfikacji grodzisk w oparciu o badania na terenie województwa radomskiego*, "Biuletyn Kwartalny Radomskiego Towarzystwa Naukowego", vol. 22, 1985, no. 1–2, pp. 63–100.

Dąbrowska M., *Kominek – luksus czy konieczność?* In: Nędza czy dostatek na ziemiach polskich od średniowiecza po wiek XX, J. Sztetyłło (ed.), Warszawa 1992, pp. 177–181.

Dąbrowska M., *Oświetlenie i ogrzewanie średniowiecznych wnętrz zamkowych*, "Archaeologia Historica", vol. 14, pp. 173–188.

Dějiny hmotně kultury, vol. I (2) Kultura každodenního života od 13. do 15. století, J. Petráně (ed.), Praha 1985.

Długoszewska W., *Petrykozy gm. Białaczów, woj. piotrkowskie*, "Informator Archeologiczny". Badania 1990, p. 105; "Informator Archeologiczny". Badania 1991, pp. 125–6; "Informator Archeologiczny". Badania 1992, pp. 108–9.

Dobrowolski K., *Uwagi o grodach wczesno-historycznych w Polsce ze szczególnym uwzględnieniem grodziska w Piekarach*, "Sprawozdania Polskiej Akademii Umiejętności", vol. 37,1932 (1933), pp. 24–26.

Drewett P., *Rich Man, Poor Man: An Archaeological Comparison of the Economy of a Castle and a Farm, in East Sussex, England, C. 1100–1500 A.D.* In: Život v archeologii středověku, J. Kubková, J. Klápště, M. Ježek, P. Meduna (ed.), Praha 1997, pp. 160–168.

Durdík T., Kašička F., Nechvátal B., *Hrady, hrádky a tvrze na* Písecku, Písek 1995.

Durdík, *Ilustrovaná encyklopedie českých hradů*, Praha 1999, pp. 8–9.

Dworzaczek W., *Hetman Jan Tarnowski. Z dziejów możnowładztwa małopolskiego*, Warszawa 1985.

Dworzaczek W., *Leliwici Tarnowscy od schyłku XVI wieku do czasów współczesnych*, Tarnów 1996.

Dworzaczek W., *Leliwici Tarnowscy. Z dziejów możnowładztwa małopolskiego wiek XIV–XV*, Warszawa 1971.

Ericsson I., *Vom slawischen Burgwall zum deutschen Guvol. Studie zur mittelalterischen Siedlungsgenese im Raum Futterkamp*, Holstein, Lund 1984.

Florek M., *Rozpoznanie grodzisk na terenie województwa Podkarpackiego*. In: "Rzeszowska Teka Konserwatorska", vol. 2, Rzeszów 2000, pp. 7–39.

Flori J., *Rycerze i rycerstwo w średniowieczu*, Poznań 2003.

Frazik J. T., *Zamki i budownictwo obronne ziemi rzeszowskiej*, Kraków 1971.

Gajewski L., Górska J., Paderewska L., Pyrgała J., Szymański W., *Badania sondażowe grodzisk Mazowsza i Podlasia w latach 1966–1968*, "Sprawozdania Archeologiczne", vol. 22, 1970, pp. 151–172.

Gawęda S., *Początki i rola rodziny Lanckorońskich do końca średniowiecza.* „Zeszyty Naukowe Uniwersytetu Jagiellońskiego". Prace historyczne, no. 89, 1989.

Gawęda S., *Możnowładztwo małopolskie w XIV i pierwszej połowie XV wieku*, „Zeszyty Naukowe Uniwersytetu Jagiellońskiego". Prace historyczne, no. 18, 1966.

Gąssowska E., *Wojewódzki Ośrodek Archeologiczno-Konserwatorski w Kielcach. Plan działania*, "Peregrinus", nr 1, 1990, pp. 5–26.

Gedl B., *Erforschung der mittelalterlichen Wehraulangen im nördlichen Teil des schlesischkleinpolnischen Grenzgebietes*, "Zeszyty Naukowe Uniwersytetu Jagiellońskiego". Prace Archeologiczne, no. 23, 1976, pp. 97–103.

Gedl M., *Pozostałości drewnianej budowli średniowiecznym gródku w Zbrojewsku*, "Archaeologia Historica Polona", vol. 12, 2003, pp. 73–80.

Gedl M., *Studien bei die Entwicklung der Frühmittelalterlichen Besiedlung im Nordteil der kleinpolnisch-schlesischen Grenzgebiete*, Raports du IIIe Congres International d'Archelogie Slave, Bratislava 1979, vol. 1, pp. 271–276.

Gliński W., *Uwagi na temat siedziby możnowładczej Pobogów-Koniecpolskich w Chrząstowie-Koniecpolu*. In: Przemiany architektury rezydencjonalnej w XV–XVII w. na terenie dawnego województwa sandomierskiego. Wybrane przykłady, J.L. Adamczyk (ed.), Kielce 2000, pp. 145–154.

Głosek M., *Broń drzewcowa i obuchowa*. In: Uzbrojenie w Polsce średniowiecznej 1350–1450, A. Nadolski (ed.), Łódź 1990, pp. 138–139.

Głosek M., *Broń drzewcowa i obuchowa*. In: Uzbrojenie w Polsce średniowiecznej 1450–1500, A. Nowakowski (ed.), Toruń 1998, pp. 40–52.

Głosek M., Kajzer L., *Siemkowice, pow. Pajęczno*, "Informator Archeologiczny". Badania 1974, pp. 260–261.

Głosek M., Kajzer L., *Renesansowy dwór obronny w Siemkowicach (przyczynek do poznania przemian wiejskiej siedziby obronnej)*, "Kwartalnik Architektury i Urbanistyki", vol. 21, no. 2, 1976, pp. 153–166.

Głosek M., *Miecze środkowoeuropejskie z X–XV w*, Warszawa 1984.

Głosek M., *Późnośredniowieczna broń obuchowa w zbiorach polskich*, Łódź–Warszawa 1996.

Głosek M., Kajzer L., Łuk średniowieczny znaleziony w Brzegu, "Silesia Antiqua", vol. 19, 1977, pp. 243–252.

Głowacka-Fronckiewicz B., Horbacz T. J., *Późnośredniowieczne grodzisko stożkowate w Kłocku pod Sieradzem*, "Sieradzki Rocznik Muzealny", vol. 8, 1992, pp. 133–148.

Gołąb B., *Sprawozdanie z wykopalisk archeologicznych na Grojcu*, "Karta Groni", vol. 13, 1985.

Gorczyca K., *Barłogi st. 2 gm. Rzgów woj. konińskie*, "Informator Archeologiczny". Badania 1981, p. 213.

Gorczyca K., *Biskupice, pow. Grodziec, woj. konińskie*, "Informator Archeologiczny". Badania. 1983, p. 187.

Gorczyca K., *Skansen archeologiczny w Mrówkach*, "Kronika Wielkopolski", no. 4(92), 1999, pp. 97–99.

Górecki J., Łastowiecki M., Wrzesiński J., *Gródek na Ledniczce*. In: Studia Lednickie, vol. 4, Poznań–Lednica 1996, pp. 208–210.

Górska I., Paderewska L., Pyrgała J., Szymański W., Gajewski L., Okulicz Ł., *Grodziska Mazowsza i Podlasia (w granicach dawnego województwa warszawskiego)*, Wrocław 1976 (Review, A. Gieysztor, „Kwartalnik Historii Kultury Materialnej", vol. 25, no. 4, pp. 550–551.

Gradowski M., *To też są zabytki*, "Spotkania z Zabytkami", 1985, no. 2, pp. 34–35.

Grążawski K., *Późnośredniowieczny gródek rycerski w Radoszkach gmina Grążawy w świetle badań archeologicznych*. In: Szkice brodnickie, vol. 1, S. Bilski (ed.), Brodnica–Toruń 1988, pp. 45–66.

Grążawski K., *Średniowieczny gródek rycerski w Bachotku na ziemi chełmińskiej w świetle badań archeologicznych*, "Sprawozdania Archeologiczne", vol. 40, 1988, pp. 317–341.

Grundmann G., *Burgen, Schlösser und Gutshäuser in Schlesien*. Bd. 1, Die mittelalterischen Burgruinen, Burgen und Wohntürme, Breslau 1939 (reprint 1982).

Grygiel R., *Dzieje rezydencji*. In: Grygiel R., Jurek T., Doliwowie z Nowego Miasta nad Wartą, Dębna i Biechowa. Dzieje rezydencji i ich właścicieli, Łódź 1996, pp. 11–284.

Grygiel R., Jurek T., *Doliwowie z Nowego Miasta nad Wartą, Dębna i Biechowa. Dzieje rezydencji i ich właścicieli*, Łódź 1996.

Grygiel R., Jurek T., *Zduny. Późnośredniowieczne i nowożytne rezydencje właścicieli miasta*, Łódź 1999.

Grygiel R., *Wyniki badań archeologicznych rezydencji*. In: R. Grygiel, T. Jurek, Zduny Późnośredniowieczne i nowożytne rezydencje właścicieli miasta, Łódź 1999, pp. 28–29.

Grygiel R., *Zarębowie z Jarocina w świetle źródeł archeologicznych i historycznych*, Łódź 1992, pp. 27–28.

Guerquin B., *Zamki w Polsce*, Warszawa 1984.

Gurba J., *Grodziska Lubelszczyzny*, Lublin1976.

Habovštiak A., *Stredoveká dedina na Slovensku*, Bratislava 1985.

Hadamik C., *Średniowieczne dwory obronne w powiecie włoszczowskim*, Włoszczowa 2005.

Hadamik C., *Bebelno koło Włoszczowy. Wieś i siedziba rycerska w wiekach średnich*, Kielce 2004.

Hejna A., *České tvrze*, Praha 1961.

Hellmich M., *Schlesische Burghügel und Burgwalle, Der Oberschiesier*, 1930 (non vidimus).

Hensel W., Hilczer-Kurnatowska Z., Łosińska A., *Studia i materiały do osadnictwa Wielkopolski wczesnohistorycznej*, vol. 7, Poznań 1995.

Hensel W., Kurnatowska Z., *Studia i materiały do dziejów Wielkopolski wczesnohistorycznej*, vol. 4–6, 1972, 1980, 1987.

Hensel W., *Studia i materiały do osadnictwa Wielkopolski Wczesnohistorycznej*, vol. 1–3 Poznań 1950, 1953, 1959.

Herrnbrodt A., *Die Ausgrabungen auf der Motte Hoverberg bei Birgelen, Kreis Geilenkirchen-Heinsberg*, "Bonner Jahrbücher" 155–56, 1955–1956.

Herrnbrodt A., *Der Husterknup. Eine niederrheinische Burganlage des frühen Mittelalters*, Beihefte Bonner Jahrbücher, 6 Köln–Graz 1958.

Hilczerówna Z., *Rogownictwo gdańskie w X–XIV w.* In: Gdańsk wczesnośredniowieczny, vol. 4, Gdańsk 1961, pp. 41–144.

Horbacz T. J., *Dwór na kopcu w Kłóbce, gm. Lubień Kujawski, woj. włocławskie.* In: T. J. Horbacz, L. Kajzer, T. Nowak, L. Wojda, Siedziby obronno-rezydencjonalne w powiecie kowalskim na Kujawach w XIII–XVIII wieku. Łódź 1991, pp. 144–159.

Horbacz T. J., *Fragment późnośredniowiecznej akwamanili z Bobrownik, woj. włoc*ławskie, "Acta Universitatis Lodziensis". Folia Archaeologica, vol. 4, 1983, pp. 123–129.

Horbacz T. J., Kajzer L., Nowak T., Wojda L., *Siedziby obronno-rezydencjonalne w powiecie kowalskim na Kujawach w XIII–XVIII wieku*, L. Kajzer (ed.), Łódź 1991.

Horbacz T. J., *Nowożytny dwór w Brodni Dolnej koło Łasku.* In: Między północą a południem. Sieradzkie i Wieluńskie w późnym średniowieczu i czasach nowożytnych, T. J. Horbacz i L. Kajzer (ed.), Sieradz 1993, p. 303-307.

Horbacz T. J., *O niektórych „kopcach historycznych" w Sieradzkiem w kilkadziesiąt lat później*, "Archaeologia Historica Polona", vol. 5, 1997, pp. 69–82.

Horbacz T. J., Z. Lechowicz, *Fikcja czy rekonstrukcja? (w związku z artykułem A. Pawłowskiego)*, "Z Otchłani Wieków", vol. 48, 1982, no. 4, pp. 175–177.

Hunicz A., *Katalog wczesnośredniowiecznych i średniowiecznych grodzisk południowo-wschodniej Lubelszczyzny*, "Biuletyn Informacyjny Pracowni Konserwacji Zabytków", vol. 5, no. 19, 1970, pp. 163–179.

Jakimowicz T., *Dwór murowany w Polsce w wieku XVI (wieża-kamienica-kasztel)*, Warszawa–Poznań 1979.

Jamka R., Leńczyk G., Dobrowolski K., *Badania wykopaliskowe w Piekarach w powiecie krakowskim*, "Prace Prehistoryczne", no. 2, Kraków 1939.

Janiak T., *Kafle gotyckie w zbiorach Muzeum Początków Państwa Polskiego w Gnieźnie*, Gniezno 2003

Jodłowski A., *Badania grodziska w Kopalinach, pow. Bochnia*, "Badania archeologiczne prowadzone przez Muzeum Żup Krakowskich Wieliczka" w roku 1971, Kraków 1972, pp. 11–19.

Jodłowski A., *Gródek średniowieczny w Chrostowej, pow. Bochnia*, "Sprawozdania Archeologiczne", vol. 26, 1974, pp. 317–334.

Jodłowski A., *Osadnictwo obronne w dolinie Dunajca*, "Materiały Archeologiczne", vol. 8, 1967, pp. 5–23.

Jurek T., *Właściciele rezydencji*. In: R. Grygiel, T. Jurek, Zduny. Późnośredniowieczne i nowożytne rezydencje właścicieli miasta, Łódź 1999.

Kajzer L., *Archeologia a historia kultury materialnej*, „Kwartalnik Historii Kultury Materialnej", vol. 42, 1994, no. 2, pp. 173–175.

Kajzer L., *Dwory obronne wieluńskiego w XIII–XVII w.*, "Acta Universitatis Lodziensis". Folia Archeologica, nr 6, 1984.

Kajzer L., [Review:] M. Szope, Grodziska i zamczyska województwa tarnowskiego, 1981, "Z Otchłani Wieków", vol. 48, 1982, no. 4, pp. 191–192.

Kajzer L., *Archeologiczny rodowód dworu. Przemiany siedzib obronno-rezydencjonalnych Polski centralnej w późnym średniowieczu i czasach nowożytnych*, Łódź 1988.

Kajzer L., *Czy akwamanila mogileńska pochodzi z XII wieku?*, "Kwartalnik Historii Kultury Materialnej", vol. 29, 1981, no. 1, p. 79–81.

Kajzer L., *Czy tzw. gródki stożkowate były fundacjami „średniego rycerstwa"?* In: Średniowieczne siedziby rycerskie w na tle badań podobnych obiektów na ziemiach polskich, A. Kola (ed.), Toruń 1987, p. 105–126.

Kajzer L., *Głuszynek, gm. Topólka, woj. włocławskie*, "Informator Archeologiczny". Badania 1986, p. 179.

Kajzer L., *Grodziska średniowieczne i nowożytne*, "Prace i Materiały Muzeum Archeologicznego i Etnograficznego w Łodzi" , nr 36, 1989–90, pp. 33–43.

Kajzer L., *O budownictwie obronnym województwa łęczyckiego w późnym średniowieczu i czasach nowożytnych – w piętnaście lat później*, "Acta Universitatis Lodziensis", Folia Archaeologica, vol. 20, 1996, pp. 111–122.

Kajzer L., *Orenice gm. Piątek, woj. płockie* „Informator Archeologiczny". Badania 1986, p. 190; B 1987, p. 201–202.

Kajzer L., *Pałace i dwory w dawnym województwie sieradzkim*, vol. 2, Materiały do dziejów rezydencji w Polsce, T. S. Jaroszewski (ed.), Warszawa 1994, pp. 139–152.

Kajzer L., *Pełczyska, stan. 2, gm. Wartkowice, woj. sieradzkie, AZP 61–47/2* "Informator Archeologiczny". Badania 1996, p. 274.

Kajzer L., *Studia nad świeckim budownictwem obronnym województwa łęczyckiego w XIII–XVII wieku*, "Acta Universitatis Lodziensis", Folia Archaeologica, vol. 1, Łódź 1980.

Kajzer L., *Średniowieczna i nowożytna Kościelna Wieś w świetle archeologicznych badań terenowych*. In: Kościelna wieś na Kujawach. Studium osadnicze, L. Kajzer (ed.), Łódź 1994, p. 107–158.

Kajzer L., *Średniowieczny drewniany dwór obronny w Orłowie nad Bzurą*, "Slavia Antiqua", vol. 32, 1990, pp. 241–290.

Kajzer L., *Uwagi o ewolucji wiejskich siedzib rycerskich w ziemiach łęczyckiej i sieradzkiej w XIII–XVI wieku*, "Kwartalnik Historii Kultury Materialnej", vol. 23, 1975, no. 4, pp. 589–603.

Kajzer L., *W sprawie genealogii wiejskiej siedziby obronnej w Polsce*, "Kwartalnik Historii Kultury Materialnej", vol. 20, 1972, no. 3, pp. 451–465.

Kajzer L., *W sprawie waloryzacji masowych zbiorów ceramiki późnośredniowiecznej i nowożytnej*, "Kwartalnik Historii Kultury Materialnej", vol. 39, 1991, no. 4, pp. 467–483;

Kajzer L., *Wstęp do archeologii historycznej w Polsce*, Łódź 1996, pp. 33–34.

Kajzer L., *Wstępna informacja o zbiorze późnogotyckich kafli z zamku w Ujeździe koło Tomaszowa Mazowieckiego*, "Łódzkie Sprawozdania Archeologiczne", vol. 10, 2006–2007, pp. 259–273.

Kajzer L., *Z badań nad budownictwem rezydencjalno-obronnym ziemi łęczyckiej i sieradzkiej w XVI w.*, "Kwartalnik Architektury i Urbanistyki", vol. 24, 1979, no. 4, pp. 373–382.

Kajzer L., *Z zagadnień genezy tzw. gródków stożkowatych (Uwagi na marginesie lektury VI tomu Początków Polski prof. Henryka Łowmiańskiego)*, "Kwartalnik Historii Kultury Materialnej", vol. 34, 1986, no. 2, pp. 331–339.

Kajzer L., *Zamki i społeczeństwo. Przemiany architektury i budownictwa obronnego w Polsce w X–XVIII wieku*, Łódź 1993.

Kajzer L., Augustyniak J., *Wstęp do studiów nad świeckim budownictwem obronnym sieradzkiego w XIII–XVII/XVIII wieku*, Łódź 1986.

Kajzer L., Horonziak A., *Archeologiczna weryfikacja grodzisk i kopców podworskich na obszarze Kujaw Brzeskich i ziemi dobrzyńskiej*, "Zapiski Kujawsko-Dobrzyńskie", vol. 11, 1997.

Kajzer L., Horonziak A., *Budownictwo obronne Ziemi Dobrzyńskiej*, Włocławek 1995.

Kajzer L., Kołodziejski S., Salm J., *Leksykon zamków w Polsce*, Warszawa 2001.

Kałagate S., *Średniowieczny materiał zabytkowy z przypadkowego odkrycia na stacji meteorologicznej w Radzyniu gm. Sława, woj. zielonogórskie, stan. 10 (AZP 63–19/74)*, "Wielkopolskie Sprawozdania Archeologiczne", vol. 3, 1995, pp. 233–234.

Kamińska J., *Siedlątków, obronna siedziba rycerska z XIV wieku*, "Prace i Materiały Muzeum Archeologicznego i Etnograficznego w Łodzi", Seria Archeologiczna, no. 15, 1968, pp. 15–88.

Kamińska J., Golczyńska A., *Kopiec w Witowie*. In: Rozwój osadnictwa w rejonie Burzenina nad Wartą VI–XIV w., J. Kamińska (ed.), Wrocław 1970, pp. 162–165.

Kamińska J., *Grody wczesnośredniowieczne ziem Polski środkowej na tle osadnictwa*, Łódź 1953, (Rev. M. Młynarska, "Kwartalnik Historii Kultury Materialnej", vol. 4, 1956, pp. 131–140 (Rev. Z. Hilczerówna, "Studia i materiały do dziejów Wielkopolski i Pomorza", vol. 2, no. 1, 1956, pp. 307–313).

Kamińska J., *Grodziska stożkowate śladem posiadłości rycerskich XIII–XIV w.*, "Prace i Materiały Muzeum Archeologicznego i Etnograficznego w Łodzi", Seria Archeologiczna, no. 13, 1966, pp. 43–78.

Kamińska J., Gupieńcowa R., *Sprawozdanie z badań archeologicznych, przeprowadzonych w 1964 roku na terenie ziemi* sieradzkiej, "Sprawozdania Archeologiczne", vol. 19, 1968, pp. 222–225.

Kamińska J., Kajzer L., *Grodzisko z XIII–XIV w. w Podłężycach, pow. Sieradz*, "Sprawozdania Archeologiczne", vol. 21, 1969, pp. 203–207.

Kamińska J., *Radomsko-Dobryszyce*. In: Na granicach archeologii, A. Nadolski (ed.), Łódź 1968, pp. 67–72.

Kamińska J., *Sprawozdanie z badań archeologicznych na grodziskach typu „stożkowatego" w pow. Poddębickim, w 1965 r.*, "Sprawozdania Archeologiczne", vol. 6, 1968, pp. 216–219

Kamińska J., *Sprawozdanie z badań nad grodami i osadnictwem otwartym wczesnego średniowiecza na terenie Polski środkowej w 1955 r.*, "Sprawozdania Archeologiczne", vol. 5, 1959 pp. 185–188;

Kastek T., Limisiewicz A., Mruczek R., *Domniemane ofiary zakładzinowe z terenu folwarku w Sobótce*, "Śląskie Sprawozdania Archeologiczne", vol. 43, 2001, pp. 461–472.

Kaźmierczyk J., *Podkowy na Śląsku. Studia z dziejów kultury materialnej*, Wrocław 1978.

Kaźmierczyk J., *Z badań nad grodami i miastami wczesnego średniowiecza na Śląsku*, "Archeologia Polski", vol. 10, 1966, no. 2, pp. 655–700.

Kiersnowska T., *„Słupy" rycerskie w Polsce średniowiecznej*, "Kwartalnik Historii Kultury Materialnej", vol. 20, 1972, no. 3, pp. 437–450.

Kirschke B., Prinke A., *Grodziska w województwie poznańskim. Katalog stanowisk archeologicznych*, "Poznańskie Zeszyty Archeologiczno-Konserwatorskie", nr 2, Poznań 1995.

Kobyliński Z., *Antypozytywizm a ochrona dziedzictwa archeologicznego*. In: Archeologia w teorii i praktyce, A. Buko, P. Urbańczyk (ed.), Warszawa 2000, pp. 167–186.

Kochanowski M., *Elementy odzieży i sprzęt gospodarstwa domowego z grodziska w Plemiętach*. In: Plemięta. Średniowieczny gródek w ziemi chełmińskiej, A. Nadolski (ed.), Poznań 1985, p. 165–183.

Kociński M., *Późnośredniowieczna siedziba obronna w Trzemszach, gm. Przykona, pow. Turek*, "Konińskie Zeszyty Muzealne", vol. 7, 2011, pp. 29–105.

Kočka-Krenz H., *Biżuteria średniowieczna na ziemiach polskich jako wyznacznik chronologiczny*, "Archaeologia Historica Polona", vol. 6, 1997, pp. 69–75.

Kočka-Krenz H., Sikorski A., *Góra, gm. Pobiedziska, woj. poznańskie, stan. 1. Wstępne wyniki badań z lat 1985–1991*, "Wielkopolskie Sprawozdania Archeologiczne", vol. 1, 1992, pp. 135–148.

Kola A., *Żelazny osprzęt średniowiecznej wieży mieszkalnej w Plemiętach i jej wyposażenia*. In: Plemięta. Średniowieczny gródek w ziemi chełmińskiej, A. Nadolski (ed.), Poznań 1985, pp. 63–83.

Kołaczyk M., *Gródek stożkowaty w Orenicach gm. Piątek, woj. płockie w świetle badań z lat 1986–1987*, Łódź 1990 (Master's dissertation in the archives of the Institute of Archaeology at the University of Łódź).

Kołodziejski A., *Trzciel pow. Międzyrzecz w świetle wykopalisk*, Zielona Góra 1967 (Informator Muzealny).

Kołodziejski A., *Wstępne badania archeologiczne grodziska w Rybojadach, pow. Międzyrzecz*, "Rocznik Lubuski", vol. 3, 1962, pp. 298–311.

Kołodziejski S., *La problmatique des tudes sur les rsidences fortifies feodales sur le territoire de la Petite-Pologne occidentale*, "Acta Archaeologica Carpathica", vol. 22, 1983, pp. 161–198.

Kołodziejski S., *Obronne rezydencje Lisów w północnej Małopolsce. Uwagi do problematyki badań*, "Acta Universitatis Lodziensis". Folia Archaeologica, vol. 18, 1994, pp. 59–76.

Kołodziejski S., *Sprawozdanie z badań przeprowadzonych w roku 1987 w Kozłowie, gm. loco, woj. kieleckie*, Kielce 1988 (mpip. W archiwum ROBiDZ w Kielcach).

Kołodziejski S., Średniowieczne budownictwo obronne na pograniczu Małopolski z województwem sieradzkim i ziemią wieluńską. In: *Między północą a południem w późnym średniowieczu i czasach nowożytnych. Materiały z sesji naukowej w Kościerzynie koło Sieradza (4–6 grudnia 1991 r.)*, T. J. Horbacz, Kajzer L., (ed.), Sieradz 1993, p. 145–158.

Kołodziejski S., *Średniowieczne rezydencje obronne możnowładztwa na terenie województwa krakowskiego*, Kraków 1994.

Kołodziejski S., *Średniowieczne rezydencje obronne w zachodniej Małopolsce.* In: Średniowieczne siedziby rycerskie w ziemi chełmińskiej na tle badań podobnych obiektów na ziemiach polskich. Materiały z sesji archeologiczno-historycznej. Bachotek 3–4 maja 1985, A. Kola (ed.), Toruń 1987, pp. 167–179.

Koppány A., *Középkori Magyarország kastélyai*, Budapest 1999, (Manorhouses and Castles in Medieval Hungary, pp. 261–267).

Kornecki M., *Gotyckie kościoły drewniane na Podhalu*, Kraków 1987.

Kornecki M., *Kościoły drewniane w Małopolsce zagadnienia do uwarunkowań oraz systematyki typów i form architektury (od średniowiecza do XX wieku)*, Kraków 1999.

Kosiorek A., *„Dwór na kopcu" w Borówku wyniki badań archeologicznych*, "Prace i Materiały Muzeum Miasta Zgierza", vol. 3–4, 2002, p. 232.

Kosiorek A., *Z najnowszych badań archeologicznych nad założeniami obronnymi dawnego województwa skierniewickiego*, "Acta Universitatis Lodziensis". Folia Archaeologica, vol. 23/2, 2001, p. 85–92.

Kosmala T., *Sosnowiec-Zagórze, woj. katowickie. Stanowisko 5*, „Informator Archeologiczny". Badania 1986, p. 199.

Kosmala T., *Zagórze svol. 13, gm. Mucharz, woj. bielskie, AZP 107-53*, "Informator Archeologiczny". Badania 1993, pp. 103–4.

Kotowicz P. N., *Problematyka „Zamczyska" w Mymoniu w świetle zabytków archeologicznych ze zbiorów Muzeum Historycznego w Sanoku*. In:

Seminarium Trepczańskie, (eds.) P. N. Kotowicz, W. Banach, E. Kasprzak, Sanok 2007, pp. 51–67.

Kowalczyk E., *„Nazwy Obronne" Słup, Samborza i Zawada a zagadnienie obrony stałej ziem polskich w średniowieczu*, Warszawa 1992.

Kowalski A. P., *Archeologia kulturoznawcza. Projekt dyskursu „negatywistycznego"*. In: Archeologia w teorii i praktyce, A. Buko, P. Urbańczyk (ed.), Warszawa 2000, pp. 115–136.

Kowalski K.M., *Artefakty jako źródło poznania*, Gdańsk 1996.

Kozak J., *Wieruszyce, pow. Bochnia*, „Informator Archeologiczny". Badania 1968, p. 407; "Informator Archeologiczny". Badania 1969, p. 405; „Informator Archeologiczny". Badania 1971, p. 299–300; „Informator Archeologiczny". Badania 1972, p. 289; "Informator Archeologiczny". Badania 1973, p. 297; "Informator Archeologiczny". Badania 1974, p. 291.

Kozierowski S., *Studia nad pierwotnym rozsiedleniem rycerstwa wielkopolskiego*, published successively in "Miesięcznik Heraldyczny" in the years 1913–1920.

Kramarek J., *Pierwsze wykopaliska archeologiczne na Śląsku*, "Z Otchłani Wieków", vol. 24, 1958, no. 1, pp. 25–333.

Kramarkowie I. J., *U źródeł archeologii*, Wrocław 1972.

Krause E., *Badania archeologiczne grodziszczka w Szamotułach w woj. poznańskim*. In: Średniowieczne siedziby rycerskie w ziemi chełmińskiej na tle podobnych obiektów na ziemiach polskich, Toruń 1987, pp. 131–135.

Krause E., *Średniowieczne siedziby rycerskie w Wielkopolsce i Polsce środkowej*. In: "Rocznik Przedsiębiorstw Państwowego Pracownie Konserwacji Zabytków", no. 2, 1987, Warszawa 1988, pp. 44–60.

Krause E., *Nowe źródła archeologiczne o siedzibie rycerskiej w Siedlątkowie w woj. sieradzkim*. In: Średniowieczne siedziby rycerskie w ziemi chełmińskiej na tle badań podobnych obiektów na ziemiach polskich. Materiały z sesji archeologiczno-historycznej. Bachotek 3–4 maja 1985 roku, A. Kola (ed.), Toruń 1987, p. 127–130.

Kruppé J., *Garncarstwo późnośredniowieczne w Polsce*, Wrocław 1981.

Kuczyński J., *Dębno, pow. Kielce*, "Informator Archeologiczny". Badania 1972, p. 244.

Kuczyński J., *XIV-wieczny gródek w Dębnie woj. kieleckie, gmina Nowa Słupia*, "Rocznik Muzeum Narodowego w Kielcach", vol. 12, 1982, p. 211–233.

Kunysz A., *Grodziska w województwie rzeszowskim*, "Materiały i Sprawozdania Rzeszowskiego Ośrodka Archeologicznego", 1966, 1968, pp. 25–87.

Kurczab J., *O działalności Karpackiej Ekspedycji Archeologicznej*. In: Polonia Minor Medii Aevi. Studia ofiarowane Panu Profesorowi Andrzejowi Żakiemu w osiemdziesiątą rocznicę urodzin, Z. Woźniak, J. Gancarski (ed.), Kraków–Krosno 2003, p. 83–120.

Kurnatowska Z., Łosińska A., *Weryfikacja grodzisk wielkopolskich na półmetku*, "Fontes Archaeologici Posnanienses", vol. 32, 1981(1983), pp. 25–62.

Kurnatowska Z., Łosińska A., *Sprawozdanie z weryfikacji grodzisk wielkopolskich w latach 1983–1984*, "Fontes Archaeologici Posnanienses", vol. 34 (1982–1985), pp. 77–84.

Kurtyka J., *Tęczyńscy. Studium z dziejów polskiej elity możnowładczej w średniowieczu*, Kraków 1997.

Kwaśniewski K., *Paleniska i piece w polskim budownictwie ludowym*, Warszawa 1963.

Labuda G., *Uwagi o przedmiocie i metodzie geografii historycznej*, "Przegląd Geograficzny", vol. 25, 1953, pp. 5–56.

Lalik T., *Budowa dworu drewnianego w Jadownikach w roku 1394*, "Kwartalnik Historii Kultury Materialnej", vol. 19, 1971, no. 3, pp. 463–468.

Lechowicz Z., *Gniazdków gm. Chotcza woj. radomskie*, "Informator Archeologiczny". Badania 1986, p. 180.

Lechowicz Z., *Wyniki badań na stanowisku 1 w Gniazdkowie gm. Chotcza, woj. radomskie w latach 1985–86*, "Materiały Konserwatorskie. Badania archeologiczne w woj. radomskim - 1986", cz. II, Radom 1987, pp. 5–7.

Leńczyk G., *Trzecie sprawozdanie z badań archeologicznych w woj. krakowskim w r. 1935*, "Sprawozdania Polskiej Akademii Umiejętności", vol. 40, 1935, pp. 317–319.

Leńczyk G., *Drugie sprawozdanie z inwentaryzacji i planowania grodzisk w woj. krakowskim w r. 1933*, "Sprawozdania Polskiej Akademii Umiejętności", vol. 39, 1934, pp. 28–33.

Leńczyk G., *Elementy obronne w miejscach umocnionych*, "Studia Archeologiczne", vol. 2, 1967, pp. 73–116.

Leńczyk G., *Grodzisko w Piekarach w powiecie krakowskim*, "Z Otchłani Wieków", vol. 7, 1932, pp. 77–85.

Leńczyk G., *Katalog grodzisk i zamczysk z terenu Małopolski*, oprac. S. Kołodziejski, Kraków 1983.

Leńczyk G., *Kopce historyczne w powiecie sieradzkim*, "Sprawozdania Polskiej Akademii Umiejętności", vol. 42, 1937, no. 8, pp. 229–231.

Leńczyk G., *Na śladach miejsc obronnych*, "Dawna Kultura", vol. 3, 1956, pp. 122–127.

Leńczyk G., *Na śladach miejsc umocnionych*, "Z Otchłani Wieków", vol. 27, 1961, pp. 108–109.

Leńczyk G., *Rozmieszczenie grodzisk i zamczysk w województwie wołyńskim*, "Sprawozdania Polskiej Akademii Umiejętności", vol. 42, 1937, no. 8, pp. 227–229.

Leńczyk G., *Sprawozdanie z inwentaryzacji i planowania grodzisk w okolicy Krakowa*, "Sprawozdania Polskiej Akademii Umiejętności", vol. 37, 1932, pp. 36–40.

Leńczyk G., *Tymczasowe sprawozdanie z badań terenowych na grodzisku w Piekarach pod Krakowem*, "Sprawozdania Polskiej Akademii Umiejętności", vol. 37, 1932, pp. 23–24.

Leńczyk G., *W sprawie atlasu grodzisk. Uwagi na marginesie doświadczeń w woj. krakowskim*, "Z Otchłani Wieków", vol. 19, 1950, pp. 130–132.

Leńczyk G., *Zamki i grodziska nad Wisłokiem*, "Z Otchłani Wieków", vol. 13, 1938, pp. 99–104.

Lewandowski M., *Puginały średniowieczne z ziem polskich*. In: Mediaevalia Archaeologica. "Acta Archaeologica Lodziensia", nr 31, 1986, A. Nadolski (ed.), pp. 101–119.

Lodowski J., *Relikty późnośredniowiecznych rezydencji obronnych w Chróścinie i Żuchlowie, pow. Góra*, "Śląskie Sprawozdania Archeologiczne", vol. 43, 2001, p. 565.

Lodowski J., *Ryczeń, gm. Góra, woj. leszczyńskie, stanowisko* 1, "Informator Archeologiczny". Badania 1981, p. 250.

Łaszkiewicz T., Wawrzyniak P., *Popów – przyczynek do dyskusji nad funkcją niektórych gródków stożkowatych*. In: Średniowieczne siedziby rycerskie w ziemi chełmińskiej na tle badań podobnych obiektów na ziemiach polskich. Materiały z sesji archeologiczno-historycznej. Bachotek 3–4 maja 1985, A. Kola (ed.), Toruń 1987, pp. 137–145.

Łęga W., *Kultura Pomorza we wczesnym średniowieczu na podstawie wykopalisk*, vol. II, part. II, "Rocznik Towarzystwa Naukowego w Toruniu", vol. 36, 1930, pp. 295–327.

Łowmiański H., *Początki Polski*, vol. 3, Warszawa 1967.

Machnik J., *Legenda Karpackiej Ekspedycji Archeologicznej*. In: Polonia Minor Medii Aevi. Studia ofiarowane Panu Profesorowi Andrzejowi Żakiemu w osiemdziesiątą rocznicę urodzin, Z. Woźniak, J. Gancarski (ed.), Kraków-Krosno 2003, pp. 65–82.

Makiewicz T., *Średniowieczne grodzisko stożkowate na stanowisku 5 w Kunowie*, pow. Mogilno, "Slavia. Antiqua", vol. 19, 1972, p. 227–240.

Mamzer H., Ostoja-Zagórski J., *Orientacje badawcze w polskiej archeologii*, "Nauka", 1/2007, pp. 131–148.

Mapa grodzisk w Polsce, W. Antoniewicz, Z. Wartołowska (ed.), Wrocław 1964.

Marciniak-Kajzer A., *Dwór obronny w Proboszczewicach*, "Acta Universitatis Lodziensi". Folia Archaeologica, vol. 18, 1994, pp. 25–58.

Marciniak-Kajzer A., *Palenisko, kominek czy piec – urządzenia ogniowe w średniowiecznych dworach*. In: Rzeczy i ludzie. Kultura materialna w późnym średniowieczu i w okresie nowożytnym. Studia dedykowane Marii Dąbrowskiej, M. Bis, W. Bis (ed.), Warszawa 2014, p. 63–74.

Marciniak-Kajzer A., *Średniowieczny dwór rycerski w Polsce. Wizerunek archeologiczny*, Łódź 2011.

Marciniak-Kajzer A., *Badania nad kulturą materialną średniowiecznego dworu rycerskiego w optyce archeologa*. In: Polska i Europa w średniowieczu. Przemiany strukturalne. Podmioty i przedmioty w badaniach historycznych, M. Adamczewski (ed.), Warszawa 2011, p. 115–123.

Marciniak-Kajzer A., Horbacz T. J., *Sprawozdanie z badań archeologicznych przeprowadzonych w roku 1995 w miejscowości Gruszczyce gm. Błaszki woj. sieradzkie*, "Sieradzki Rocznik Muzealny", vol. 10 (1995–96), pp. 121–125.

Marciniak-Kajzer A., *Jak wyglądały późnośredniowieczne kuchnie?*, "Vox Patrum" 33, vol. 59, 2013, p. 449–161.

Marciniak-Kajzer A., *Kilka słów o średniowiecznej złotej ostrodze z pogranicza krzyżacko-polskiego*, "Acta Militaria Mediaevalia", vol. 3, 2007, pp. 201–208.

Marszałek J., *Katalog grodzisk i zamczysk w Karpatach*, Warszawa 1993.

Menclová D., *České hrady*, vol. 1, 2, Praha 1972.

Měřínský Z., *Provoz a vybavení domácnosti ve vyšším sociálním prostředí (měšťanstvo a šlechta) na základě pramenů archeologických*, "Archaeologia Historica", vol. 15, 1990, pp. 19–42.

Měřínský Z., *Střédovéké hrádky a tvrze na jihozápadní Moravě*, "Archaeologia Historica", vol. 2, 1977, pp. 37–43.

Michalik P., *Późnośredniowieczne i wczesnonowożytne noże z zamku w Pucku*, Warszawa 2000.

Minta-Tworzowska D., *Postmodernizm, myśl poststrukturalistyczna a archeologia (zarys problematyki)*. In: Archeologia w teorii i praktyce, A. Buko, P. Urbańczyk (ed.), Warszawa 2000, pp. 87–95.

Mitteilungen der Residenzen–Kommission der Akademie der Wissenschaften zu Göttingen, Kiel from 1995 year

Moszyński K., *Kultura ludowa Słowian*, vol. 1, Kultura materialna, Warszawa 1967, pp. 373–4.

Müller-Wille M., *Mittelalterliche Burghügel im nördlichen Rheinland*, Köln/ Gratz 1967.

Muzolf B., *Stryków, st. 5 – siedziba obronna właścicieli miasta Strykowa*, "Prace i Materiały Muzeum Miasta Zgierza", vol. 5, 2003, pp. 80–83.

Nadolski A., *Hełm i fragmenty zbroi z Siedlątkowa*, "Prace i Materiały Muzeum Archeologicznego i Etnograficznego w Łodzi", no 15, 1963, pp. 89–93;

Nadolski A., *Hełm i fragmenty zbroi z XIV wieku znalezione w Siedlątkowie nad Wartą*, "Studia do Dziejów Dawnego Uzbrojenia i Ubioru Wojskowego", vol. 4, 1969, pp. 5–23.

Naumowicz-Śmigielska E., *Chłapowo, gm. Dominowo, woj. poznańskie*, "Informator Archeologiczny". Badania 1977, p. 218; "Informator Archeologiczny". Badania 1979, p. 208

Naumowicz-Śmigielska E., Grabska M., *Iwno pow. Środa. Stanowisko 2 i 3*, "Informator Archeologiczny". Badania 1974, pp. 228–9.

Naumowicz-Śmigielska E., *Wstępne sprawozdanie z badań wykopaliskowych na gródku średniowiecznym w Dąbrówce pow. Poznań*, "Fontes Archaeologici Posnanienses", vol. 24, 1973, pp. 250–251.

Nekuda V., Unger J., *Hrádky a tvrze na Moravé*, Brno 1981.

Niedźwiadkowie A. and R., Rozwałka A., *Wyniki badań gródka stożkowatego w Brzezinach-Trójni, stan. 26, woj. lubelskie*, "Archeologia Polski Środkowowschodniej", vol. 3, 1998, pp. 227–233.

Niegoda J., *Naczynia ceramiczne*. In: Wratislavia Antiqua, vol. 1, Ze studiów nad życiem codziennym w średniowiecznym mieście. Parcele przy ulicy więziennej 10–11, we Wrocławiu, C. Buśko, J. Piekalski (ed.), Wrocław 1999, p. 157–182.

Nierychlewska A., *Budownictwo obronne powiatu radomskiego w okresie od XIII do XVIII wieku*, Radom 2002, pp. 60–65.

Nosek E., *Czternastowieczna kuźnia w Siedlątkowie*, "Prace i Materiały Muzeum Archeologicznego i Etnograficznego w Łodzi", no. 15, 1968, pp. 95–131.

Nowak T., *Własność ziemska w ziemi łęczyckiej w czasach Władysława Jagiełły*, Łódź 2003.

Nowakowie Ł. i A., *Mrówki, pow. Konin*, "Informator Archeologiczny". Badania 1971, p. 254.

Nowakowski A., *Uzbrojenie średniowieczne w Polsce (na tle środkowo-europejskim)*, Toruń 1991.

Nowakowski D., *Siedziby książęce i rycerskie księstwa głogowskiego w średniowieczu*, Wrocław 2008.

Nowakowski P. A., *Arsenały domowe rycerstwa polskiego w średniowieczu*, Toruń 2006.

Olczak J., Siuchniński K., *Typologische Klassifikation der frühmittelalterlichen Burganlagen in Mittelpommern*, "Ethnografisch-Archäologische Zeitschrift", vol. 16, 1975, pp. 443–474.

Ostoja-Zagórski J., *W kwestii znaczeniowych treści kultury materialnej*, "Kwartalnik Historii Kultury Materialnej", vol. 42, 1994, no. 2, pp. 177–179.

Pałubicka A., *Archeologia jako nauka historyczna o kulturze. O badaniach formy i funkcji znalezisk archeologicznych*. In: Archeologia w teorii i praktyce, A. Buko, P. Urbańczyk (ed.), pp. 177–179.

Parczewski M., *Jędrychowice, pow. Głubczyce*, "Informator Archeologiczny". Badania 1972, pp. 250–251.

Pauk M. R., *Funkcjonowanie regale fortyfikacyjnego w Europie Środkowej w średniowieczu*, "Kwartalnik Historii Kultury Materialnej", vol. 51, 2003, no. 1, p. 3–16.

Pawłowski A., *Wiejskie siedziby obronne na tle podziału politycznego Śląska w 1 połowie XIV wieku*, "Silesia Antiqua", vol. 26, 1984, pp. 111–118.

Pawłowski A., *Grody stożkowate, ostrosłupowe i wieże mieszkalno-obronne na Śląsku w średniowieczu*, Wrocław 1978.

Pawłowski A., *Jak budowano obronne siedziby rycerskie?*, "Z Otchłani Wieków", vol. 46, 1980, no. 1, p. 80.

Pawłowski A., *Z badań grodzisk średniowiecznych województwa wrocławskiego*, "Sprawozdania Archeologiczne", vol. 30, 1978, pp. 241–257.

Piasek D., *Rycerskie i szlacheckie siedziby obronne na Pomorzu Gdańskim w XIII–poł. XVII w.*, Gdańsk 2006

Piekalski J., *Problem genezy budowli typu kemenate w miastach środkowoeuropejskiej strefy nadmorskiej.* In: Archaeologia et historia urbana, R. Czaja, G. Nawrolska, M. Rębkowski, J. Tandecki (ed.), Elbląg 2004, pp. 227–236.

Piekalski J., *Wczesne domy mieszczan w Europie Środkowej. Geneza-funkcja-forma*, Wrocław 2004.

Piekalski J., Wiśniewski A., *Akwamanila z mieszczańskiej parceli przy ul. Nożownicze 13 we Wrocławiu*, "Śląskie Sprawozdania Archeologiczne", vol. 33, 1992, pp. 175–182.

Piekalski J., Żurek A., *Ze studiów nad siedzibami obronnymi północno-wschodniego pogranicza Śląska w XIII–XVII w.*, "Acta Universitatis Vratislaviensis". Studia Archeologiczne, vol. 24, 1993, pp. 139–187.

Piepers W., *Die Ausgrabungen auf Burg Garsdorf. Kreis Bergheim*, "Bonner Jahrbücher" 162, 1962, pp. 433–444.

Pierzak J., Rozmus D., *Gródek rycerski w Kozłowie, gm. Sośnicowice*, "Rocznik Muzeum w Gliwicach", vol. 11/13, 1997, pp. 21–37.

Pierzak J., Rozmus D., *Średniowieczny gródek rycerski w Krzykawce gm. Bukowno, woj. Katowice*, "Śląskie Prace Prahistoryczne", vol. 3, 1994, p. 125.

Plemięta. Średniowieczny gródek w ziemi chełmińskiej, A. Nadolski (ed.), Warszawa–Poznań–Toruń 1985.

Polla B., *Hrady a kaštiele na Východnom Slovensku*, Košice 1980.

Proksa M., *Studia nad zamkami i dworami ziemi przemyskiej od połowy XIV do początków XVIII wieku*, Przemyśl 2001.

Prusicka-Kołcon E., *Drugi sezon badań na tzw. gródku stożkowatym w Gozdowie stan. 1, pow. Hrubieszów*, "Archeologia Polski Południowowschodniej", vol. 6, 2001, pp. 142.

Prusicka-Kołcon E., *Wyniki badań tzw. gródka stożkowatego w Gozdowie, stan. 1, pow. Hrubieszów*, "Archeologia Polski Środkowowschodniej", vol. 4, 1999, pp. 191–196.

Pyrgała J., *Badania sondażowe wczesnośredniowiecznych grodzisk w powiecie płońskim przeprowadzone w 1965 roku przez Zakład Polskiego Atlasu Archeologicznego IHKM PAN*, "Sprawozdania Archeologiczne", vol. 19, 1968, pp. 192–194.

Pyzik Z. W., *Grodzisko stożkowate w Kiełbowie Starym, pow. Białobrzegi*, "Rocznik Muzeum Świętokrzyskiego", vol. 6, 1970, pp. 461–485.

Pyzik Z. W., *Grodzisko średniowieczne we Włoszczowie*, "Rocznik Muzeum Narodowego w Kielcach", vol. 19, 1998, pp. 157–175.

Pyzik Z. W., *Szczekociny, pow. Włoszczowa*, "Informator Archeologiczny". Badania 1969, pp. 396–397.

Ratzel F., *Antropogeographie*, Bd. 1–2, Stuttgart 1921 (non vidimus).

Reguła K., *Badania archeologiczne na grodzisku wczesnośredniowiecznym w Sobolowie–Sieradze, pow. Bochnia*, "Badania Muzeum Żup Krakowskich w r. 1967", pp. 61–63;

Reyniak J., *Dawne miejsca obronne w dorzeczu górnej Wisły*, "Karta Groni", no. 9–10, 1980, pp. 55–74.

Reyniak J., *Osadnictwo obronne w dorzeczu górnej Wisły*, "Acta Archaeologica Carpathica", vol. 20, 1980, pp. 73–92.

Rębkowski M., *Średniowieczna ceramika miasta lokacyjnego w Kołobrzegu*, Kołobrzeg 1995.

Romanowska-Grabowska O., *Izdebno pow. Żnin. Jezioro Wolskie. Stanowisko 1*, "Informator Archeologiczny". Badania 1974, p. 230.

Rutkowska-Płachcińska A., *Mieszkanie, higiena*. In: Historia kultury materialnej Polski, Rutkowska-Płachcińska A. (ed.) vol. 2, pp. 312–357.

Rzeźnik P., Stosik H., *Ceramika grafitowa z Raciborza (XII–XIII w.) w świetle pierwszych analiz specjalistycznych*. In: Początki i rozwój miast Górnego Śląska. Studia interdyscyplinarne, D. Abłamowicz, M. Furmanek, M. Michnik (ed.), Gliwice 2004, pp. 171–185.

Rzeźnik P., Trzciński M., *Późnośredniowieczna ceramika ze wsi Rusko, gm. Strzegom, z badań w 1994 roku*, "Śląskie Sprawozdania Archeologiczne", vol. 37, 1996, pp. 301–314.

Rzeźnik P., *Przemiany wytwórczości garncarskiej średniowiecznego Wrocławia w czasie wielkiej reformy miejskiej*. In: Kultura średniowiecznego Śląska i Czech „Rewolucja" XIII wieku, K. Wachowsk (ed.) i, Wrocław 1998, pp. 121–153.

Sachs R., *Tak zwane „fibule w kształcie sowy" i ich znaczenie. Z badań nad treściami ideowymi ozdób w państwie krzyżackim.* In: Niemcy–Polska w średniowieczu, J. Strzelczyk (ed.), Poznań 1986, pp. 355–365.

Sachs R., *Witków woj. zielonogórskie. Stanowisko 6*, "Informator Archeologiczny". Badania 1983, p. 222.

Samsonowicz H., *Struktura społeczna późnego średniowiecza w Polski w badaniach historycznych.* In: Społeczeństwo Polski średniowiecznej, P. K. Kuczyński (ed.), vol. 7, Warszawa 1996, pp. 267–282.

Sedlaček A., *Hrady, zámky a tvrze království českeho*, vol. 1–15, Praha 1880–1927, (2 edition. Praha 1927–1937).

Semkowicz W., *Ród Pałuków*, Kraków 1907.

Semkowicz W., *Ród Awdańców w wiekach średnich*, "Roczniki Towarzystwa Przyjaciół Nauk Poznańskiego", vol. 44, 1917.

Slivka M., *Veže ako dominanty domínií (Symbolika a geneticko-typologický vývoj na Slovensku)*, "Archaeologia Historica Polona", vol. 12, 2002, pp. 9–29.

South S., *Method and Theory in Historical Archaeology*, New York 1977.

Stępnik T., Dębski A., *Sprawozdanie z badań archeologicznych późnośredniowiecznej osady rycerskiej w Żernikach–Jaryszkach, gm. Kórnik, woj. wielkopolskie*, "Wielkopolskie Sprawozdania Archeologiczne", vol. 10, 2009, pp. 207–217.

Strzyż P., *Broń palna w Europie Środkowej w XIV–XV w.*, Warsaw 2014.

Strzyżewski C., *Jankowo Dolne gm. Gniezno, woj. poznańskie*, "Informator Archeologiczny". Badania 1990, p. 98; "Informator Archeologiczny". Badania 1991, p. 119; "Informator Archeologiczny". Badania 1992, pp. 100–101.

Strzyżewski C., *Strzyżewo Paczkowe, svol. 37, gm. Gniezno woj. poznańskie*, "Informator Archeologiczny". Badania 1994, pp. 105–6.

Suchodolski S., *Kopytów, pow. Pruszków*, "Informator Archeologiczny". Badania 1972 p. 251

Svoboda L., *Stavební vývoj českých tvrzí.* In: Encyklopedie českých tvrzí, vol. 1, Praha 1998, p. 11–33.

Svoboda L., Úlovec J., Chotébor P., Procházka Z., Fišera Z., Anderle J., Slavík J., Rykl M., Durdík T., Brych V., *Encyklopedie českých tvrzí*, vol. 1, Praha 1998, vol. 2, 2000, vol. 3, 2005.

Szope M., *Grodziska i zamczyska województwa tarnowskiego*, Tarnów 1981.

Szwed A., *Ród Grzymałów w Wielkopolsce*, Toruń 2001.

Szydłowska E., *Średniowieczny gródek w Krzykawce, woj. Katowice*, "Śląskie Prace Prahistoryczne", vol. 1, 1989, pp. 138–163.

Szymański W., *Przyczynek do badań nad problematyką grodzisk stożkowatych (Orszymowo i Wilkanowo w pow. płockim)*, "Kwartalnik Historii Kultury Materialnej", R. 16, 1968, no. 1, pp. 55–72.

Szymański W., *Sprawozdanie z badań sondażowych grodzisk w miejscowościach: Biała, Orszymowo, Parzeń, Wilkanowo i Wyszogród (D. Drwały), pow. Płock w 1966 roku*, "Sprawozdania Archeologiczne", vol. 20, 1966, pp. 231–235.

Szymczak A., *Budzynek gm. Dalików woj. sieradzkie. Stanowisko 1*, "Informator Archeologiczny". Badania 1976, p. 260; "Informator Archeologiczny". Badania. 77 p. 215–216.

Szymczak J., *Ostrogi żelazne i pozłociste*. In: Archeologia i starożytnicy. Studia dedykowane Profesorowi Andrzejowi Abramowiczowi w 70 rocznicę urodzin, Łódź 1997, pp. 275–284.

Szymczak J., *Początki broni palnej w Polsce (1383–1533)*, Łódź 2004.

Szymczak J., *Produkcja i koszty uzbrojenia rycerskiego w Polsce XIII–XV w.*, Łódź 1989.

Szymczakowa A., *Szlachta sieradzka w XV wieku. Magnifici et generosi*, Łódź 1998.

Szymczakowa A., *Urzędnicy łęczyccy i sieradzcy do połowy XV wieku*, "Acta Universitatis Lodziensis". Folia Historica, vol. 20, 1984.

Śliwiński B., *Lisowie Krzelowscy w XIV–XV w. i ich antenaci*, Gdańsk 1993.

Ślusarski Z., *Horodysko, pow. Chełm*, "Informator Archeologiczny". Badania 1967, pp. 331–332.

Śniady P., *Krajkowo, gm. Mosina, woj. poznański*, "Informator Archeologiczny". Badania 1991, p. 121.

Świątkiewicz P., *O średniowiecznej lampie ze Zgierza*. In: Od pradziejów do współczesności. Archeologiczne wędrówki. Studia dedykowane Pani Profesor Marii Magdalenie Blombergowej, Łódź 2007, pp. 59–61.

Świątkiewicz P., *Późnośredniowieczne grodzisko w Karsznicach, woj. płockie*, "Prace i Materiały Muzeum Archeologicznego i Etnograficznego w Łodzi", Seria Archeologiczna, no 35, 1988, pp. 137–157.

Thullie C., *Zabytkowe dzwonnice drewniane w Polsce*, "Teka Komisji Architektury i Urbanistyki", vol. 3, 1969, pp. 119–133.

Timpel W., *Gommerstedt bei Bösleben, Kr. Arnstadvol. Burghügel und Siedlung des Mittelalters*, "Ausgrabungen und Funde", Bd. 21, 1976, pp. 142–144.

Tomala J., *Budownictwo obronne powiatu kaliskiego w XIV-XVIII wieku*, Poznań 1995.

Tomala J., *Nowe odkrycia zabytków średniowiecznych z terenu Mazowsza*, "Kwartalnik Historii Kultury Materialnej" vol. 34, 1986, no. 2, pp. 281–28.

Tomala J., *Późnośredniowieczne i nowożytne założenia obronne między Krotoszynem a Żerkowem*, "Archaeologia Historica Polona", vol. 15/1, 2005, pp. 235–255.

Tomala J., *Ktery gm. Krzyżanów, woj. płockie*, "Informator Archeologiczny". Badania 1983, p. 200.

Tomaszewski A., *Romańskie kościoły z emporami zachodnimi na obszarze Polski, Czech i Węgier*, Wrocław 1974.

Topolski J., *Fernand Braudel a koncepcja historii kultury materialnej*, "Kwartalnik Historii Kultury Materialnej", vol. 42, 1994, no. 2, pp. 159–165;

Tyszkiewicz J., *Człowiek w środowisku geograficznym Polski średniowiecznej*, Warszawa 1981.

Úlovec J., *Hrady, zámky a tvrze na Chebsku*, Cheb 1998.

Unger J., *Hmotná kultura středověké šlechty v archeologických pramenech na Moravě*, "Archaeologia Historica", vol. 10, 1985, pp. 323–329.

Unger J., *Koválov, šlechtické sídlo z 13. století na jižní Moravé*, Brno 1994.

Unger J., *Život na lelekovickém hradě ve 14. století. Antropologická sociokulturní studie*, Brno 1999.

Urbański M., *Grodzisko stożkowate w Zawalowie stan. 1 gm. Miączyn - XIV-XVII w.*, "Sprawozdania z badań terenowych w województwie zamojskim", z. 1, 1986, p. 36.

Vidal de la Blache P., *Principes de geographie humaine*, Paris 1948 (1 edition 1922).

Wachowski K., *Militaria z grodu na Ostrówku w Opolu*. In: Studia nad kulturą wczesnopolskiego Opola, Wrocław 1984, pp. 11–112.

Wawrzonowska Z., *Uzbrojenie i ubiór Piastów Śląskich od XII do XIV w.*, Łódź 1976.

Wawrzyniak P., *Dobrzyca gm. loco woj. kaliskie*, "Informator Archeologiczny". Badania 1991, p. 131.

Wawrzyniak P., *Średniowieczna rezydencja biskupów poznańskich w Głównej w świetle badań archeologicznych w latach 2004–2005*. In: Nie tylko archeologia, E. Cnotliwy, A. Janowski, K. Kowalski, S. Słowiński (ed.), Szczecin 2006, pp. 317–330.

Wdowiszewski Z., *Ród Bogoriów w wiekach średnich*, "Rocznik Polskiego Towarzystwa Heraldycznego", vol. 9, 1928/1929.

Wędzki A., *Ze studiów nad rezydencjami możnowładczymi i rycerskimi na ziemiach polskich w XI–XII wieku*, "Slavia Antiqua", vol. 25, 1978, pp. 173–187.

White H., *Metahistory. The Historical Imagination of Nineteenth Century Europe*, Baltimore 1973.

Wilke G., *Średniowieczne wieże w miastach Toskanii zasiedlane okresowo*, "Archaeologia Historica Polona", vol. 12, pp. 31–46.

Wohntürme, Veröffentlichungen der Deutschen Burgenvereinigun .e.V, H. Müller (ed.), Langenweiβbach 2002.

Wojda L., *Rozdrażew, woj. kaliskie*, "Informator Archeologiczny". Badania 1988 p. 134.

Wroniszewski J., *Ród Rawiczów. Współrodowcy Warszowiców i Grotowiców*, Toruń 1994.

Wroniszewski J., *Ród Rawiczów. Warszowice i Grotowice*, Toruń 1992.

Wrzosek W., *Braudelowska idea kultury materialnej*, "Kwartalnik Historii Kultury Materialnej", vol. 42, 1994, no. 2, pp. 167–172.

Wyrobisz A., *Szkło w Polsce od XIV do XVII w.*, Wrocław 1968.

Zaitz E., *Sprawozdanie z badań archeologicznych przy pałacu Decjusza na Woli Justowskiej w Krakowie*, "Materiały Archeologiczne", vol. 20, 1980, pp. 131–157.

Zajączkowski S. M., *O wielowioskowej własności szlacheckiej w województwie łęczyckim w XV i pierwszej połowie XVI w.*, „Zeszyty Naukowe UŁ" seria I, no. 60, 1969, pp. 79–104.

Zajączkowski S. M., *Sieć osadnicza i struktura własnościowa osadnictwa dawnych ziem łęczyckiej i sieradzkiej w początkach XVI wieku*, "Slavia Antiqua", vol. 19, 1972, pp. 19–80.

Zajączkowski S. M., *Studia nad wielowioskową własnością szlachecką w Łęczyckiem i Sieradzkiem i jej rolą w osadnictwie*, "Kwartalnik Historii Kultury Materialnej", vol. 14, 1966, no. 2, pp. 179–208.

Zajączkowski S. M., *Wielowioskowa własność szlachecka w województwie sieradzkim (XV i pierwsza połowa XVI w.)*, "Rocznik Łódzki", vol. 18 (21), 1973, pp. 23–50.

Zalewska A., *Teoria źródła archeologicznego i historycznego we współczesnej refleksji metodologicznej*, Lublin 2005.

Zin W., Radwański K., Kadłuczka A., *Wstępne wyniki badań prowadzonych w Pałacu Decjusza na Woli Justowskiej*, "Sprawozdania z posiedzeń Komisji Naukowych", Polska Akademia Nauk, Oddział w Krakowie, vol. 23/1, 1981, pp. 163–166.

Život v archeologii středověku, J. Kubková, J. Klápště, M. Ježek, P. Meduna (ed.), Praha 1997.

Żaki A., *Fortalicjum średniowieczne w Sromowcach Wyżnich (Pieniny polskie)*, "Acta Archaeologica Carpathica", vol. 11/2, 1970, pp. 231–238.

Żaki A., *Mrukowa i Żmigród Stary – dwa górskie fortalicja w Beskidzie Niskim*, "Acta Archaeologica Carpathica", vol. 5, 1963, pp. 77–84.

Żaki A., *Sprawozdanie z prac badawczych prowadzonych w Wietrznie–Bóbrce pow. Krosno i okolicy*, "Przegląd Zachodni", vol. 7, vol. 2, z. 12, p. 499–509.

Żaki, *Starożytne i średniowiecze warownie karpackie*, "Acta Archaeologica Carpathica", vol. 8, 1966, p. 5–55.

Крадин Н. П., *Русское деревянное еборoнoе зодчество*, Москва 1988.